RETHINKING FIELD EXPERIENCES IN PRESERVICE TEACHER PREPARATION

The focus of this book is the centrality of clinical experiences in preparing teachers to work with students from diverse cultural, economic and experiential backgrounds.

Organized around three themes—learning teaching through the representation and approximation of practice; learning teaching situated in context; and assessing and improving teacher preparation—*Rethinking Field Experiences in Preservice Teacher Preparation* provides detailed descriptions of theoretically grounded, research-based practices in programs that prepare preservice teachers to contextualize teaching practices in ways that result in a positive impact on learning for traditionally underserved students. These practices serve current demands for teacher accountability for student learning outcomes and model good practice for engaging teacher educators in meaningful, productive dialogue and analysis geared to developing local programs characterized by coherence, continuity and consistency.

Etta R. Hollins is professor and Kauffman Endowed Chair for Urban Teacher Education at the University of Missouri-Kansas City, USA.

RETHINKING FIELD EXPERIENCES IN PRESERVICE TEACHER PREPARATION

Meeting New Challenges for Accountability

Edited by Etta R. Hollins

Routledge
Taylor & Francis Group

NEW YORK AND LONDON

First published 2015
by Routledge
711 Third Avenue, New York, NY 10017

and by Routledge
2 Park Square, Milton Park, Abingdon, Oxon OX14 4RN

*Routledge is an imprint of the Taylor & Francis Group, an
informa business*

© 2015 Etta R. Hollins

Library of Congress Cataloging in Publication Data

A catalog record for this book has been requested.

ISBN: 978-1-138-82385-3
ISBN: 978-1-138-82386-0
ISBN: 978-1-315-74181-9

Typeset in Bembo
by Apex CoVantage, LLC

This book is dedicated to *accomplished teaching* that supports each student in meeting the highest potential.

CONTENTS

PREFACE

Failure of public education in urban communities is a familiar reality. Low-performing schools far exceed the number of high-performing schools in urban settings. However, it is the existence of high-performing urban schools and individual high-performing teachers in low-performing schools that provide evidence of what is possible for students in urban school settings. This evidence has not led to the identification of practices or ways of thinking about practice that result in our ability to foster consistently high outcomes for traditionally underserved students.

The academic performance of underserved students depends on access to high-quality teaching and learning experiences. The quality of teaching practices determines the quality of learning experiences provided for students. Thus, classroom teachers have a powerful influence on student learning outcomes. Darling-Hammond (2004) pointed out that "the fact that the least qualified teachers typically end up teaching the least advantaged students is particularly problematic, given recent studies that have found that teacher quality is one of the most important determinants of student achievement" (p. 1056). The quality of teaching practices provides one explanation for the general quality of academic performance of P–12 students in public schools and some of the variation in performance among sub-groups (Darling-Hammond, 2000).

The extent to which teaching practices provide meaningful and productive learning experiences for students is influenced by the interrelationship among learner characteristics, including background experiences, language and values; and teaching practices; and learning outcomes. Further, teachers' ability to provide learning experiences for students that generate the expected outcome is influenced by their knowledge of learning, particular learners, pedagogy and subject matter. This basic principle is supported in findings from a developing body of research indicating that it is especially important for teachers to have specific knowledge of the students they teach and that productive teaching practices are tapered to the characteristics of the students. One example is a study by Carol Lee (1995) in which a specific aspect of African American high school students' everyday language referred to as "signifying" was used to facilitate their learning to interpret complex literary text. In another example, Moses, Kamii, Swap, & Howard (1989) combined students' everyday language and shared experience to facilitate learning basic concepts in algebra. Moll (1986) and McCarty (2002) demonstrated the importance of embedding learning experiences within the values and practices of students' home culture. This research brings attention to particular aspects of students' background experiences that can be used to develop meaningful and productive learning experiences. However, more importantly, this research illuminates the need for teachers to be able to contextualize practice for particular students when learning distinct skills and subject matter under specific conditions. Learning to contextualize teaching practices in this way requires carefully guided experiences in classrooms with real students.

Learning to contextualize teaching practices in a preservice teacher preparation program suggests a significant departure from traditional conceptualizations of student teaching and related clinical experiences. According to the National Council for Accreditation of Teacher Education (NCATE) Blue Ribbon Panel on Clinical Preparation and Partnerships for Improved Student Learning (2010),

> this demanding, clinically based approach will create varied and extensive opportunities for candidates to connect what they learn with the challenge of using it while under the expert tutelage of skilled clinical educators. Candidates will blend practitioner knowledge with academic knowledge as they learn by doing. They will refine their practice in the light of new knowledge acquired and data gathered about whether their students are learning.
> (p. ii)

This idea of "learning by doing" described by the NCATE Blue Ribbon Panel can also be described as guided practice within a professional community. It is a type of apprenticeship that is significantly different from traditional conceptualizations of student teaching.

Guided practice can be understood from a sociocultural theoretical perspective on learning teaching. In this conceptualization, candidates learn how to participate in a community of practice where the primary activity is to facilitate learning based on the cultural, social and historical context of school, themselves and that of the students they teach. In this process, candidates are actively engaged in co-constructing contextualized knowledge of teaching practice with peers and more experienced practitioners through focused inquiry, directed observation, guided practice, dialogue and reflection on practice. Focused inquiry is a way of collecting data about learners and the learning context, and determining what teaching practices might provide the most meaningful and productive learning experiences for students. Directed observation is a process for bringing attention to a particular aspect of teaching and learning in order to develop deeper under-standing. Guided practice engages candidates in the enactment and assessment of learning experiences that have been specifically designed for particular learners. This contextualization of practice brings together academic knowledge of subject matter and pedagogy with knowledge of particular students and engages candi-dates in constructing deep understanding of how to best facilitate learning for the particular students being taught. Guided practice in a sociocultural clinical context engages candidates in learning with and from peers, expert practitioners and the students they teach.

Developing carefully guided clinical experiences of the kind needed for learn-ing to contextualize teaching practices will require significant changes in many preservice teacher preparation programs. According to the NCATE Blue Ribbon Panel, "First, the very focus of teacher education programs needs to be redesigned from beginning to end" (p. 2). The NCATE Blue Ribbon Panel emphasized the need for making a direct and explicit connection between preservice teacher preparation and P–12 student learning outcomes. Subsequently, the NCATE/ Council for the Accreditation of Educator Preparation (CAEP) in new standards for the accreditation of educator preparation programs have incorporated the requirement that candidates provide evidence of a positive impact on P–12 stu-dent learning during clinical practice and that preservice program providers pres-ent evidence that program graduates demonstrate a positive impact on student learning as classroom teachers. New preservice teacher performance assessments adopted by states across the nation require that candidates demonstrate readiness for teaching by providing evidence of the ability to contextualize knowledge of theory, pedagogy and subject matter in planning and enacting learning expe-riences for particular students. Most new systems of teacher evaluation being implemented in school districts require the use of some measure of impact on student learning outcomes as an indication of teaching effectiveness. This new accountability brings a paradigm shift in our thinking about teaching and preser-vice teacher education from a focus on inputs to a focus on evidence for P–12 student learning outcomes.

In the research and scholarly literature, there are very few models for designing *preservice teacher education programs* that are focused on direct and explicit evidence of the impact on student learning outcomes. Further, Cochran-Smith and Zeich-ner (2005) pointed out that one of the shortcomings in existing research is the dearth of thick and rich descriptions of preservice teacher preparation programs. Many of the studies described in the literature review in the American Educa-tional Research Association's publication *Studying Teacher Education* (2005) were self-studies focused on individual courses or isolated practices within a program. These studies provided important insights into the process of learning teaching practices but did not provide insight into the dynamic interaction among the different parts of the program. Redesigning preservice teacher preparation programs to meet new standards of accountability, especially the impact on P–12 student learning, requires a level of coherence, continuity and consistency not previously expected or typically found in many teacher preparation programs. Examples of factors influencing the stability of the curriculum in preservice teacher preparation include the dependence on adjuncts and part-time faculty, inadequate training for part-time university supervisors for student teaching and different instructors teaching different sections of the same course, with each making personal decisions about the content and learning experiences.

Transforming preservice teacher preparation from where it is to where it needs to be is a very complex process. There is a great deal of research on learning to teach in university-based and alternative teacher preparation programs. However, we have very few examples of how the evidence from these studies and theoretical conceptualizations of aspects of learning to teach have been intentionally linked together or combined in *designing and testing* new models of programs in preservice teacher preparation. *In essence, findings from disparate studies of learning to teach and teacher education practices have not had the level of impact on the design of teacher preparation programs necessary for improving learning outcomes in P–12 schools.* Further, preservice teacher preparation involves participants and stakeholders with different academic and experiential backgrounds, various levels of preparation for professional teaching practice and varying levels of academic knowledge of the research and practice in teacher education. Some of the stakeholders are subject matter specialists, while others have expertise in subject matter pedagogy, and others are practitioners in the field who guide clinical experiences. The NCATE Blue Ribbon Panel (2010) stated that "Clinically based approaches must have the commitment and support of the full complement of stakeholders who need to be involved" (p. 8).

Additionally, while there are very few well-documented examples of excellent preservice programs found in the research and scholarly literature, there is also a shortage of faculty members with the expertise necessary for *leading* the redesign of preservice programs to meet the most recent demands for accountability (Loughran, 2006; Zeichner, 2005). This means that it is very important to develop and make widely available to teacher educators pedagogies, practices and prototypes that will guide the transformation of preservice teacher preparation programs. In this edited volume, the authors provide well-thought-out and theoretically grounded detailed descriptions of preservice teacher preparation programs and theoretical conceptualizations characterized by coherence, continuity and consistency.

The authors provide evidence that the design of each program and each theoretical conceptualization has been carefully crafted on the basis of research on learning to teach and on evidence from practice within each program. In describing each program, the emphasis is on clinical field experiences because this is the particular aspect of the program where candidates learn to integrate academic knowledge with knowledge about P–12 students for the purpose of designing meaningful and productive learning experiences for the students in their charge. Further, guided practice in clinical experiences provides opportunities for faculty to gain insight into the strength of candidates' academic preparation and the propensity for interpreting and translating academic knowledge and knowledge about students into productive teaching practices.

The clinical experiences described in this edited volume are models of good practice in the design of preservice teacher preparation that are presented for more than a contribution to the scholarly literature. These models are not intended for direct replication based on an attempt to preserve some level of fidelity for research purposes. Rather, the purpose of presenting models of good practice is to engage *teacher educator practitioners* in meaningful and productive dialogue in analyzing the design of preservice programs and in developing carefully thought-out and theoretically grounded *local designs* based on research and evidence from practice that take the local context into consideration. The preservice clinical approaches presented in this book provide exemplars for application of the design principles described in the NCATE Blue Ribbon Panel report and research findings from studies of learning to teach.

Organizational Structure of Book

This book is organized into three parts: (1) learning teaching through the representation and approximation of practice, (2) learning teaching situated in context and (3) assessing and improving teacher preparation. In Part I, the authors present three different ways of identifying, representing and examining models of competent teaching and making sense of the essential aspects of the teaching process and the interconnectedness that enables and supports student learning. Each chapter presents a different approach for engaging candidates in observing, planning and enacting aspects of teaching practice and for analyzing student responses to particular practices. In the approaches in this part of the book, the authors describe the experiences candidates need for learning teaching, how the experiences are organized, how the experiences are situated or positioned in relationship to the context and competent teaching practice, and how the experiences are guided and facilitated.

In Part II of this book, the authors focus on learning teaching situated in a particular context. The authors in this part of the book situate learning teaching within the context of classrooms and communities serving urban and low-income students. This situated learning is grounded in a sociocultural perspective on learning and a social justice philosophical stance for envisioning the future for urban and low-income students. This perspective takes into consideration how students learn; how candidates learn teaching; and the sociopolitical relationship among schools, communities and the larger society. This perspective takes into consideration the influence of candidates' early socialization on the ways in which they will appropriate knowledge in practice when facilitating learning for students from cultural and experiential backgrounds different from their own. The authors in Part II present a situated process approach to learning teaching that is historical—where knowledge is cumulative over an interrelated sequence of experiences—and collaborative—where candidates learn from and with peers, expert teachers, students, parents and community members.

In Part III of this book, the authors are concerned with (1) assessing candidates' readiness for teaching and teaching competence, (2) using teaching performance assessments to improve preservice teacher preparation and (3) developing networked improvement communities to advance teacher preparation across the field. The purpose of this part of the book is to carefully examine the demands for accountability for PK–12 student learning and the implications for the assessment of readiness for teaching and teaching competence, along with the potential of teaching performance assessments for improving practices within and across preservice teacher preparation programs. This part of the book builds upon and extends discussions in previous chapters supporting the need for increasing the use of theoretically grounded approaches that provide a carefully designed and developmental sequence of learning experiences that result in candidates having the ability to facilitate learning that generates the expected learning outcomes for students from different cultural and experiential backgrounds.

The second chapter in Part III of this book presents an approach to building a networked improvement community (NIC) for the purpose of addressing the challenges faced by teacher educators in preparing candidates for the first years of teaching. This NIC is focused on capturing practitioner knowledge and placing it into the professional knowledge base, describing the challenges faced in providing adequate preparation for quality teaching, developing an improvement map for preservice teacher preparation, developing a research agenda for improving teacher preparation and developing prototypes for practices in preservice teacher preparation.

The chapters in each part of this book contribute to developing deep knowledge about ways to facilitate learning the teaching process and practices through clinical field experiences that are theoretically grounded, conceptually developed, well-articulated, strategically designed and consistently enacted based on shared understanding among all participants. Each chapter presents a different approach to developing deep knowledge for guiding candidates' growth and development in teaching competence. These different approaches are clearly described and supported with examples from practice. Each chapter clearly delineates the challenges faced in providing carefully guided, meaningful and productive clinical field experiences that are addressed through the approach described.

References

Cochran-Smith, M., & Zeichner, K. (2005). *Studying teacher education: The report of the AERA panel on research and teacher education.* Washington, DC: American Educational Research Association (AERA) and Routledge.

Darling-Hammond, L. (2000). Teacher quality and student achievement: A review of state policy evidence. *Education Policy Analysis Archives, 8*(1). Retrieved from http://epaa.asu.edu/epaa/vol18.html.

Darling-Hammond, L. (2004). Standards, accountability, and school reform. *Teachers College Record, 106*(6), 1047–1085.

Lee, C.D. (1995). A culturally based cognitive apprenticeship: Teaching African American high school students skills in literary interpretation. *Reading Research Quarterly, 30*(4), 608–630.

Loughran, J. (2006). *Developing a pedagogy of teacher education.* New York, NY: Routledge.

McCarty, T. (2002). *A place to be Navajo: Rough Rock and the struggle for self-determination in indigenous schooling.* Mahwah, NJ: Lawrence Erlbaum.

Moll, L.C. (1986). Writing as communication: Creating strategic learning environments for students. *Theory into Practice, 25*(2), 102–108.

Moses, R.P., Kamii, M., Swap, S.M., & Howard, J. (1989). The Algebra Project: Organizing in the spirit of Ella. *Harvard Educational Review, 59*(4), 423–443.

National Council for Accreditation of Teacher Education (NCATE) (2010). Transforming teacher education through clinical practice: A national strategy to prepare effective teachers. Washington, DC: Author.

Zeichner, K. (2005). Becoming a teacher educator: A personal perspective. *Teaching and Teacher Education, 21*(2), 117–124.

ACKNOWLEDGMENTS

This book was initiated through dialogue and collaboration among participants at the Annual Summit on Teacher Education organized and sponsored by the American Educational Research Association (AERA), Division K—Teaching and Teacher Education. The Summit on Teacher Education was originally conceptualized by Etta Hollins when she was AERA vice president-elect for Division K. The intent was to develop collaboration among AERA scholars and researchers whose work focused on teaching and teacher education and constituent organizations focused on policy, practice and setting standards for teaching and teacher education. Arnetha Ball graciously agreed to organize and chair the first two meetings of the summit during her term as AERA vice president for Division K. The Summit on Teacher Education brings together scholars and researchers from AERA and the leaders of constituent organizations for the purpose of identifying and implementing research-based approaches to addressing highly salient issues and problems in teaching and teacher education. The following organizations have been active participants at the Annual Summit on Teacher Education:

American Educational Research Association
American Association of Colleges for Teacher Education
American Federation of Teachers
Association of Teacher Educators
Council for the Accreditation of Educator Preparation
National Association for Alternative Certification
National Board for Professional Teaching Standards
National Education Association
Stanford Center for Assessment, Learning and Equity (SCALE)

U.S. Department of Education
Office of Elementary and Secondary Education
Academic Improvement and Teacher Quality Programs

We wish to express special appreciation to the AERA executive director, Felice Levine, for supporting and hosting the summit at the AERA headquarters and for participating in the dialogue at the summit. Also, we wish to express appreciation to the AERA staff for their work in planning and coordinating the logistics for the summit.

1

URBAN SCHOOLS AS A CONTEXT FOR LEARNING TEACHING

Magaly Lavadenz and Etta R. Hollins

The past two decades have brought increasing public demands and legislative mandates for teacher accountability for student learning and more rigorous curriculum standards at all grade levels in elementary and high schools. These more strident demands for accountability are based on the belief that the condition of public education in the United States has reached the level of a national crisis that threatens the economy and the quality of life for all citizens. This belief is based on evidence from national and international assessments of educational progress and the inability of public schools to prepare students with the necessary competency for jobs in science, technology, engineering and mathematics (STEM).

For example, results from the 2013 National Assessment of Educational Progress showed that only 38% of 12th-grade students scored at or above the proficient level in reading and 26% scored at or above the proficient level in mathematics. Results from the 2012 Program for International Student Assessment (PISA) showed that 15-year-old students in the United States scored lower than their peers in 29 countries in mathematics and scored lower than their peers in 18 countries in literacy (Kelly & Xie, 2013). Further, the failure of public schools in critical areas is evident in the recent action taken by the United States Senate to increase the limit for the number of H-1B guest worker visas from 85,000 to 300,000 for immigrants with at least a college degree and to exempt foreign graduates of U.S. universities with degrees in STEM fields from annual statutory limits on employment-based permanent immigrant visas (green cards). The fact that this legislation was passed at a time when the economy was fluctuating and the unemployment rate was especially high among U.S. citizens fuels this concern (Costa, 2012).

Public schools in the United States have faced an even greater challenge in educating students from low-income groups, ethnic minority groups and students living in urban areas. The National Assessment of Educational Progress (NAEP) 2011 reported results for Grades 4 and 8 in reading as average scores on a 0–500 scale. Only five large-city school districts met or exceeded the national average score of 220 in reading at Grade 4. Only two urban school districts met or exceeded the national average score of 264 in reading at Grade 8. These data showed that African American and Latino students as a group scored well below the national average and well below their white peers in the same school setting. These data are particularly troublesome given present demographic trends indicating an increase in the percentage of underserved and underperforming students across the nation. Data from the NAEP showed that there were over 5 million students attending the nation's elementary and secondary schools. One-fifth of these students were concentrated in five states (California, Florida, Illinois, New York and Texas). In these five states, almost half of the students were low-income and of an ethnic minority.

Demographic shifts in the makeup of the student population in public schools have resulted in a mismatch between the cultural and experiential backgrounds of the students and their teachers. A recent report from the National Center for Education Information (2011) reported that there are 3.2 million teachers educating 49.4 million students in PK–12 schools in the United States (Feistritzer, 2011). This report indicates that 84% of all teachers are white and female and that 31% of all teachers are employed in large-city school districts, where more than half of their students are low-income and of an ethnic minority. Additionally, there is considerable evidence that graduates of preservice teacher preparation programs across the nation feel underprepared for the diverse students in their classrooms (Hollins & Guzman, 2005).

The central challenge facing teacher educators is that of developing learning experiences that are powerful enough to prepare candidates for facilitating excellence in academic performance for students from different cultural and experiential backgrounds. This challenge is grounded in the extent to which teacher educators have (a) deep knowledge of the particular context in which schools are located and the social and academic context within different school settings, especially those serving low-income and urban communities; (b) a shared understanding among faculty within a teacher preparation program of what constitutes competent teaching practice; (c) a deep understanding of the knowledge and skills that support competent teaching practice; and (d) the ability to develop a well-designed and well-articulated approach to learning competent teaching. The focus of this chapter is on making sense of urban schools as the context for learning teaching and introducing approaches to clinical and field experiences that support learning to teach diverse students in different school settings.

The Conditions in Urban Schools

The life conditions for children living in large cities are very different from those for middle-class white children living in the suburbs or small towns—a lifestyle more familiar to the majority of those who enter teacher preparation programs. Children living in large cities are often faced with poverty, homelessness, living outside the home or in foster care placements, acting as caregivers for younger siblings and working to help support the family, and one or both parents may be incarcerated. Many children attending urban schools have cumulative deficits in their academic knowledge and skills due to lack of opportunities for meaningful learning experiences within and outside school. Teachers in large-city schools are often the least experienced and least prepared for teaching students with a different cultural and experiential background than their own. Further, many beginning teachers who have completed typical preservice programs acknowledge feeling unprepared for the complexity of the academic and social context in urban schools. Often, beginning teachers find themselves unable to provide meaningful and productive learning experiences for urban students and unable to keep the students focused on learning (Hollins & Guzman, 2005).

Academic Performance Challenges

While there is concern about the underachievement of the general population of elementary and high school students in the United States, the crisis in urban schools is of much greater concern for many reasons, including the fact that poor academic preparation contributes to widespread poverty, unemployment and crime in urban communities. The poor quality of education provided for urban and low-income students often develops into a persistent multi-generational condition where parents lack the competency for monitoring, participating in or contributing to the educational process for their children. Teachers' ability to facilitate learning for children whose parents lack the skills to contribute to their education varies greatly. A few exceptional teachers are able to foster high outcomes for urban students, regardless of their life situation, their parents' inability to participate or the cumulative deficits in their academic knowledge and skills (MacGillivray, 2009). However, many teachers are unable to facilitate even literacy acquisition and development for the most prepared and eager urban students (Hollins, 2012).

An essential aspect of the problem in schools serving low-income and urban students is limited access to high-quality learning experiences. This situation, which has a devastating impact on student learning, is in part attributable to the content and/or quality of preservice teacher preparation. The disproportionate impact of school conditions on learning outcomes for urban and low-income ethnic minority students when compared with their white middle-class peers is evident in NAEP scores. A comparison of NAEP 2012 reading scores for Grade 8 shows that, on a scale of 0–500, white students had a mean score of 270, while African American and Hispanic students had scores of 247 and 249, respectively (NAEP, 2013). The impact is even greater for English-language learners (ELLs), who now comprise nearly 20% of the nation's student population. National data reveal achievement gaps of 43 points for eighth-grade ELLs when compared with white eighth graders, with ELLs mean score at 233 and their white counterparts' mean score at 266 (Hemphill & Vanneman, 2011). The now-prevalent practice of placing students in special education when they fall behind in developing literacy skills or display behaviors that indicate frustration further limits their access to quality learning experiences and increases their risk of dropping out of school (Artiles, Harry, Reschy, & Chinn, 2002; Artiles, Rueda, Salazar, & Higareda, 2005).

The Social Context in Urban Schools

First-year beginning teachers often find themselves in classrooms with urban students who have a cumulative deficit in their knowledge and skills and who display behaviors indicating high levels of frustration. Some urban students distrust adults and have lost respect for teachers and school administrators. When caught in this situation, it is difficult for novice teachers to figure out how to build relationships with and among students, provide meaningful and productive learning experiences and provide the support students need to begin to correct the deficits in their knowledge base. The results of this situation can be disastrous for the students and the novice teachers (Sipe, 2004).

Sipe (2004) described his experience as a first-year beginning teacher in a dysfunctional urban middle school where the physical and social environments reflected a climate of more a jail than a school and projected oppositional relationships of control and authority. Teachers and students were pitted against each other, and the stress level was high among all participants. Some of the teachers exchanged insults with the students. Most seemed insensitive to the students' life situations or seemed to feel that the students did not deserve better. Most teachers at the school showed little or no commitment to changing the situation or perhaps possessed little knowledge of how to do so. Sipe described the dilemma he faced as "1) . . . falling prey to the inhumanity of the 'us vs. them' mentality and act accordingly; 2) you insulate yourself by refusing to care and bide your time until you can transfer or retire; or 3) the stress gets to you and your mental health suffers" (p. 6). Simultaneously, the district and the state struggled with a litigation appeals process regarding the inadequacy of funding that threatened closure of the school. Ultimately, the court ruled in favor of the district; the school remained open, but Sipe left.

Many first-year beginning teachers face a similar dilemma as that described by Sipe (2004). In this situation, novice teachers and their students are engaged in an ongoing socialization process for induction into the culture of a low-performing school. This means that novice teachers are being socialized into the profession by their colleagues at a low-performing urban school where they are learning to teach and to develop relationships with and among their students. The lessons many of these novice teachers learn will perpetuate the situation in urban schools that promotes a negative social climate and denies access to high-quality learning experiences for the students. The students fail to develop academic knowledge and skills, learn to resent those who denied them access to high-quality opportunities for learning and recognize that the quality of their adult life has been severely and negatively impacted by those they were supposed to trust and respect. This resentment of school and school practitioners may be passed from one generation to the next.

The socialization process that happens in low-performing urban schools is part of the function of schools as the primary socializing institution for the nation. Schools serve as complex microcosms of the macro-level historical patterns of ideologies and practices that intersect in the daily interactions between teachers and students. These ideologies and practices incorporate societal values associated with race, class and gender. For example, Lewis (2011), in a year-long ethnographic study in three schools in southern California, found that schools serve as "race-making institutions through actions that explicitly or implicitly ascribe status, position and power to some students and not others" (p. 190).

Lewis (2011) described a situation in which a teacher denied access to the restroom for one child and not another based on race. This researcher used Bourdieu's theory of cultural capital to explain how schools carry out the function of socialization of the young into existing social norms. Cultural capital refers to socially valued assets that provide access to benefits and privileges available in society. Those with less cultural capital have limited access. Based on this theory, students with high levels of cultural capital have greater access to meaningful and productive learning experiences and thus outperform their peers with less cultural capital. The process of schooling can increase the cultural capital provided for urban and low-income ethnic minority students.

Productive Teaching Practices for Diverse Students

A few school districts and individual schools serving low-income and minority students meet or exceed national and state standards, and there are examples among these schools that perform as well as or better than those with a majority of middle-class white students. There are a few teachers in every low-performing school who elicit excellence in academic performance from their students. These high-performing schools and effective teachers serving urban and low-income students are engaged in everyday practices not found in low-performing schools or in the classrooms of less effective teachers. The everyday practices in high-performing urban schools and classrooms include providing access to high-quality education, such as meaningful and productive learning experiences, building relationships with and among students, building collaborative relationships among colleagues and learning teaching in urban school settings (Hollins, 2012).

The teaching practices that hold promise for providing access to high-quality learning experiences for urban and other underserved students incorporate a particular ideological perspective and related epistemic practices that are grounded in teachers assuming responsibility for the quality of the learning experiences they provide and for the learning outcomes that result. This ideological perspective embraces *differences* among learners as assets for enhancing the depth and breadth of learning rather than as deficits that present barriers to learning. Teachers using this ideological perspective get to know their students well, including the everyday activities in which they engage outside of school, their interests, their values and their cultural practices. This knowledge becomes the fabric for developing meaningful and productive learning experiences that enable students to meet the expected curriculum standards.

There are good examples that apply the assets-based ideological perspective. One example was reported by Moll (1988) in a study of two teachers facilitating literacy acquisition and development for Latino students in an elementary school. These teachers worked from the assumption that the children they taught had the capability to master the curriculum grade-level skills and competencies when supported by appropriate pedagogical practices and social arrangements. The teachers provided the children with a challenging, innovative and intellectually rigorous curriculum where the pedagogy focused on helping the children make meaning from text, regardless of the subject matter. The teachers replaced skills-based basal readers with trade books and allowed the children to choose books that were the most interesting to them. The children were guided in making connections between their personal experiences and what was read in the texts as a way to facilitate reading comprehension. Further, the children were guided in analyzing the strategies they used to understand the text and the strategies the authors used to convey meaning and to elicit particular responses. These metalinguistic and metacognitive activities enabled the students to interpret symbolic language, make inferences based on the texts and to extrapolate.

Moll (1988) found that the teachers' social mediation encouraged the children to be actively engaged in their own learning and supportive of their peers' learning. Children had a great deal of autonomy. They were not grouped by ability; rather, children worked collaboratively on projects and learning tasks with others based on personal interest and choice. Moll (1998) concluded that the teachers were able to provide appropriate, high-quality and meaningful learning for the students because they had managed to create autonomy for themselves as well. These teachers were able to establish such autonomy for themselves because they used theoretically and philosophically grounded approaches that they could explain. The teachers could present persuasive arguments to the school administration that allowed them to make decisions for their classrooms. Additionally, teachers engaged in regular dialogue and collaboration with colleagues and university faculty as a way to analyze and improve their classroom practices.

Robert Moses and his colleagues (1989) faced a similar challenge to that with Latino children in their efforts to make algebra accessible to African American students who had frequently underperformed in math and were denied access to algebra. The approach used in this situation was two-pronged: first, parents were engaged in a process for gaining access to the algebra classes for their students and, second, developing a pedagogical approach that provided access to meaningful and productive learning experiences for African American students that included teaching students to set and achieve learning goals. The students and their parents were frustrated with the lack of access to higher-level mathematics and high-quality instruction. The epistemic practices related to this type of ideological perspective are based on learning experiences that build on what learners know, what they have experienced and what they value. For example, Moses and his colleagues (1989) used techniques from the Civil Rights Movement to engage African American parents in challenging the denial of access to high-quality learning experiences in algebra for students who were traditionally underserved. The result was that traditional requirements for enrolling in an algebra course, such as prior achievement and performance in math, were replaced with motivation to learn and empowering students to engage in self-regulated learning. Traditional teaching practices were replaced with epistemic practices that took advantage of the knowledge that students had already acquired in their everyday experiences.

Teaching practices for introducing sixth graders to algebra involved a five-step process that moved students from the concrete representation of a concept or process to the abstract or symbolic:

1. Physical event
2. Picture or model of this event
3. Intuitive (idiomatic) language description of this event
4. A description of this event in regimented English
5. Symbolic representation of the event.

(Moses, Kamii, Swap, & Howard, 1989, p. 433)

In this approach, a familiar situation or event created a shared experience through which students could learn the new concept and that teachers could use to guide understanding and correct misunderstandings. The students created a picture or model of this event, which served as a concrete illustration of the concept to which they could refer to support their understanding and application of the new concept. In the third step, the children used their everyday language to describe or explain the concept. This allowed the teacher and the students to check understanding and monitor progress. Children were supported in moving from their everyday language usage to a more regimented language, as used in the discipline. Finally, the children were ready to construct a symbolic representation of the concept or process. This represents a very structured and cognitively guided process for constructing mathematical understanding and engaging in mathematical thinking.

McCarty and colleagues (1991) described the implementation of a social studies curriculum that employed an inquiry-based pedagogy with structured questions. This curriculum and pedagogical approach actively engaged Navajo students in learning, whereas they had been previously disengaged and nonresponsive. The researchers concluded that:

> Among the most significant factors in any curriculum's effectiveness is the degree to which it enables students, through their interactions and explorations of content, to use what they know to learn something new. The Rough Rock curriculum does this in two ways. First, its obvious content—the concepts, ideas, and information the curriculum develops—directly reflect and validate students' experiences, encouraging them to draw upon prior knowledge to solve new problems.
>
> (McCarty, Lynch, Wallace, & Benally, 1991, p. 50)

Additionally, the Rough Rock curriculum and instructional practices incorporated Navajo cultural practices, values and perspectives. The approach employed for this social studies curriculum was inquiry-based, with structured open-ended questions. In one fourth-grade class, the students studied the local community by researching local institutions and interviewing community members. In the process, much of the conventional social studies curriculum was addressed. However, the use of an inquiry-based and structured questioning approach mirrored practices for learning experienced by the students in their Navajo community outside of school. For example, when children were first learning to herd sheep, they began by making careful observations, and adults asked specific questions that helped the children make sense of their observations and ensure that important concepts were understood. Further, "in the Navajo view knowledge is not a linear hierarchy, nor a set of skills from which learners and teachers may at any given time pick and choose. Instead, knowledge is a spiraling body of integrated concepts, ideas, and information which support and reinforce each other, continuously expanding to higher levels of complexity and abstractness" (McCarty et al., 1991). This Navajo perspective on the nature of knowledge is well supported in this inquiry approach. This approach supports the Navajo perspective on the communal value of knowledge acquired by individuals as well.

In another example, Lee (1995) investigated having African American high school students use a linguistic pattern from the vernacular commonly found in African American informal language to improve their ability to read and interpret complex literary text. This was a two-step cognitive process that involved, first, recognizing the characteristics and function of the particular language pattern in everyday informal language and, second, learning to apply knowledge of this linguistic pattern when interpreting complex literary text. The particular language pattern chosen for this experience was "signifying"—a form of discourse where the speaker uses figurative and metaphorical language to deliberately elicit a particular response from listeners.

In this study, Lee (1995) first engaged the students in learning to recognize the use of the informal linguistic form of signifying in literature written by African American authors. Texts written by African American authors using the vernacular enabled students to use their background knowledge of cultural expressions and contexts as a basis for making inferences from figurative and metaphorical language. This pedagogical approach was based on a cognitive apprenticeship and employed modeling, coaching and self-monitoring to facilitate student learning. In describing the cognitive apprenticeship, Lee (1995) pointed out that:

> In a cognitive apprenticeship, the teacher models for the student, often verbally, the kind of thinking she or he uses to solve the problem. As the apprentice is engaged in practice, the expert or teacher coaches by commenting on the novice's performance by evaluating, encouraging, and making specific suggestions for improvement or efficiency.
>
> (Lee, 1995, p. 622)

This approach enabled underachieving African American high school students to learn the skills and strategies necessary for interpreting complex literary text written by many different authors.

Mutually Respectful and Supportive Relationships

An important part of teaching in any school setting is developing relationships with students. This is sometimes more challenging in situations where the teacher and students are from different cultural and experiential backgrounds and the teacher knows little about the students. This was the case with Gregory Michie when he accepted his first job as a classroom teacher. Most of the students were African American, and their teacher, Michie, was white. He knew little about the students. Michie (1999/2009) found ways to learn about the students through listening in on their public conversations and engaging the students in dialogue about their own lives and experiences. Michie (1999/2009) described his practice as emphasizing ". . . with one eye all of the hope and possibility I saw in my students and the other on a school system and larger society that seemed intent on 'shutting them in, shutting them down, and shutting them up'" (p. 8). Showing interest in the students and sharing his own life experiences with them enabled Michie to develop mutually respectful and caring relationships.

Other scholars have emphasized listening to students as an important aspect of understanding their perspectives and their needs and as part of building positive relationships and a supportive social context for learning (Hemmings, 2003; Nasir, Jones, & McLaughlin, 2011).

Curriculum Content That Increases Access and Opportunity

Meaningful and productive learning experiences build upon what students know, what they have experienced and what they value. Examples of teachers using knowledge about their students were discussed in a previous section of this chapter that included research conducted by Lee (1995), Moses et al. (1989), McCarty et al. (1991) and Moll (1988). In these studies, teachers used aspects of students' everyday language and social discourse, cultural practices and daily experiences to frame the curriculum and develop learning experiences. These teachers framed the curriculum in ways that allowed students to use what was familiar and of value to them to construct school-required knowledge. These practices are consistent with recommendations made by many conceptual theorists, including Gay (2002), Delpit & Dowdy (2008) and Banks & Banks (1995).

Other scholars have advocated for a more direct use of students' voices in framing the curriculum and developing learning experiences. For example, Nieto (2000) presented an approach for documenting and reporting students' voices in her own work. Nieto (2000) emphasized the use of students' voices as a learning tool for academic, psychological and social development. Thompson (2007) emphasized the value of the authentic student voice in representing their own experiences and ways of constructing and representing new knowledge and re-conceptualizations. Thompson (2007) further argued for the importance of teachers accepting a wide variation in students' language usage and the development of linguistic proficiency.

Finally, teaching urban and underserved students can be challenging when teachers do not have a deep understanding of the cultural and experiential backgrounds of those they teach or when teachers are not attentive to how this knowledge can be used to facilitate learning for their students. The promising practices presented here provide insights into what teachers know and how they use that knowledge to facilitate learning for urban and underserved students. This is essential knowledge for learning to teach students from different cultural and experiential backgrounds.

Learning Teaching in Urban Schools

Learning teaching is a complex process. Differences in the background experiences of teachers and students increase the complexity in learning to teach. Part of the problem with traditional practices for learning to teach is that not enough attention has been given to helping preservice teachers gain a deep understanding of the relationship among teaching practices, student characteristics and learning outcomes. This deep understanding is especially important in developing teaching competence for students from urban and low-income communities. Developing this type of deep knowledge and understanding will require new approaches in preservice teacher preparation. The National Council for the Accreditation of Teacher Education (NCATE) Blue Ribbon Panel (2010) indicated that the process for learning teaching practice needs to be grounded in well-conceptualized and well-designed clinical field experiences and that this requires a total rethinking of present practices in preservice teacher preparation.

Rethinking and redesigning preservice teacher preparation requires examining what is known based on the existing research and scholarly literature. An important resource for examining the research is the American Education Research Association (AERA) Panel on Research on Teacher Education's report on the state of research in the field in its publication titled *Studying Teacher Education* (Cochran-Smith & Zeichner, 2005). The general findings from this analysis of the research in teacher preparation are that results are mixed and inconclusive concerning the most persistent and systemic problems and issues in the field; the majority of the studies were qualitative and tended to be located within a single course or field experience; most did not provide a rich description of the program in which the course or field experience was located; most did not account for the interaction among different program components, courses or experiences across the program; and many of the studies were weak in methodological approaches and theoretical perspectives.

The authors of the AERA Blue Ribbon Panel report further pointed out that research on clinical field experiences shared the weaknesses described in other areas of research in teacher education, but in addition did not provide adequate descriptions of school settings for field experiences, approaches to selecting and preparing cooperating teachers and the relationship between cooperating teachers and university-based faculty supervisors or faculty teaching methods courses. Often, the specific approach to facilitating learning teaching in field experiences was unclear. Particular research on the preparation of teachers for teaching diverse students was similar to that in other areas. Research on prejudice reduction among teacher candidates showed mixed results, and there were very few studies that followed candidates into the field as novice teachers to determine the interplay and impact of their attitudes and beliefs on planning and enacting learning experiences for underserved students. Research on providing candidates with knowledge about teaching diverse students did not include evidence of application in classrooms during clinical field experiences or in their classrooms as novice teachers. These findings make clear that there is a basic need for a theoretically based conceptualization of quality teaching and quality teacher preparation, without which much of the research will continue to fail in advancing the field.

In specifically addressing the research on teaching diverse students, Arnetha Ball and Cynthia Tyson (2011) published an edited volume titled *Studying Diversity in Teacher Education*. This volume builds upon and extends the work of the AERA Panel on Research on Teacher Education. This volume differs from *Studying Teacher Education* in that it presents a historical perspective on teacher education; explains the relationship between research on teaching diverse students and research on teacher education; presents frameworks, perspectives and paradigms for reframing research on teacher education; and presents a new research agenda. Several authors make explicit the entrenchment of traditional perspectives and practices in teacher education. The format used by most authors in this volume is that of synthesizing the literature as the basis for presenting a framework, perspective or paradigm for redesigning teacher education programs and as a way to reframe a research agenda for the field. The authors in this volume clearly delineate the need for clarity on the meaning of quality teaching and learning for students from diverse and traditionally underserved groups.

Re-Conceptualizing Teaching and Learning Teaching

Preparing teachers for urban and underserved student populations requires re-conceptualizing the process for learning teaching and locating clinical/field experiences in schools and communities serving these students. In re-conceptualizing teacher preparation for quality teaching, Hollins (2011) described an active practice-based process that can serve as a model for preparing teachers for urban and underserved students. This practice-based process includes focused inquiry, directed observation and guided practice.

The focused inquiry aspect of Hollins' practice-based approach provides candidates with opportunities for engaging in carefully reading selected texts and in dialogue with practitioners in the field as part of constructing a conceptual framework for making sense of how schools work and for understanding specific aspects of teaching practice. Focused inquiry provides the conceptual framework for directed observations where candidates focus attention on and document particular aspects of the school and classroom context and the related practices that support student academic, psychological and social development. During directed observation, candidates develop habits of mind that support attending to learner characteristics and responses that enable making adjustments in teaching practices to better facilitate student learning. When combined, focused inquiry and directed observation form the framework for and are integral parts of guided practice. Guided practice provides opportunities for candidates to integrate and apply knowledge about subject matter, pedagogy, learning and their students under the careful supervision of a more knowledgeable and experienced practitioner. Hollins (2011) refers to focused inquiry, directed observation and guided practice as epistemic practices for facilitating the process of learning to teach.

These epistemic practices—carried out in an authentic context and guided by a theoretical perspective and a philosophical stance—enable candidates to learn the teaching process. The teaching process consists of planning instruction, enacting learning experiences, interpreting and translating students' responses, adjusting learning experiences as necessary and (re)enacting learning experiences. This re-conceptualization of teaching and learning teaching is an example of the work being done by many scholars and researchers in an attempt to move the field forward in developing high-quality preservice teacher preparation with greater coherence, continuity and consistency. The authors in this book move the discussion forward by introducing more nuanced approaches to learning teaching.

References

Artiles, A., Harry, B., Reschy, D. J., & Chinn, P. C. (2002). Overrepresentation of color in special education. *Multicultural Perspectives, 4*, 3–10.

Artiles, A.J., Rueda, R., Salazar, J.J., & Higareda, I. (2005). Within-group diversity in minority disproportionate representation: English language learners in urban school districts. *Exceptional Children, 71*(3), 283–300.

Ball, A., & Tyson, C.A. (Eds.). (2011). *Studying diversity in teacher education.* Lantham, MD: Rowman & Littlefield.

Banks, C.A.M., & Banks, J.A. (1995). Equity pedagogy: An essential component of multicultural education. *Theory into Practice, 34*(3), 152–158.

Cochran-Smith, M., & Zeichner, K. (2005). *Studying teacher education: The report of the AERA Panel on Research and Teacher Education.* Washington, DC: American Educational Research Association (AERA) and Routledge Press.

Costa, D. (November 19, 2012). *Stem labor shortages: Microsoft report distorts reality about computing occupations.* Washington, DC: Economic Policy Institute (EPI).

Delpit, L., & Dowdy, J.K. (Eds.). (2008). *The skin we speak: Thoughts on language and culture in the classroom.* New York, NY: New Press.

Feistritzer, C.E. (2011). *Profile of teachers in the U.S., 2011.* Washington, DC: National Center for Education Information.

Gay, G. (2002). Preparing for culturally responsive teaching. *Journal of Teacher Education, 53*(2), 106–116.

Hemmings, A. (2003). Fighting for respect in urban high schools. *Teachers College Record, 105*(3), 416–437.

Hemphill, F.C., & Vanneman, A. (2011). *Achievement gaps: How Hispanic and white students in public schools perform in mathematics and reading on the national assessment of educational progress* (NCES 2011–459). Washington, DC: National Center for Education Statistics, Institute of Education Sciences, U.S. Department of Education.

Hollins, E.R. (2011). A vision for teaching practice. *Teacher Education and Practice, 24*(4), 455–457.

Hollins, E.R. (2012). An interpretive process for teaching and learning teaching. A paper presented at the American Educational Research Association, Division K, Summit on Teacher Education, Washington, DC.

Hollins, E.R., & Guzman, M.T. (2005). Research on preparing teachers for diverse populations. In M. Cochran-Smith & K. Zeichner (Eds.), *Studying teacher education: The report of the AERA Panel on Research and Teacher Education* (pp. 477–548). Washington, DC: American Educational Research Association (AERA) and Routledge.

International Association for the Evaluation of Educational Achievement (2012). TIMSS & PIRLS assessments. Chestnut Hill, MA: International Study Center, Lynch School of Education, Boston College.

Kelly, D., & Xie, H. (2013). *Performance of U.S. 15-year-old students in mathematics, science, and reading literacy in an international context: First look at PISA 2012.* Washington, DC: U.S. Department of Education, National Center for Educational Statistics.

Lee, C.D. (1995). A culturally based cognitive apprenticeship: Teaching African American high school students skills in literary interpretation. *Reading Research Quarterly, 30*(4), 608–630.

Lewis, A. (2011). *Race in the schoolyard: Negotiating the color line in classrooms and communities.* New Brunswick, NJ: Rutgers University Press.

MacGillivray, L. (2009). *Literacy in times of crisis: Practices and perspectives.* New York, NY: Routledge.

McCarty, T.L., Lynch, R.H., Wallace, S., & Benally, A. (1991). Classroom inquiry and Navajo learning styles: A call for reassessment. *Anthropology and Education Quarterly, 22*, 42–59.

Michie, G. (2009). *Holler if you hear me: The education of a teacher and his students.* New York, NY: Teachers College Press.

Moll, L.C. (1988). Some key issues in teaching Latino students. *Language Arts, 65*(5), 465–472.

Moses, R.P., Kamii, M., Swap, S.M., & Howard, J. (1989). The Algebra Project: Organizing in the spirit of Ella. *Harvard Educational Review, 59*(4), 423–443.

Nasir, N.S., Jones, A., & McLaughlin, M. (2011). School connectedness for students in low-income urban high schools. *Teachers College Record, 113*(8), 1755–1793.

National Assessment of Educational Progress (NAEP) (2013). *The nation's report card: Are the nation's 12th-graders making progress in mathematics and reading?* Washington, DC: Institute of Education Sciences, U.S. Department of Education.

National Center for Education Statistics (2013). *The nation's report card: Trends in academic progress 2012* (NCES 2013 456). Washington, DC: Institute of Education Sciences, U.S. Department of Education.

National Council for Accreditation of Teacher Education (NCATE) (2010). *Transforming teacher education through clinical practice: A national strategy to prepare effective teachers.* Washington, DC: Author.

National Center for Education Information. Profile of teachers in the U.S. 2011. Washington, DC.

Nieto, S. (2000). Placing equity front and center: Some thoughts on transforming teacher education for a new century. *Journal of Teacher Education, 51*(3), 180–187.

Sipe, P. (2004). Newjack: Teaching in a failing middle school. *Harvard Educational Review, 74*(3), 330–339.

Thompson, G. (2007). *Through ebony eyes: What teachers need to know but were afraid to ask about African American children.* San Francisco, CA: Jossey-Bass.

PART I

Learning Teaching through the Representation and Approximation of Practice

Designing clinical and laboratory experiences for learning teaching requires careful attention to ways of thinking about and making sense of teaching practice, ways of taking it apart and putting it together, ways of representing actions and behaviors that are characteristic of the process and ways of creating meaningful and productive experiences for learning the rules of engagement in teaching practice. Planning productive clinical experiences for candidates requires that teacher educators have a shared understanding of the meaning of essential concepts such as teaching, teaching practice and learning teaching (Lampert, 2010). In this book, *teaching* refers to facilitating the growth and development of students academically, socially and psychologically using conceptual and theoretical knowledge developed for professional practice. Teaching practice refers to the application of a wide range of approaches that facilitate learner growth and development found in the everyday work of academically and clinically prepared classroom teachers. The academic preparation of teachers refers to subject matter knowledge, theory and pedagogical content knowledge that guides teaching practice. Clinical preparation refers to opportunities to apply conceptual and theoretical knowledge to practice in a real classroom setting under the guidance of an experienced and knowledgeable mentor.

Designing clinical and field experiences for candidates in a preservice teacher preparation program requires deep knowledge of teaching, teaching practices and learning to teach coupled with understanding how to make decisions about the nature and sequence of experiences that best facilitate learning teaching. Ultimately, the understanding of teaching practice candidates construct depends on how teaching is represented, the approximations of teaching practice observed and the approaches they enact. Several scholars in the field have addressed issues related to the representation and approximation of approaches for learning teaching. For example, Grossman et al. (2009), in a study across three different professions (the clergy, clinical psychology and teaching), identified three key conceptual elements in pedagogies for the preparation of candidates for professional practice: representations, decomposition and approximations of practice. The central issue is how to make professional practice visible to the novice. In the Grossman et al. (2009) study, decomposition referred to taking practice apart to reveal the essential elements and the relationship among multiple elements that constitute an aspect of professional practice for careful examination by novices. Representation refers to the depiction of an aspect of practice from a particular perspective in terms of approach, form or function for the purpose of examination or enactment. Approximations of practice refer to the extent to which an iteration of a novice's enactment of an approach resembles competent or proficient practice in the field.

The taking apart and representation of practice have been addressed in the scholarly literature in different ways. Lampert and Graziani (2009) described an approach to *ambitious teaching* that supported both teacher educator and teacher candidate learning located within the context of teaching Italian to speakers of other languages. This approach involved several well-designed instructional activities that teacher educators demonstrated and candidates learned to plan and enact. Learning teaching in this way involved videotaping and reviewing candidates' lessons on a closed-circuit television network and "a daily cycle of presentation, demonstration, scaffolded planning, coached rehearsal, teaching, and debriefing" (p. 496). In describing this process, these scholars pointed out particular characteristics:

> These activities embodied the rules of engagement of ambitious teaching by structuring instructional relationships around routines of interaction. The instructional activities specified how teacher, content, and diverse students would interact within work on authentic problems, how materials of instruction would be used, how the space would be arranged, and how the teacher would move around the room. These specifications served as a stable and rehearsable backdrop for the dynamic work of responding to student thinking.
>
> (Lampert & Graziani, 2009, p. 493)

The approach to learning the rules of engagement in the study by Lampert and Graziani (2009) was characterized by collective knowledge building, balancing flexibility and stability and addressing authentic problems of practice. The candidates had opportunities for observation, planning, rehearsing and enacting short segments of instruction and receiving feedback from peers, teacher educators and cooperating teachers. A basic premise for the approach advocated by Lampert and Graziani (2009) is that employing a standard design allows more time for attention to learning teaching practice and to the specific needs of students. The authors in this section of the book address this conceptualization of learning teaching using different approaches. However, one counterargument is that constructing learning experiences based on knowledge of the students, pedagogy, subject matter and a particular theoretical perspective is a more powerful way to support the development of deep knowledge and to meet the needs of particular learners. This second conceptualization of learning teaching is addressed in Part II of this book.

Part I of this book is organized such that one chapter introduces two or more factors that are involved in or that influence clinical experiences for learning teaching, and the next chapter extends the discussion of at least one of these factors, provides a different perspective and introduces two or more related factors not discussed in the previous chapter. Each of the approaches in this part of the book is based on a *cognitive apprenticeship perspective* for learning teaching, where the essential tools are coaching, demonstration, modeling, observation, reflection, rehearsal and self-monitoring.

Chapter 2 in Part I extends the discussion presented in the introduction in Chapter 1 by addressing the historical and contemporary practices, models and structures in preservice teacher preparation, which serve as background information for subsequent chapters. Following a discussion of the variety of approaches to making clinical experiences the focus of teacher preparation that are currently underway across the nation and the issues and problems for which solutions are sought, the discussion turns to the practice of situating coursework in the schools and communities for which teacher candidates are being prepared to teach. In doing so, the authors discuss the rationale used for a greater emphasis on learning to teach in and from practice and some of the potential pitfalls in moving down this path. The authors describe an approach to clinical field experiences that includes the location of university methods classes within the context of urban schools. Rich examples are provided for connections between the methods taught in university-based courses, teaching practices observed in classrooms and opportunities for candidates to plan, rehearse and enact specific practices. This approach is grounded in extensive collaboration and teamwork among faculty and classroom teachers. Further, the authors describe community-based clinical experiences linked to university courses. Examples are presented of the ways that university faculty engage in collaboration with leaders in community-based organizations to develop partnerships for planning and supporting candidates' learning in different contexts within the community.

The authors in Chapter 3 argue for moving beyond partnership arrangements with schools for clinical experiences toward symbiotic and interdependent social and structural arrangements involving entire teacher preparation programs rather than individual courses. These authors describe four teacher preparation programs that situate discussions of learning from coursework, clinical practice and assessment within a system for learning to teach. Rich examples are presented for the clinical experiences provided for learning teaching practice in these programs.

Further, the authors describe how particular approaches such as Montessori and Reading Recovery can form the basis for *focused* clinical practice rather than learning from models of good practice that may be unique to individual teachers, as described in Chapter 2.

In Chapter 4, authors who are representatives of the National Association for Alternative Certification describe five different alternative preservice teacher preparation programs. There is great variability in what might be described as an alternative teacher preparation program. However, the authors of Chapter 4 describe the strengths of many non-traditional programs as "blending practitioner and academic knowledge through intensive clinical experiences; fostering partnerships between districts, schools, program providers and certifying agencies; and promoting rigorous accountability, including the examination of teacher retention, particularly in high-needs areas, student achievement and even students' value-added gains in the classroom." The particular programs described in this chapter subscribe to the Martin Haberman (2011) approach to teacher preparation, which relies on recognizing functions and behaviors of effective teachers and on-the-job mentoring by outstanding teachers rather than relying on educational theories.

In summary, the discussion in Part I is about designing clinical and laboratory experiences as a cognitive apprenticeship for learning teaching that hones and strengthens teaching practice and that enhances and enriches student learning outcomes. At the core of this discussion is the conceptualization of purposeful, powerful and productive experiences for learning teaching. Each conceptualization presents a particular perspective on the process for learning teaching that addresses the representation and approximation of teaching practice needed in experiences for learning teaching, how the experiences are to be organized, how the experiences are to be situated or positioned in relation to the context and shared vision for competent teaching practice, and how the experiences are to be guided and facilitated.

Each chapter presents a different perspective on the essential element(s) in the process of learning teaching. In Chapter 2, the essential element is situating experiences in authentic contexts where methods courses and classroom practices are purposefully linked such that candidates learn the application and adjustment of practice to meet individual and group needs. In Chapter 3, the essential element is the modeling and practice of an established approach to teaching that enables learning the rules of engagement and frees candidates to attend to individual and group needs. The essential element in Chapter 4 is an apprenticeship where candidates attend to the functions and behaviors of effective teachers and in this process learn to adjust practice for individual and group needs. Each of these conceptualizations forms a basis for thinking about the design of clinical and laboratory experiences for learning teaching.

References

Grossman, P., Compton, C., Igra, D., Ronfeld, M., Shahan, E., & Williamson, P.W. (2009). Teaching practice: A cross-professional perspective. *Teachers College Record, 111*(9), 2055–2100.

Haberman, M. (2011). The beliefs and behaviors of star teachers. *Teachers College Record*, www.tcrecord.org ID Number 16504.

Lampert, M. (2010). Learning teaching in, from, and for practice: What do we mean? *Journal of Teacher Education, 61*(1–2), 21–34.

Lampert, M., & Graziani, F. (2009). Instructional activities as a tool for teachers' and teacher educators' learning. *The Elementary School Journal, 109*(5), 491–509.

2

OPPORTUNITIES AND PITFALLS IN THE TURN TOWARD CLINICAL EXPERIENCE IN U.S. TEACHER EDUCATION[1]

Kenneth Zeichner and Marisa Bier

The Current Landscape of Teacher Education in the United States

A teaching force of around 3.6 million teachers teaches in about 90,000 public schools in the United States. Throughout the formal history of teacher education in the United States, there have been a variety of pathways into teaching both inside and outside colleges and universities (Fraser, 2007). Approximately 1,400 colleges and universities are authorized to offer teacher education programs, and despite the tremendous growth in non-college and university programs since the 1980s, about two-thirds of teachers in the United States continue to be prepared by colleges and universities (National Research Council, 2010). Increasingly, a variety of other non-profit and for-profit programs, including school district programs, currently prepare about one-third of the new teachers in the nation each year (Chubb, 2012; Schorr, 2012; Zeichner, 2014). In some parts of the country, however, nearly as many teachers enter the field through non-college and university pathways as through college and university programs (Feistritzer & Haar, 2008), and in at least one state (Florida), school districts are required to have their own teacher education programs (Emihovich, Dana, Vernetson, & Colon, 2011).

Today, despite a growing variety of specific program structures for teacher education (Zeichner & Conklin, 2008), there are three basic ways to become a public school teacher in the United States. First, between 1960 and 1990, colleges and universities had a virtual monopoly on the preparation of teachers. With the exception of emergency credentialed teachers in subjects or geographical areas where enough qualified teachers could not be found (e.g., special education, remote rural schools), almost all teachers entering U.S. public schools entered the teaching force through *college-recommending* programs sponsored by a college or university after completing an undergraduate or post-graduate teacher education program of at least a year in length (Grossman & Loeb, 2008). In these programs, candidates complete the requirements for initial certification prior to becoming teachers of record. Beginning in the 1980s, an increasing number of teachers began to enter the teaching force through *early entry* programs and completed most of their teacher education programs after becoming the teacher of record in a public school classroom fully responsible for students (Grossman & Loeb, 2008).[2] Recently, a third and *hybrid* form of teacher education has re-emerged that is more school-based than the traditional university model, but where there is still a significant amount of preparation and mentoring support before candidates enter the teaching force as teachers of record. The urban teacher residency (UTR)[3] that involves shared responsibility for teacher preparation by different institutions and may or may not involve a substantive role for colleges and universities (Berry et al., 2008) is an example of a hybrid program model (also see Zeichner & Payne, 2013; Zeichner, Payne, & Brayko, 2015). In urban teacher residencies, residents work under the supervision of a mentor teacher and become teachers of record after they complete their residency year.

All of the early entry, hybrid and some of the college-recommending programs occur at the post-graduate level and are 1 or 2 years in length. Most of the preparation of teachers in college-recommending programs takes place at the undergraduate level in 4- or 5-year programs. Education and teacher education in the United States is controlled at the state level, and despite the existence of voluntary national program accreditation requirements and some degree of cooperation among the states, there is significant variation among the states in their requirements for teacher education programs (Levine, 2006; Zeichner, 2011). For example, although most states require some amount of clinical experience before individuals become teachers of record legally responsible for classrooms, the amount of clinical experiences varies greatly (American Association of Colleges for Teacher Education [AACTE], 2013).

In this chapter, we discuss examples of the various kinds of practice-centered models for preservice teacher education that exist in the United States today in the three basic forms of teacher education (early entry, hybrid and college-recommending) and identify some of the central issues that teacher educators are working on in the United States in relation to clinical experiences for prospective teachers. In doing so, we draw on work in which we have been involved at the University of Washington in Seattle (UW) and discuss the practice of moving college and university courses into schools and communities in order to more strategically access the expertise of teachers, community-based educators and local community members in the preparation of urban teachers. Although it is clear that some of what teacher candidates need to learn to begin teaching can be acquired outside the elementary and secondary classrooms for which they are being prepared, it is also clear from several decades of research on teacher learning that a number of critical elements of professional practice can only be learned in the context of real or simulated classrooms under the guidance of strong mentoring (Ball & Cohen, 1999; Feiman-Nemser, 2010).

In 2010, the National Council for Accreditation of Teacher Education (NCATE) Blue Ribbon Panel on Clinical Preparation and Partnerships issued a widely discussed report calling for teacher education to be turned *upside down* and for making clinical practice the central focus of preparation (NCATE, 2010). This was followed by similar calls from the national organization of the Council of Chief State School Officers (CCSSO, 2012) and the two national teacher associations (American Federation of Teachers, 2012; National Education Association, 2011). In response, there have been a number of efforts involving programs throughout the country to improve the quality of clinical teacher education and its connections to the rest of the preparation programs. Before examining some of these efforts, we will provide a brief overview of some of the major issues that teacher educators have tried to address in this work.[4]

Issues and Problems in U.S. Clinical Teacher Education

The clinical education for teachers that exists today in the United States is highly varied in its characteristics and quality (Clift & Brady, 2005; NCATE, 2010; National Research Council, 2010). It consists of experiences for varying lengths of time in schools, in designed settings such as virtual classrooms and in community settings (Grossman, 2010). The quality of school placements, the frequency and quality of mentoring, supervision and coaching, the degree of connection between the clinical experiences and the other parts of the preparation program and the overall degree of monitoring of the quality of the experiences varies greatly within and across programs (Grossman, 2010; Zeichner, 2010a).[5]

The Lack of Coordination of Coursework and Clinical Experiences

Historically, one of the major problems in teacher education within the dominant college-recommending model has been the lack of coordination between coursework and clinical experiences. Although most college-recommending programs include multiple clinical experiences over the length of their programs and often situate these experiences within some type of school and university (and sometimes community) partnership, the disconnect between what teacher candidates are taught in their courses and their opportunities to learn to enact these practices in their clinical placements is often very great, even within professional development and partner schools (Bullough, Hobbs, Kauchak, Crow, & Stokes, 1997; Zeichner, 2010b).[6]

For example, it is very common for the cooperating/mentor teachers with whom teacher candidates are placed to know very little about the specifics of the courses that teacher candidates take in their program, and the instructors of the courses often know very little about the classrooms where teacher candidates are placed for their clinical work (Zeichner, 1996). Even when school and university teacher educators are aware of each other's worlds, they do not necessarily share a vision of quality teaching and teacher preparation. As a result of this lack of a shared vision and common goals, the usual ways in which placements are determined and the structure of the cooperating/mentor teachers' roles, teacher candidates frequently do not have opportunities to observe, try out and receive detailed feedback on their teaching of the methods they learn about in their coursework.[7] Even if the teaching practices that are taught in the courses exist in the classrooms where candidates are placed, candidates do not necessarily gain access to the thinking and adaptive decision-making processes of their experienced mentors (Hammerness et al., 2005; Zeichner, 1996), who are usually greatly undercompensated and underprepared and supported for the complex and important work they are expected to do in mentoring prospective teachers (Zeichner, 2010b).

The frequent lack of opportunities to practice and receive feedback on teaching methods that are addressed in courses is, in part, a reflection of the power and knowledge relations that exist in many programs that devalue the role of teachers and other K–12 educators in defining the meaning of good teaching practice (Cochran-Smith, 1991). In some of the newly re-emerged hybrid forms of teacher education where responsibility for teacher preparation is shared to varying degrees by schools and universities, there is sometimes more of a joint construction of the meaning of good teaching practice, and the "gap" is smaller (Zeichner & Payne, 2013).

The hybrid models such as teacher residencies that focus on preparing teachers for specific school districts and claim to "wrap coursework around practice" do not necessarily lead to the kind of shared vision and cohesiveness that is an important element of good teacher education programs (Gatti & Catalano, 2015).[8] There are dangers associated with too much congruency between coursework and clinical work that should be kept in mind, including limiting the ability of teacher candidates to envision alternatives to current practices (Buchmann & Floden, 1990).

Uneven Mentoring and the Under-Resourcing of Clinical Experiences

In addition, the quality of mentoring and assessment of the work of teacher candidates in school and community placements is highly variable, and it is more common than not that very little preparation and continuing support are provided to cooperating/mentor teachers and program supervisors (Grossman, 2010; Hamel & Jaasko-Fisher, 2011; Valencia, Martin, Place, & Grossman, 2009). Even when this professional development is provided, the underfunding of clinical teacher education often undermines the capacity of supervisors and mentors to support teacher candidates. This under-resourcing of clinical teacher education leads to higher numbers of candidates being supervised by mentors/supervisors and has become a greater problem in recent years, as the public universities where most teachers in the United States are still educated have lost significant amounts of financial support from their states (Newfield, 2008).

Although there have been some opportunities over the years for teacher educators to obtain external funding from state and federal governments and private foundations to support innovation in clinical teacher education (e.g., Sykes & Dibner, 2009), the long-term investment in carefully planned clinical teacher education prior to the assumption of responsibility for a classroom is disappearing. With the exception of the teacher residency model, the federal government and foundations have increased support to *fast-track* programs, where there is often little or no *preservice* clinical experience (Levine, 2012; Rotherham, 2008; Suggs & deMarrais, 2011).

Over time, and especially in recent times with the disinvestment of states in public universities[9] where most teachers in the United States are prepared, there is little evidence of programs being able to sustain the innovations that were initially supported by external funding. Because the federal government has seriously considered phasing out the Teacher Quality Partnership grant program that has supported many innovative efforts in clinical teacher education, including urban teacher residencies (AACTE, 2010; Rennie Center for Education Research & Policy, 2009), the extent to which these efforts will be sustained is not clear.

There are clearly links between efforts to shorten initial teacher education through early entry and UTR programs and efforts to reduce the role of colleges and universities in teacher preparation and to open the preparation of teachers up to other providers. These efforts to deregulate teacher education and to create a market economy (Chubb, 2012; Gatlin, 2009) are closely linked with efforts by the federal government and venture philanthropists to deregulate and privatize K–12 education (Saltman, 2010; Zeichner, 2014; Zeichner & Pena-Sandoval, 2015). A number of new non-university teacher education programs like the Relay Graduate School of Education and MATCH Teacher Residency (Burris, 2012; Schorr, 2012) have recently emerged to prepare teachers specifically for charter schools.[10]

One prominent feature of a number of these new non-university teacher education programs like Relay that have been funded by venture philanthropists to "disrupt the teacher education market"[11] and to provide space for new programs is that they focus on a narrowly defined vision of teaching as management that is primarily aimed at raising student standardized test scores. In fact, in some of these programs like Relay and the Urban Teacher Center, candidates cannot complete the program until they are able to raise student test scores by at least 1 year. Absent from these programs that focus heavily on classroom management moves (e.g., from Lemov, 2010) is attention to a more professional vision of teaching that involves preparation to help students achieve a broader range of outcomes beyond good scores on standardized tests in literacy and mathematics. The preparation of teachers to know the communities in which they teach, to develop their relational and cultural competence and how to thoughtfully adapt their teaching to meet the constantly changing needs of their students are not discussed in the literature on these "new-generation" teacher education programs (e.g., Kronholz, 2012; Schorr, 2012).

The Marginal Status of Clinical Teacher Educators

In university programs, the educators who currently provide the mentoring and assessment of teacher candidates' work in the field are often adjunct faculty or doctoral students with low status and little decision-making authority in the institution. There is frequent turnover among these supervisors, and they often feel that they are accorded second-class status in the program in comparison with research faculty (Bullough, Draper, Smith, & Burrell, 2004). When permanent tenure-line faculty are involved in field supervision, this work often does not count in their teaching load and is not valued highly in the reward system that exists in most universities (Labaree, 2004).

Additionally, the elementary and secondary teachers who serve as school-based mentors for teacher candidates in many clinical experiences are expected to do the important work of mentoring in addition to their full-time teaching loads, and this work is not usually highly valued in the reward systems in many school districts.

Building the capacity of schools to host teacher candidates for their clinical experiences and developing the capacity of teachers to be high-quality mentors must be priorities if we are serious about making clinical experiences the central aspect of teacher education. In 1963, James Conant, in his widely influential study of teacher education in the United States, identified clinical experiences as the "one indisputably essential element in professional education" (p. 142). In outlining what he felt was needed to achieve high quality in these experiences, Conant emphasized the need to carefully select, prepare and develop the mentoring abilities of the K–12 teachers in whose classrooms teacher candidates are placed for their clinical work. He also advocated that these teachers be adequately compensated and that their workloads reflect the additional responsibilities they have assumed as teacher educators.

> Public school systems that enter into contracts with a college or university for practice teaching should designate, as classroom teachers working with practice teaching, only those persons in whose competence as teachers, leaders, and evaluators they have the highest confidence, and should

give such persons encouragement by reducing their work loads and raising their salaries.

(Conant, 1963, p. 212)

As Conant (1963) suggested, careful attention must be paid to both the selection of mentor teachers and the ways in which they are compensated in order to elevate their professional status and the rigor of their work. A number of countries, such as Australia, Finland and the Netherlands, provide additional resources and supports to the schools and teachers that work with teacher candidates during their clinical experiences and provide models for what can be done in the United States to enhance the capacity of both schools and mentors to support high-quality clinical teacher education (Darling-Hammond & Lieberman, 2012). None of the reform initiatives in teacher education in the United States since Conant's 1963 analysis (e.g., professional development schools, urban teacher residencies) has yet addressed these structural and resource issues in clinical teacher education in ways that can be sustained beyond temporary grant funding. The UTR literature discusses the potential of program sustainability beyond initial grant funding through the reallocation of school district funds that will allegedly become available as a result of greater alignment between the initial preparation and district frameworks and initiatives and greater teacher retention (e.g., Berry et al., 2008), but residencies have not been around long enough to determine if these predictions will be realized.

A further issue involved in undermining the opportunities for teacher candidate learning during clinical experiences is the frequent lack of a curriculum (similar to the curriculum that exists for all courses) that lays out a well-thought-out plan for how opportunities to learn for teacher candidates will be created over the course of the clinical experience and how the needs of teacher candidates for learning to teach can be addressed over the course of a clinical experience and coordinated with the primary classroom mission of promoting pupil learning (Feiman-Nemser & Buchmann, 1985; Turney, Eltis, Towler, & Wright, 1985).

There is also widespread consensus that the selection of classrooms as sites for clinical experiences has not been very effectively carried out in many programs (Greenberg, Pomerance, & Walsh, 2011; NCATE, 2010) and that the increased accountability pressures on schools around pupil test scores, together with the meager compensation provided for mentoring, have complicated the task of locating high-quality placements for many teacher candidates (Anderson & Stillman, 2011). For example, Ronfeldt (2012) refers to the growing movement to use student standardized test scores as a part of teacher evaluation and compensation that has resulted in a growing reluctance among teachers and principals in schools affected by these policies to turn over responsibility of their classrooms to teacher candidates.

Despite all of these problems, there is evidence of a great deal of activity across the country to focus attention on improving the quality of clinical teacher education in all three pathways into teaching. We now provide an overview of some of the major aspects of the current turn toward teaching practice and clinical experience and reflect upon the future for clinical teacher education in the United States.

Examples of Efforts to Raise the Quality of Clinical Teacher Education in the United States

The 2010 NCATE report asserts that the preparation of teachers must "move to programs that are fully grounded in clinical practice and interwoven with academic content and professional courses" (p. ii). A variety of models for practice-based teacher education exist in which attempts are made to more closely link coursework with school-based experiences. They include programs that: (a) create designed settings to provide "a sheltered opportunity for prospective teachers to engage in targeted practice of clinical skills" (Grossman, 2010, p. 2),[12] (b) provide early entry into the classroom in an effort to prepare teachers largely on the job, (c) include hybrid university-based teacher education programs like urban teacher residencies that focus on preparation for specific contexts and that are largely situated in schools and (d) shift college-recommending programs into schools and communities.

One of the major aspects of the current turn toward clinical teacher education in the United States is a return to a focus in all of the various pathways into teaching on more strategically teaching prospective teachers how to enact particular teaching practices that are thought to enhance student learning (Zeichner, 2012). One strand of these efforts in the United States is to identify and teach *core* teaching practices associated with particular conceptions of *ambitious teaching* as the central focus of a teacher education program. The teaching of these practices is often embedded in relation to the teaching of specific school subjects (e.g., Ball & Forzani, 2009; Windschitl, Thompson, & Braaten, 2011) and claims to draw on research that has identified certain teaching practices that enhance student learning. Other strands of this work focus on teaching particular instructional and classroom management strategies that are not tied to particular subject matter areas or grade levels (e.g., Danielson, 2007; Lemov, 2010). In reality, there is a great deal of variability in the empirical warrant for these various models of effective teaching (Pianta, 2011).

There is also a big difference in the conceptions of teaching that are associated with these different efforts to teach core teaching practices. Some of this work is focused solely on equipping teachers with classroom management skills to foster better student performance on standardized tests (e.g., Gatti & Catalano, 2015), while other aspects of this work are focused more broadly on supporting richer and more successful student learning in a broader way. Anderson and Stillman (2013) contrast three alternative views of teaching in relation to clinical teacher education: teaching as management, teaching as the performance of particular pedagogies and strategies and teaching as the facilitation of student learning. All of these varieties are found within the current movement to teach teacher candidates how to enact core teaching practices in teacher education programs.

Periodically, throughout the history of formal teacher education in the United States, there has been a renewed focus on the enactment of particular teaching practices in American teacher education programs. Although the current incarnation of this trend differs in a number of significant ways from efforts of the past, it shares the intent to make teaching practice the center of teacher education (Zeichner, 2013).

Clinical Experience in Designed and Virtual Settings

In addition to placing teacher candidates in school and community settings for clinical experiences, teacher educators have also been involved in creating simulations of classroom practice within courses or connecting their courses to the practices of good teachers through technology. Grossman (2005, 2010, 2011) discusses various aspects of this work to create "laboratories" for clinical teacher education (Berliner, 1985), including the "microteaching" movement in the 1970s (Grossman, 2005) and current efforts to make the thinking and practices of teachers who are using particular teaching practices more visible to teacher candidates through technology. The Carnegie Foundation–funded Quest Project, where teacher educators used the Web pages created by K–12 teachers in their teacher education methods courses, (insideteaching.org) is an example of this work.

In the Quest Project, Pam Grossman, a teacher educator at Stanford University, created a website where she documented how she incorporated the website of an experienced Los Angeles high school English teacher (Yvonne Divans Hutchinson) in her English methods course. One aspect of this work focused on the task of engaging students in text-based discussions of literature. In addition to reading academic literature on this topic, teacher candidates utilized Hutchinson's website, which includes images of her leading discussions around text in which students were very engaged, interviews with Hutchinson and statements by her students, as well as examples of student work and methods and materials that Hutchinson used to prepare her students for discussions. This utilization of the work of a master Los Angeles teacher is an example of how Grossman made explicit connections between what teacher candidates were learning in theory and how it was enacted in practice in an actual classroom. The experience allowed teacher candidates to understand student learning related to the effective use of particular teaching practices.

The Rise of Early Entry Programs

Over the last two decades, there has been tremendous growth in *early entry* programs that place novices in classrooms as teachers of record with very little preparation beforehand. Most teacher learning in these programs takes place while teachers are fully responsible for classrooms and relies heavily on the quality of mentoring that is provided by the program and the school district. Examples of early entry programs that have received substantial support from foundations and the federal government include Teach for America (TFA)[13] and the New Teacher Project (now TNTP) founded by Michele Rhee, a graduate of TFA and a former superintendent of the Washington, DC, schools. This project sponsors *teaching fellows* programs in over 25 major U.S. cities. Early entry teachers typically receive full beginning teacher salaries while they complete their preparation program.

These and other early entry programs typically include a brief summer institute for a few weeks prior to the beginning of the academic school year and then the assumption of full responsibility as a teacher for 1 or 2 years. During the 1 or 2 years in the program, the novice teachers who usually do not have any background in education continue to complete coursework that will qualify them for a state teaching license, and an experienced teacher mentor provides on-site support and guidance.[14] Early entry teachers complete their certification requirements in college and university or school district programs or in those sponsored by other non-profit or for-profit entities. In New York State, New Orleans, Houston, Chicago and Newark, NJ, for example, many TFA teachers currently complete their certification requirements through the Relay Graduate School of Education, an independent, normal, school-like program that prepares teachers. The Relay Graduate School of Education (Kronholz, 2012) is part of a growing trend throughout the nation for charter school networks to prepare their own teachers in new, largely school-based programs that operate outside of the dominant university teacher education system.[15]

In early entry programs, individuals are usually required to make a commitment to teach in an urban or rural school in a high-poverty community for 1 or 2 years. For most of the teachers who enter the teaching force through one of the *fast-track* or early entry programs, most of the preparation occurs while these novice teachers are teachers of record fully responsible for a classroom in poor urban and rural communities (Darling-Hammond, 2004; Peske & Haycock, 2006). They are not found in public schools teaching students from the middle and upper-middle classes—the children of many of the advocates of the deregulation of teacher education.

Although the research on the effects of different pathways to teaching is not conclusive and has shown greater variability within types of pathways than across pathways (e.g., Constantine et. al., 2009; Decker, Mayer, & Glazerman, 2006; Heilig & Jez, 2010; National Research Council, 2010; Zeichner & Conklin, 2005), there is some evidence of a "learning loss" by pupils, as underprepared beginning teachers of record are catching up with teachers who completed all of their preparation for an initial teaching license prior to becoming responsible for classrooms (Zeichner & Conklin, 2005). Although there is a diversity of perspectives about the meaning of the research on different pathways into teaching, it is clear, given the high turnover of teachers in the most poverty-impacted schools (e.g., American Federation of Teachers, 2007; Lankford, Loeb, & Wyckoff, 2002), that the communities in which the schools staffed by many early entry teachers are located have become dependent on a constant supply of early entry teachers who stay for a few years and then leave.

The current teacher education system does not help these communities to develop the capacity to have access to a more experienced teaching staff in its schools and to lessen their dependence on inexperienced and underprepared teachers. Given the documented importance of teacher experience in teaching quality (e.g., Ronfeldt, Loeb, & Wyckoff, 2013), this is a serious problem of injustice for many poor communities. There is evidence that there are alternative approaches to preparing teachers for high-needs schools that are effective in bringing more fully prepared teachers into these schools and keeping them there over longer time than is typical (e.g., Berry et al., 2008; Skinner, Garreton, & Schultz, 2011). Any effort to assess the efficacy of different teacher education programs needs to take into account a full range of learning outcomes, including, but not limited to, standardized test scores and the retention records of teachers from different programs.

Urban Teacher Residency Programs

In 2004, Tom Payzant, then-superintendent of public schools in Boston, gave an invited plenary address at the national meeting of the major teacher education organization in the U.S.: the American Association of Colleges for Teacher Education. The title of his talk was "Should teacher education take place at colleges and universities?" In this talk, Payzant complained about the quality of the teachers his district was getting from the many colleges and universities in the Boston area and threatened that if college and university teacher education did not improve the quality of their programs, he would start his own program within the Boston schools. Soon after, the largely school-based Boston Teacher Residency Program was opened as one of the first UTR programs in the United States (Berry et al., 2008). As pointed out previously, however, the UTR is a new name for a type of program rather than a new program model. Largely school-based programs that prepare teachers to teach in specific school districts with a supervised year-long clinical experience have been around for many years and have re-emerged rather than emerged in urban teacher residencies.

Currently, the U.S. Education Department is promoting the UTR model, and many teacher residencies are starting up across the country with federal and private financial support. In 2009–2010, the U.S. Education Department allocated $143 million to support the start-up of 40 new teacher residencies. Additional teacher residency programs were funded in the 2014 Teacher Quality partnership awards of 35 million dollars. In addition, a new organization has emerged with significant funding from private sources to support the development of residencies: Urban Teacher Residencies United.[16]

Although the specific designs of UTR programs across the country differ, they all provide a structure that falls between the fast-track program that places novices in classrooms as teachers of record with little preparation and traditional college and university programs where candidates complete all of their initial preparation before assuming responsibility for classrooms. Aspiring teachers—known as residents—are selected according to rigorous criteria aligned with the needs of particular school districts to participate in a 1- or 2-year program. During the program, the goal is to integrate coursework with an intensive, full-year classroom residency alongside an experienced mentor. According to an Aspen Institute report (Berry et al., 2008), "UTRs seek to:

- Tightly weave together education theory and classroom practice
- Focus on residents learning alongside an experienced, trained mentor
- Group candidates in cohorts to cultivate professional learning communities and foster collaboration
- Build effective partnerships among school districts, higher education institutions and nonprofit organizations
- Serve school districts by recruiting and training teachers to meet specific district needs
- Support residents once they are hired as teachers of record
- Establish and support differentiated career goals for experienced teachers" (p. 4).

The UTR model can potentially contribute to urban schools where teacher attrition is high and student learning and teacher experience are low by providing teachers who are well-prepared to work in those communities and committed to staying in them for a longer duration than is typically reported for graduates of early entry and college-recommending programs. Berry et al. (2008) propose that residencies are an important approach that policymakers, practitioners and the public should consider in their efforts to ensure that they have a teaching workforce that is ethnically and racially diverse and prepared to succeed. They suggest that districts need to consider the full array of options and make informed decisions about how they invest in teachers and teaching.

UTRs are currently based in many cities across the nation (e.g., New York, Los Angeles, Chicago, Denver) and look different in different places in terms of how they are designed and implemented. Yet they are guided by a common set of principles that define the components of a high-quality residency program, inform the design of new residencies and distinguish teacher residencies from other kinds of preparation programs. These principles include tightly woven clinical experiences as the central program element, with a focus on wrapping coursework around this practice, learning alongside an experienced mentor, and alignment between the curriculum of the residency program and the frameworks and practices used in particular districts. In addition, support is provided to residents in the first few years following the completion of their residency. Guided by these principles, programs such as those in Newark, New York and Chicago offer different applications of the UTR model, but all pair master's-level pedagogical training and education content with a rigorous full-year classroom practicum under the supervision of expert teachers who have been trained to mentor novices and are compensated at a much higher level than is common in college-recommending programs.

Thus far, there is some research that has demonstrated that urban teacher residences help create a more ethnically and racially diverse teaching force and increase teacher retention in urban schools impacted by poverty. There is very limited evidence to date, however, about the ability of UTR-prepared teachers to raise student achievement (e.g., Papay, West, Fullerton, & Kane, 2011).

Moving College-Recommending Teacher Education into Schools and Communities

Following about a decade of activity to develop school–university partnerships in teacher education through the development of "professional development schools" (Boyle-Baise & McIntyre, 2008)[17] and in response to recent national calls to place more emphasis on school-based teacher learning (e.g., National Commission on Teaching and America's Future, 2010), there are currently a number of university-based programs that are adopting a more situated approach to teacher education and moving instruction more into schools and communities where university instructors work side by side with practicing teachers in preparing teacher candidates (e.g., Noel, 2013). With a focus on context, courses are situated in schools, are planned around existing school curriculum and draw on the expertise that exists within the schools. This structure is not common in typical university-based courses, which are often disconnected from schools and from practices candidates may encounter in their individual field experiences.

At UW, where we both have worked for the past 5 years, some of the methods and foundations courses in the elementary and secondary teacher education programs (both post-baccalaureate certification programs) are taught in local public schools where instructors strategically attempt to connect academic and school-based practices. For example, in addition to the usual practice of professors providing teacher candidates with the theoretical basis for particular teaching strategies, teacher candidates also have opportunities in these courses to observe a classroom in which particular teaching strategies teacher candidates are learning are used with students. They may also have time to plan and rehearse[18] lessons using these strategies that they then go and teach to students. In some cases, there is an opportunity to debrief their teaching with their teaching peers, as well as with the professor and teachers in the school (Lampert et al., 2013).

For example, each section of the elementary mathematics methods class at UW is taught by a faculty member and an experienced teacher in an elementary school classroom in a public school that is partnered with the university. In this course, teacher candidates regularly use small video cameras to record their attempts to try out the teaching strategies they are learning about with individual and small groups of pupils, and they review these tapes as part of the debriefing process. They also submit the tapes to their university instructor, who provides each candidate with feedback several times per quarter. This enables the instructor, who usually is not able to get around to see all of the candidates trying out the teaching strategies each week, to gain an understanding of how each candidate is using the strategies and what they need to work on. When the instructor, her teaching assistants or the classroom teacher are in a small group directly observing candidates practicing specific teaching strategies, they also strategically intervene at times to model particular ways of asking pupils questions to accomplish such goals as eliciting students' reasoning in solving problems.

In this math methods course, the focus is on instructional practices that enable teachers to learn how to teach toward instructional goals as they learn to elicit and respond to students' mathematical ideas, treating students as sensemakers. The goal is to prepare teachers to create classroom learning environments where students are oriented toward each other's ideas and to produce disciplinary practices such as mathematical modeling, reasoning and justification. Teacher educators also want to disrupt long-standing ideas embedded in urban schools about who can and cannot do mathematics and that mathematical success is an exception rather than a rule (Cornbleth, 2010).

The entry point for novice teachers to learn these instructional practices involves supporting them to lead instructional activities that embody the principles, practices and disciplinary knowledge that are important in elementary mathematics teaching. Examples of instructional activities that foster the development of principled practice are: (a) counting and number tasks that engage K–5 students in reasoning about the base-10 structure of the number system and the meaning of the four operations, and (b) posing cognitively demanding word problems so that K–5 students have entry into the task, monitoring student work and orchestrating discussions to meet a specified mathematical goal.

The elementary literacy class at UW is also taught by a faculty member and a teacher in the teacher's partner school classroom. During each session, teacher candidates work with individual children and groups of children, many of whom are English learners. Teacher educators in this course focus on instructional practices that support children's learning in the areas of comprehension, word work and vocabulary. The overarching approach is to help teacher candidates learn to assess children's reading needs, design lessons to meet those needs and then engage in adaptive instruction. Through modeling, simulations, videotapes and classroom observations, teacher educators help teacher candidates build deep conceptual understandings of reading processes and reading instruction and develop a variety of teaching strategies to promote children's learning.

Two teaching practices that are particularly useful in promoting teacher candidate learning in school-based courses are: (a) small-group guided reading, and (b) explicit instruction in word work and comprehension. Both practices require teacher candidates to simultaneously consider students' abilities to decode words and make sense of text. Candidates must also teach in a way that helps students learn to become strategic readers who are able to apply their skills and strategies to new text; at the same time, candidates must develop their own abilities to become teachers who can adapt their practices to meet students' evolving needs.

To learn about children's literacy abilities and development, teacher candidates support classroom teachers by administering *high-leverage* literacy assessments and closely observing students as they engage with reading and writing. In collaborative peer groups and with the support of the course instructor, students analyze children's literacy abilities and then plan and implement appropriate instruction. Debriefing with instructors and colleagues, teacher candidates continually analyze their own teaching and students' learning, using those insights to plan follow-up lessons. They provide feedback to the children's classroom teachers to support the instruction they are designing for children in their classrooms.

The secondary math methods course at UW meets at least six times over a 10-week quarter at a local high-needs partner high school, where teacher candidates, in groups, observe teachers as they instruct their ninth-grade algebra classes. These teachers implement many of the same equity-oriented teaching practices as those taught in the methods course and are often graduates of the UW program. Following the observations, the teacher candidates, university course instructor and classroom teachers meet to debrief the lesson, during which time they examine the relationship between students, mathematics and particular teaching practices. Further, during these debriefing meetings, the teacher candidates have opportunities to ask questions of the teachers about the students they observed and about particular teaching decisions that may have been made. In this particular version of a practice-based methods course that comes in the first quarter of a four-quarter master's program, teacher candidates do not have opportunities to try out the practices themselves. This comes during the second methods course, when teacher candidates enact the strategies with students in their practicum classroom and then carefully analyze them with their mentors and supervisors and in their campus-based methods course (Campbell, 2008, 2012).

For several years, secondary language arts methods at UW were taught entirely in a partner middle school. The class is completely immersed in the culture of the school and exposed to the typical occurrences that randomly happen during a school day (fire drills, people walking in and out of their classroom), as well as being privy to frequent discussions with expert educators within the school. The course also provides multiple structured opportunities for teacher candidates to learn about particular teaching practices. Typically, teacher candidates are instructed in particular reading and writing strategies and then work with small groups and individual students in a language arts classroom in the school, making use of those strategies to support students. The candidates then come back together as a group to debrief the experience of implementation.

In looking specifically at understanding text, teacher educators engage candidates in a diverse set of activities that they can use in their own classrooms to provide all students with access to text. One practice that is focused on is eliciting and responding to student ideas. Teacher educators engage candidates in this core practice through think-aloud/read-aloud activities. They show candidates representations, model, collaboratively plan with them and engage candidates in rehearsals before enactment in their placement classrooms. After the enactment, teacher educators support teacher candidates in reflecting about their practice and student learning.

Teacher candidates also learn multiple ways to support student meaning-making through text discussions. In discussions, teacher educators model for candidates how to ask questions that probe student understanding and support student participation. Candidates learn how to create a discourse community where students feel comfortable disagreeing, agreeing and furthering others' ideas by using the text and their lived experiences. The teacher candidates prepare for whole-class discussions by using a mentor text. Each candidate develops questions that support the deeper understanding of a particular chapter, and each candidate presses his or her peers to develop further questions.

Thus far, there is limited evidence about the value of these school-based courses and collaborative teaching by university and K–12 educators. There is some evidence that the learning and ability to enact the teaching practices by candidates is greater in this model than when coursework is offered in university classrooms. There is also some evidence of the power of situating instruction in the context of a classroom to disrupt teacher candidates' low expectations for the learning of students in high-needs urban schools (e.g., Campbell, 2012).

Clinical Experiences in Communities

In addition to teacher candidate learning in school-based clinical experiences, for many years some teacher educators in the United States have advocated for placing teacher candidates for periods of time in the broader communities in which schools are situated (e.g., Flowers, Patterson, Stratemeyer, & Lindsey, 1948). These experiences have varied greatly in their purposes and in the activities in which teacher candidates are engaged. For example, some experiences have focused on service learning or on learning about how students learn in settings outside of school, while others have emphasized learning about the resources and practices in the community and learning from adults in the community (e.g., Boyle-Baise & McIntyre, 2008; Mahan, 1982; Zeichner & Melnick, 1996) so that candidates can learn to teach in more culturally responsive ways (Lucas & Villegas, 2011).

These experiences can be short-term in a single course and/or community that may be characterized as visiting a community, or they can be longer and more intensive, which may be thought of as immersing preservice teachers in local communities. Some programs are elective, such as Indiana University's cultural immersion programs, which provide opportunities for student teachers to work in local schools in other countries and within diverse communities in the United States (Longview Foundation, 2008). Other community experiences are required portions of teacher education programs in addition to or linked to school-based experiences (e.g., Zeichner, Payne, & Brayko, 2015). Despite repeated calls over many years for clinical teacher education to be broadened into local communities, very few early entry, college-recommending and now hybrid programs like urban teacher residencies have done so. Some empirical evidence exists about the transformative power of community-based learning for prospective teachers in helping teacher candidates become more interculturally competent and teach in culturally responsive ways (Boyle-Baise & McIntyre, 2008; Sleeter, 2008).

At UW, we are developing community strands in our elementary, secondary and teacher residency programs that include a variety of clinical experiences in the communities in which teacher candidates are teaching in their year-long program. In each quarter of both our elementary and secondary programs, the community work is linked to particular courses and school-based clinical experiences, and although the specific purposes of the community work vary each quarter, the goal underlying the work across the programs is to develop "community teachers" who are knowledgeable of the communities in which they teach and are aware of the resources and funds of knowledge in those communities that can be accessed in their teaching (Murrell, 2001). In partnering with community-based organizations (CBOs), we are deepening relationships with CBO leaders and building an understanding of their work as educators in out-of-school settings. We are also working with local community members, leaders and civil rights activists as teacher educators and asking them to share their diverse perspectives on the schools where they send their kids and grandchildren and the kind of teachers they hope they experience. These and other community experiences (e.g., training and experience in home visits) for teacher candidates have provided them with insights that can support the enactment of more culturally relevant teaching practices and support the development of the kind of teacher commitment to the urban neighborhoods in which they work that is important to school success for urban students (Ladson-Billings, 1994).

Conclusion

There is widespread agreement in the United States that providing high-quality clinical experiences to teacher candidates is the key element in providing effective teacher preparation and that many individuals entering the teaching force in the United States do not have access to it now (NCATE, 2010; National Research Council, 2010). While current efforts to build new, more clinically based models for teacher preparation in the United States are needed, there are cautions that should be heeded as this widespread effort moves forward. First, one of us warned in 1980 that the then-national effort to add additional field experiences to largely campus-based university programs needed to give careful attention to the nature and quality of this additional time in schools and its relation to the rest of the preparation program (Zeichner, 1980). What was seen at that time—uncritical glorification of school-based experience and a lack of attention to illuminating the particular design features of these experiences that make them educative—is also characteristic of the current movement. This concern is similar to the concern raised by Ellis (2010) referred to previously that the push to move teacher education more into schools in the UK has often been characterized by impoverished views of the role of experience in learning to teach.

The current literature is filled with discussions of programs that involve more school-based experience in university programs, the development of new school-based programs like urban teacher residencies, hundreds of early entry programs and discussions of the movement of teacher education coursework to school and community settings that imply that merely moving teacher education to schools and communities is necessarily beneficial (Zeichner, 2010b). This literature often does not clearly illuminate the specific ways in which these school- and community-based experiences operate (e.g., what co-teaching between university and school-based teacher educators looks like) and the ways in which particular features of these experiences are connected to various desired outcomes for teacher candidates and the schools. One hopeful sign in this regard is some recent research that seeks to identify the features of clinical placement sites and clinical experience design characteristics that support teacher candidate learning and pupil learning in schools (e.g., Anderson & Stillman, 2011; Cornbleth, 2010; Ronfeldt, 2012).[19]

A second caution has to do with what is eliminated from teacher education programs as they move more to the field. There is some historical evidence that as programs have become more school-based, the focus of the preparation narrows to a more technical focus on the mastery of teaching skills and that important elements of a teacher's education such as multicultural education and the social foundations of education are reduced or eliminated (Greene, 1979; Zeichner,

2014). While the mastery of teaching and classroom management skills and practices is among the most important aspects of teacher preparation, teachers also need to have a clear sense of the social, political, community and cultural contexts in which they work to be able to build and sustain strong relationships with their students, adapt their practice in response to the changing needs of their students and accomplish a host of other things that go beyond the mastery of specific teaching and classroom management practices (Bartolome, 1994; Bransford & Darling-Hammond, 2005). There is a danger that the current wave of emphasizing school-based experience in teacher education in the United States will contribute to further deprofessionalizing teaching rather than strengthening teachers' abilities to teach in culturally responsive ways and to acquire the adaptive expertise that is needed to successfully teach in today's U.S. public schools (Banks et al., 2005; Hammerness et al., 2005).

Finally, as briefly mentioned earlier, one of the major problems in U.S. teacher education in the last 50 years has been the inability to institutionalize and sustain innovations that have initially been funded by private foundations, states or the federal government. There is a whole litany of major efforts to transform teacher education throughout the country, ranging from the National Teacher Corps of the 1960s and 1970s, the Professional Development School movement of the 1980s and 1990s, and the over–$100 million effort led by the Carnegie Corporation Teachers for a New Era that have failed to achieve this transformation to any significant degree (Fraser, 2007). As the public universities and public schools where the majority of teacher education in the United States still takes place have continued to lose their state and federal funding, private foundations have shifted toward funding alternatives to college and university teacher education and promoting charter schools (Levine, 2012; Suggs & deMarrais, 2011)[20] and new resources are needed to implement new and intrusive accountability requirements for teacher education programs (Zeichner, 2011), it is becoming harder to imagine how college and university teacher education programs will be able to transform and sustain clinical teacher education in the ways imagined by the recent national panel (NCATE, 2010).

Currently, there are strong efforts being led by the U.S. Education Department[21] to require an accountability system for teacher education programs in the United States that will involve the use of an enormous amount of resources in creating and implementing a system that rates teacher education programs according to the value analysis of the standardized test scores of the pupils taught by graduates of different teacher education programs (Duncan, 2011). Given the questionable value of this kind of data for evaluating teachers—let alone teacher education programs (Baker et al., 2010; Zeichner, 2011)—it would make more sense in our view to focus these resources on things that will enhance the quality of teacher preparation, such as building the capacity of schools and mentors to support high-quality clinical experiences.

There is a clear and growing presence of private money in steering the course of teacher education policies away from colleges and universities playing a central role and toward the deregulation and privatization of teacher education in early entry programs (Saltman, 2010; Zeichner, 2010c; Zeichner & Pena-Sandoval, 2015). The success of this growing dominance of venture philanthropy, educational advocacy organizations and education think tanks in making early entry and non-university programs the norm and the disappearance of genuine public dialogue about the future of U.S. teacher education—more than anything else—will determine the ability of the nation to achieve the lofty vision to offer a high-quality clinical education to all individuals entering the U.S. teaching force.

Notes

1 We would like to acknowledge the contributions of Elham Kazemi, Karen Mikolasy and Sheila Valencia in providing information about their school-based methods courses at the University of Washington.
2 These "early entry" teachers teach almost exclusively in urban or rural schools serving students living in poverty (Peske & Haycock, 2006).
3 The UTR is not a new model; it is a new term for a form of mostly school-based teacher education for specific school districts that has been around for many years (e.g., Fraser, 2007; Weiner, 1993). It includes working under the supervision of a mentor teacher for a year together with some coursework.
4 This increased focus on school experience in teacher education is taking place in other countries as well (e.g., Mattsson, Eilertsen, & Rorrison, 2011; Reid, 2011).
5 Although our focus here is on the enduring problems of teacher education within a U.S. context, there is a great deal of similarity to the international literature on this issue (e.g., Vick, 2006).
6 Despite repeated assertions that teachers prepared in professional development schools teach at a higher level and stay longer than those prepared in traditional clinical placements (e.g., Council of Chief State School Officers, 2012, p. 12), the great variation in the nature and quality of professional development schools (Zeichner, 2009) makes this kind of generalization problematic.
7 The point here is not that teacher candidates should learn to passively replicate teaching practices advocated either by university- or school-based teacher educators that represent an "impoverished view" of the role of experience in teacher learning (Ellis, 2010). Teacher candidates need to learn how to critically analyze and selectively utilize and adapt that which is offered to them by their programs.
8 See Darling-Hammond (2006) and Zeichner & Conklin (2008) for a discussion of the characteristics of exemplary teacher education programs.
9 This disinvestment in public higher education is part of a broader disinvestment in the public sphere that exists in some form or another in many countries (Zeichner, 2010c).
10 Both the MATCH Teacher Residency and the Relay Graduate School of Education have been authorized by their respective states (Massachusetts and New York) to offer master's degrees.
11 See www.newschools.org/venture/relay-school-of-education.

12   The Institute for Simulation and Training at the University of Central Florida, with the support of a grant from the Gates Foundation, provides virtual classrooms to about a dozen other teacher education institutions. These virtual classrooms use artificial intelligence, child avatars and a behind-the-scenes actor (Cuban, 2012). Also see http://today.ucf.edu/ucfs-virtual-classroom-software-receives-grant-for-innovative-teacher-preparation-program/.

13   Teach for America, which is the largest of the U.S. early entry programs, received a federal grant of $50 million in 2010 to expand its capacity by 80% (Zeichner, in press-a) and over the last decade has received funding of over $300 million from private foundations and the federal government (Suggs & deMarrais, 2011). There is currently a great deal of controversy about this program because of its placement of underprepared teachers with only 5 weeks of training in schools to exclusively teach students living in poverty, the ambiguity of the research about the effectiveness of these teachers (Helig & Jez, 2010), their high turnover rate after their 2-year commitment (Donaldson & Johnson, 2011) and the ties between the program and efforts to privatize public schools in the United States (Sondel, Kretchmar, & Ferrare, 2014) and to avoid state certification requirements (Heilig, 2013).

14   Current federal legislation allows these teachers still in training to be considered "highly qualified" and therefore eligible to be responsible for classrooms.

15   The Aspire, MATCH and Academy for Educational Leadership teacher residencies are examples of these emerging networks to prepare teachers for particular charter school networks.

16   http://www.utrunited.org/.

17   Despite evidence that professional development schools in some cases addressed some of the enduring problems of clinical teacher education enumerated previously (e.g., the disconnect between coursework and fieldwork), there is widespread agreement that the professional development school movement has not consistently addressed these problems, and that even when it did so, the improvements were able to be sustained (Zeichner, 2009).

18   See Lampert et al. (2013) for a detailed discussion of the pedagogy of rehearsal that is being used in the methods courses at several research universities.

19   Like most other things in teacher education, there is a long history of efforts to identify the features of good clinical sites in teacher education that should be studied by current researchers. McIntòsh (1968) made one of the earliest and most interesting efforts.

20   The U.S. Department of Education has proposed phasing out one of the major recent sources of support for innovation in college and university programs: the Teacher Quality Partnership program.

21   The proposed standards of the new national teacher accreditation body, the Council for the Accreditation of Educator Preparation (CAEP), endorse the federal vision of an accountability system for teacher education.

References

American Association of Colleges for Teacher Education (AACTE) (March 2010). *The clinical preparation of teachers: A policy brief.* Washington, DC: Author.

American Association of Colleges for Teacher Education (AACTE) (2013). *The changing teacher preparation profession: A report from AACTE's professional education data system (PEDS).* Washington, DC: Author.

American Federation of Teachers (AFT) (2007). *Meeting the challenge: Recruiting and retaining teachers in hard-to-staff schools.* Retrieved from http://www.aft.org/sites/default/files/hardtostaff_2007.pdf

American Federation of Teachers (AFT) (2012). *Raising the bar: Aligning and elevating teacher preparation and the teaching profession.* Washington, DC: Author.

Anderson, L., & Stillman, J. (2011). Student teaching for a specialized view of professional practice? Opportunities to learn in and for urban, high-needs schools. *Journal of Teacher Education, 62*(5), 446–464.

Anderson, L., & Stillman, J. (2013). Student teaching's contribution to preservice teacher development: A review of research focused on the preparation of teachers for urban and high-needs contexts. *Review of Education Research, 83*(1), 3–69.

Baker, E., Barton, P., Darling-Hammond, L., Haertel, E., Ladd, H., Linn, R., Ravitch, D., Rothstein, R., Shavelson, R., & Shepard, L. (2010). Problems with the use of student test scores to evaluate teachers. Washington, DC: Economic Policy Institute (EPI).

Ball, D., & Cohen, D. (1999). Developing practice, developing practitioners: Toward a practice-based theory of professional education. In L. Darling-Hammond & G. Sykes (Eds.), *Teaching as a learning profession* (pp. 3–32). San Francisco, CA: Jossey-Bass.

Ball, D., & Forzani, F. (2009). The work of teaching and the challenge for teacher education. *Journal of Teacher Education, 60,* 497–510.

Banks, J., Cochran-Smith, M., Moll, L., Richert, A., Zeichner, K., LePage, P., Darling-Hammond, L., & Duffy, H. (2005). Teaching diverse learners. In L. Darling-Hammond & J. Bransford (Eds.), *Preparing teachers for a changing world* (pp. 232–274). San Francisco, CA: Jossey-Bass.

Bartolome, L. (1994). Beyond the methods fetish: Toward a humanizing pedagogy. *Harvard Educational Review, 64*(2), 173–194.

Berliner, D. (1985). Laboratory settings and the study of teacher education. *Journal of Teacher Education, 36,* 2–8.

Berry, B., Montgomery, D., Curtis, R., Hernandez, M., Wurtzel, J., & Snyder, J. (2008). *Creating and sustaining urban teacher residencies.* Hillsborough, NC: Center for Teaching Quality and the Aspen Institute.

Boyle-Baise, M., & McIntyre, D.J. (2008). What kind of experience? Preparing teachers in PDS or community settings. In M. Cochran-Smith, S. Feiman-Nemser, & D.J. McIntyre (Eds.), *Handbook of research on teacher education* (3rd ed., pp. 307–330). New York, NY: Routledge.

Bransford, J., & Darling-Hammond, L. (2005). *Preparing teachers for a changing world: Report of the National Academy of Education Committee on Teacher Education.* San Francisco, CA: Jossey-Bass.

Buchmann, M., & Floden, R. (1990). *Program coherence in the U.S.: A view from the United States.* East Lansing, MI: National Center for Research on Teacher Learning. Issue Paper 90-6.

Bullough, R., Draper, M.J., Smith, L., & Burrell, J. (2004). Moving beyond collusion: Clinical faculty and university public school partnership. *Teaching and Teacher Education, 20,* 505–521.

Bullough, R., Hobbs, S., Kauchak, D., Crow, N., & Stokes, D. (1997). Long-term PDS development in research universities and the clinicalization of teacher education. *Journal of Teacher Education, 48,* 85–93.

Burris, C.C. (2012). Some scary training for future teachers. *Washington Post,* July 26. Retrieved from www.washingtonpost.com

Campbell, S.S. (2008). Mediated field experiences in learning progressive teaching: A design experiment in teacher education. Paper presented at the annual meeting of the American Educational Research Association, New York, NY.

Campbell, S.S. (2012). Taking it to the field: Teacher candidate learning about equity-oriented mathematics teaching in a mediated field experience. Unpublished doctoral dissertation, University of Washington-Seattle, College of Education, Seattle, WA.

Chubb, J. (2012). *The best teachers in the world: Why we don't have them and how we could.* Stanford, CA: Hoover Institution Press.

Clift, R., & Brady, P. (2005). Research on methods courses and field experiences. In M. Cochran-Smith & K. Zeichner (Eds.), *Studying teacher education: The report of the American Educational Research Association panel on research on teacher education* (pp. 309–424). New York, NY: Routledge.

Cochran-Smith, M. (1991). Reinventing student teaching. *Journal of Teacher Education, 42*(2), 104–118.

Conant, J. (1963). *The education of American teachers.* New York, NY: McGraw-Hill.

Constantine, J., Player, D., Silva, T., Hallgren, K., Grider, M., & Drake, J. (2009). *An evaluation of teachers trained through different routes to certification.* Washington, DC: U.S. Department of Education.

Cornbleth, C. (2010). Institutional habitus as the de facto diversity curriculum of teacher education. *Anthropology and Education Quarterly, 41*(3), 280–297.

Council of Chief State School Officers (CCSSO) (2012). *Our responsibility, our promise: Transforming educator preparation and entry into the profession.* Washington, DC: Author.

Cuban, L. (2012). *How much and what kind of teacher education do novices need?* Retrieved from http://larrycuban.wordpress.com

Danielson, C. (2007). *Enhancing professional practice.* Alexandria, VA: Association of Supervision and Curriculum Development.

Darling-Hammond, L. (2004). Inequality and the right to learn: Access to qualified teachers in California's public schools. *Teachers College Record, 106*(10), 1936–1966.

Darling-Hammond, L. (2006). *Powerful teacher education.* San Francisco, CA: Jossey-Bass.

Darling-Hammond, L., & Lieberman, A. (Eds.) (2012). *Teacher education around the world: Changing policies and practices.* London, United Kingdom: Routledge.

Decker, P. T., Mayer, D.P., & Glazerman, S. (2006). Alternative routes to teaching: The impact of Teach for America on student achievement and other outcomes. *Journal of Policy Analysis and Management, 25*(1), 75–96.

Donaldson, M. L., & Johnson, S. M. (2011). Teach for America teachers: How long do they teach? Why do they leave? *Phi Delta Kappan, 93*(2), 47–52.

Duncan, A. (2011). *Our future, our teachers: The Obama administration plan for teacher education reform and improvement.* Washington, DC: U.S. Department of Education.

Ellis, V. (2010). Impoverishing experience: The problem of teacher education in England. *Journal of Education for Teaching, 36*(1), 105–120.

Emihovich, C., Dana, T., Vernetson, T., & Colon, E. (2011). Changing standards, changing needs: The gauntlet of teacher education reform. In P. Earley, D. Imig, & N. Michelli (Eds.), *Teacher education policy in the U.S.* (pp. 47–69). New York, NY: Routledge.

Feiman-Nemser, S. (2010, March 11). *The case for strong clinical teacher education.* Remarks made at a press conference at the National Press Club. "Strong clinical teacher preparation: A must for long-term school improvement efforts." Press briefing sponsored by the American Association of Colleges for Teacher Education.

Feiman-Nemser, S., & Buchmann, M. (1985). Pitfalls of experience in teacher education. *Teachers College Record, 87,* 49–65.

Feistritzer, E., & Haar, C. (2008). *Alternative routes to teaching.* Upper Saddle River, NJ: Pearson.

Flowers, J.G., Patterson, A., Stratemeyer, F., & Lindsey, M. (1948). *School and community laboratory experiences in teacher education.* Oneata, NY: American Association of Colleges for Teacher Education (AACTE).

Fraser, J. (2007). *Preparing America's teachers: A history.* New York, NY: Teachers College Press.

Gatlin, D. (2009). A pluralistic approach to the revitalization of teacher education. *Journal of Teacher Education, 60*(5), 469–477.

Gatti, L., & Catalano, T. (2015). The business of learning to teach: A critical metaphor analysis of one teacher's journey. *Teaching and Teacher Education, 45,* 149–160.

Greenberg, J., Pomerance, L., & Walsh, K. (2011). *Student teaching in the United States.* Washington, DC: National Council on Teacher Quality.

Greene, M. (1979). The matter of mystification: Teacher education in unquiet times. In M. Greene (Ed.), *Landscapes of learning* (pp. 53–73). New York, NY: Teachers College Press.

Grossman, P. (2005). Pedagogical approaches to teacher education. In M. Cochran-Smith & K. Zeichner (Eds.), *Studying teacher education* (pp. 425–476). New York, NY: Routledge.

Grossman, P. (2010). *Learning to practice: The design of clinical experience in teacher preparation.* Policy Brief of the Partnership for Teacher Quality. Washington, DC: American Association of Colleges for Teacher Education (AACTE).

Grossman, P. (2011). A framework for teaching practice: A brief history of an idea. *Teachers College Record, 113*(12), 2836–2843.

Grossman, P., & Loeb, S. (Eds.) (2008). *Alternative routes to teaching.* Cambridge, MA: Harvard Education Press.

Hamel, F., & Jaasko-Fisher, H. (2011). Hidden labor in the mentoring of pre-service teachers: Notes from a mentor teacher advisory council. *Teaching and Teacher Education, 27,* 434–442.

Hammerness, K., Darling-Hammond, L., Bransford, J., Cochran-Smith, M., McDonald, M., & Zeichner, K. (2005). How teachers learn and develop. In L. Darling-Hammond & J. Bransford (Eds.), *Preparing teachers for a changing world* (pp. 358–389). San Francisco, CA: Jossey-Bass.

Heilig, J.V. (2013). Battle for California: TFA civil war, ELLs, and teacher quality. *Cloaking Inequity.* Retrieved from http://cloakinginequity.com/2013/03/05/battle-for-california-tfa-civil-war-ells-and-teacher-quality/

Heilig, J.V., & Jez, S. J. (2010). *Teach for America: A review of the evidence.* Boulder, CO: University of Colorado: Education and the Public Interest Center.

Kronholz, J. (2012). A new type of ed school. *Education Next, 12*(4). Retrieved from http://educatioonnext.org

Labaree, D. (2004). *The trouble with ed schools.* New Haven, CT: Yale University Press.

Ladson-Billings, G. (1994). *The dreamkeepers: Successful teachers of African American children.* San Francisco, CA: Jossey-Bass.

Lampert, M., Franke, M., Kazemi, E., Ghousseini, H., Turrou, A. C., Beasley, H., Cunard, A., & Crowe, K. (2013). Keeping it complex: Using rehearsals to support novice teacher learning of ambitious teaching in elementary mathematics. *Journal of Teacher Education, 64*(3), 226–243.

Lankford, H., Loeb, S., & Wyckoff, J. (2002). Teacher sorting and the plight of urban schools. *Educational Evaluation and Policy Analysis, 20,* 37–62.

Lemov, D. (2010). *Teaching like a champion.* San Francisco, CA: Jossey-Bass.

Levine, A. (2006). *Educating school teachers.* The Education Schools Project. Retrieved from http://www.edschools.org/pdf/Educating_Teachers_Report.pdf

Levine, A. (2012). The new normal of teacher education. *The Chronicle of Higher Education.* Retrieved from http://chronicle.com/article/The-New-Normal-of-Teacher/127430/

Longview Foundation (2008). *Teacher preparation for the global age: The imperative for change.* Silver Spring, MD: Author.

Lucas, T., & Villegas, A. M. (2011). A framework for preparing linguistically responsive teachers. In T. Lucas (Ed.), *Teacher preparation for linguistically diverse classrooms* (pp. 55–72). New York, NY: Routledge.

Mahan, J. (1982). Native Americans as teacher trainers: Anatomy and outcomes of a cultural immersion project. *Journal of Equity and Leadership, 2,* 100–109.

Mattsson, M., Eilertsen, T.V., & Rorrison, D. (Eds.) (2011). *A practicum turn in teacher education.* Rotterdam, Netherlands: Sense Publishers.

McIntosh, R. G. (1968). *An approach to the analysis of clinical settings for teacher education.* The Third Florence Stratemeyer Lecture, Annual meeting of the Association for Student Teaching, Chicago, IL.

Murrell, P. (2001). *The community teacher.* New York, NY: Teachers College Press.

National Commission on Teaching and America's Future (NCTAF) (2010). *Who will teach: Experience matters.* Retrieved from www.nctaf.org/NCTAFWhoWillTeach.pdf

National Council of Accreditation for Teacher Education (NCATE) (2010). *Transforming teacher education through clinical practice: A national strategy to prepare effective teachers.* Washington, DC: Author.

National Education Association (NEA) (2011). *Transforming teaching: Connecting professional responsibility with student learning.* Washington, DC: Author.

National Research Council (NRC) (2010). *Preparing teachers: Building evidence for sound policy.* Washington, DC: National Academies Press.

Newfield, C. (2008). *Unmaking the public university.* Cambridge, MA: Harvard University Press.

Noel, J. (2013) (Ed.). *Moving teacher education into urban schools and communities.* New York, NY: Routledge.

Papay, J., West, M., Fullerton, J., & Kane, T. (2011). *Can practice-based teacher preparation increase student achievement? Evidence from the Boston Teacher Residency.* New York, NY: National Bureau of Economic Research Working Paper #17646.

Payzant, T. (February 2004). *Should teacher education take place at colleges and universities?* Invited address presented at the annual meeting of the American Association of Colleges for Teacher Education, Chicago, IL.

Peske, H., & Haycock, K. (2006). *Teaching inequality: How poor minority students are short-changed on teacher quality.* Washington, DC: Education Trust.

Pianta, R.C. (2011). *Teaching children well: New evidence-based approaches to teacher professional development and training.* Washington, DC: Center for American Progress.

Reid, J. (2011). A practice-turn for teacher education? *South Pacific Journal of Teacher Education, 39*(4), 293–310.

Rennie Center for Education Research & Policy (2009). *Preparing tomorrow's teachers: The role of practice-based teacher preparation programs in Massachusetts.* Cambridge, MA: Author.

Ronfeldt, M., Loeb, J., & Wyckoff, J. (2013). How teacher turnover harms student achievement. *American Educational Research Journal, 50*(1), 4–36.

Ronfeldt, R. (2012). Where should student teachers learn to teach: Effects of placement school characteristics on teacher retention and effectiveness. *Education Evaluation and Policy Analysis, 34*, 3–26.

Rotherham, A. (2008). *Achieving teacher and principal excellence: A guidebook for donors.* Washington, DC: Philanthropy Roundtable.

Saltman, K. (2010). *The gift of education and venture philanthropy.* New York, NY: Macmillan Palgrave.

Schorr, J. (2012). A revolution begins in teacher prep. *Stanford Social Innovation Review.* Retrieved from http://www.ssireview.org/

Skinner, E., Garreton, M. T., and Schultz, B. (Eds.) (2011). *Grow your own teachers: Grassroots change in teacher education.* New York, NY: Teachers College Press.

Sleeter, C. (2008). Preparing white teachers for diverse students. In M. Cochran-Smith, S. Feiman-Nemser, & D. J. McIntyre (Eds.), *Handbook of research on teacher education* (3rd ed., pp. 559–582). New York, NY: Routledge.

Sondel, B., Kretchmar, K., & Ferrare, J. (2014). Mapping the terrain: Teach for America, charter school reform, and corporate sponsorship. *Journal of Education Policy, 29*(6), 742–759.

Suggs, C., & deMarrais, K. (2011). *Critical contributions: Philanthropic investment in teachers and teaching.* Atlanta, GA: Kronley & Associates.

Sykes, G., & Dibner, K. (2009). *Fifty years of federal teacher policy: An appraisal.* Washington, DC: Center on Education Policy.

Turney, C., Eltis, K., Towler, J., & Wright, R. (1985). *A new basis for teacher education: The practicum curriculum.* Sydney, Australia: University of Sydney Press.

Valencia, S., Martin, S., Place, N., & Grossman, P. (2009). Complex interactions in student teaching: Lost opportunities for learning. *Journal of Teacher Education, 60*(3), 304–322.

Vick, M. (2006). "It's a difficult matter": Historical perspectives on the enduring problem of the practicum in teacher preparation. *Asia-Pacific Journal of Teacher Education, 34*(2), 181–198.

Weiner, L. (1993). *Preparing teachers for urban schools: Lessons from thirty years of school reform.* New York, NY: Teachers College Press.

Windschitl, M., Thompson, J., & Braaten, M. (2011). Ambitious pedagogy by novice teachers. *Teachers College Record, 113*(7), 1311–1360.

Zeichner, K. (1980). Myths and realities: Field-based experiences in pre-service teacher education. *Journal of Teacher Education, 31*(6), 45–55.

Zeichner, K. (1996). Designing educative practicum experiences for prospective teachers. In K. Zeichner, S. Melnick, & M.L. Gomez (Eds.), *Currents of reform in preservice teacher education* (pp. 215–234). New York, NY: Teachers College Press.

Zeichner, K. (2009). *Teacher education and the struggle for social justice.* New York, NY: Routledge.

Zeichner, K. (June 2010a). *The importance of strong clinical preparation for teachers.* Testimony presented at a U.S. Congressional Briefing organized by the American Association of Colleges for Teacher Education, U.S. Senate Office Building, Washington, DC. Retrieved from aacte.org

Zeichner, K. (2010b). Rethinking the connections between campus courses and field experiences in college and university-based teacher education. *Journal of Teacher Education, 89*(11), 89–99.

Zeichner, K. (2010c). Neo-liberalism and the transformation of teacher education in the U.S. *Teaching and Teacher Education 26*(8), 1544–1552.

Zeichner, K. (2011). Assessing state and federal policies to evaluate the quality of teacher preparation programs. In P. Earley, D. Imig, & N. Michelli (Eds.), *Teacher education policy in the United States: Issues and tensions in an era of evolving expectations* (pp. 75–105). New York, NY: Routledge.

Zeichner, K. (2012). The turn once again toward practice-based teacher education. *Journal of Teacher Education, 63*(5), 376–382.

Zeichner, K. (2013). Two visions of teaching and teacher education for the 21st century. In X. Zhu & K. Zeichner (Eds.), *Preparing teachers for the 21st century* (pp. 3–20). Heidelberg, Germany: Springer.

Zeichner, K. (2014). The struggle for the soul of teaching and teacher education. *Journal of Education for Teaching, 40*(5), 551–568.

Zeichner, K., & Conklin, H. (2005). Teacher education programs. In M. Cochran-Smith & K. Zeichner (Eds.), *Studying teacher education* (pp. 645–746). New York, NY: Routledge.

Zeichner, K., & Conklin, H. (2008). Teacher education programmes. In M. Cochran-Smith & K. Zeichner (Eds.), *Studying teacher education* (pp. 645–746). New York, NY: Routledge.

Zeichner, K., & Melnick, S. (1996). The role of community field experiences in preparing teachers for cultural diversity. In K. Zeichner, S. Melnick, & M. L. Gomez (Eds.), *Currents of reform in preservice teacher education* (pp. 176–198). New York, NY: Teachers College Press.

Zeichner, K., & Payne, K. (2013). Democratizing knowledge in urban teacher education. In J. Noel (Ed.), *Moving teacher education into urban schools and communities* (pp. 3–19). New York, NY: Routledge.

Zeichner, K., Payne, K., & Brayko, K. (2015). Democratizing teacher education. *Journal of Teacher Education, 66*(2), 1–14.

Zeichner, K., & Pena-Sandoval, C. (2015). Venture philanthropy and teacher education policy in the U.S.: The role of the New Schools Venture Fund. *Teachers College Record, 117*(6). http://www.tcrecord.org ID Number: 17539.

3

MOVING FROM RECOMMENDATIONS TO ACTION IN PREPARING PROFESSIONAL EDUCATORS

Frances O'Connell Rust and Renée Tipton Clift

In 2010, the National Council for the Accreditation of Teacher Education (NCATE) issued a major report calling for teacher education programs to work in closer partnership with schools and school districts. They noted that such partnerships

> . . . should include shared decision making and oversight on candidate selection and completion by school districts and teacher education programs. This will bring accountability closer to the classroom, based largely on evidence of candidates' effective performance and impact on student learning. It also will ensure professional accountability, creating a platform to ensure that teachers own, and fully utilize, the knowledge base of most effective practice . . . [such a system] . . . holds great promise for advancing shared responsibility for teacher preparation; supporting the development of complex teaching skills; and ensuring that all teachers know how to work closely with colleagues, students, and community.
>
> (NCATE, 2010, p. ii)

While this thoughtful and detailed report has received much attention from current teacher educators and, in some instances, policymakers, it is not exactly a new idea. Implementing clinical practice in teacher education has long been seen as a powerful strategy for crossing institutional barriers and addressing what is perceived as the theory/practice divide. As early as 1920, the Association of Teacher Educators, then called the National Association of Directors of Supervised Student Teaching, was established as an organization distinct from the American Association of Colleges for Teacher Education in order to give primacy to field experiences and provide a national, collaborative network among school-based and university-based teacher educators (Patterson, McGoech, & Olsen, 1990). Articles on closer collaboration between schools and higher education for educator development reach back into the 1960s (Clift & Say, 1988). The Holmes Group reports (1986, 1990, 1995) made related claims.

What these reports make clear is that moving from calls for reform to actions in which schools, districts and institutions of higher education design, implement, institutionalize and assess the impact of recommended reforms in teacher education has been more difficult than achieving consensus on the necessity for reform. While studies of the types of settings best suited to field placement for preservice teachers are abundant (see, for example, Adams, Bondy, & Kuhel, 2005; Grande, Burns, Schmidt, & Marable, 2009; Guyton & McIntyre, 1990; Latham & Vogt, 2007; Ridley, Hurwitz, Davis Hackett, & Knutson Miller, 2005; Ronfeldt, 2012), there are few examples of programs that have, over time, created and sustained interdependent and mutually beneficial relationships that approach the structures and values suggested by the NCATE report.

In this chapter, we draw on studies and reports such as those cited previously; our own experiences with teacher education program design and implementation at six different research-intensive universities over a 30-year time span; research on teacher education program development; examples from existing programs and programs that are under development; and conceptions of clinical practice in other professions in order to provide a framework for moving from recommendations to action. We note that reforming teacher education with clinical practice at the core forces questions not only of "how we should conceptualize and define the outcomes of teacher education for teacher learning, professional practice, and student learning" (Cochran-Smith, 2001, p. 2) but also of how we should conceptualize the benefits of such arrangements for children, adolescents, teachers, administrators, community members and professors.

Considering Clinical Practice in Professional Education

Discussions concerning where and how to prepare educators have, historically, ranged from arguments that no preparation is necessary to creating special schools for educator (primarily teacher) preparation to locating preparation in research-intensive universities to locating preparation outside of universities and privatizing such preparation (Labaree, 2004; Joyce & Clift, 1984; Hinchey & Cadiero-Kaplan, 2005). Education for other professional fields is a bit less contentious, however. In professions ranging from law to medicine to social work to the clergy, clinical work accompanied by coursework is understood as an essential vehicle for connecting research with practice for the novice and the experienced professional. Clinical practice in most professional education is understood as a high-powered instructional strategy that is designed to enable the learner to make connections between professional coursework and the interpersonal and context-bound setting of the actual workplace.

The fields of medicine and nursing, in particular, have developed structures that depend on a readily available supply of interns, residents and nurses in training to serve patients and to assist more experienced practitioners (Benner, Sutphen, Leonard, & Day, 2010; Dyess & Sherman, 2009; Nursing Executive Center, 2005). In law, an integrated approach is being used to bring the powerful educational tradition of inculcating legal thinking together with what the Carnegie Foundation for the Advancement of Teaching describes as *civic professionalism* (Sullivan, Colby, Wegner, Bond, & Shulman, 2007) so that, as one learns about the law, one also learns about legal analysis and what it means to be a professional. Daley (2001) studied continuing professional education (CPE) in social work, law, adult education and nursing. She found that relevant practice was critical to making education meaningful, particularly with regard to interactions with clients:

> Often, it was an emotional encounter with a client that changed a professional's practice, particularly if confronted with client situations that challenged their knowledge, beliefs, and assumptions.
>
> (Daley, 2001, p. 48)

Core to each of these examples is the understanding that clinical practice is most successfully learned in environments that provide opportunities for adult learners to surface prior knowledge relative to the new information and ways of thinking that inform professional practice in a given field, engage in guided practice alongside experienced professionals and see their own practice fitting with and rising to professional standards—all essential hallmarks of adult learning (Bransford, Brown, & Cocking, 1999; Drago-Severson, 2011; Knowles, Holton, & Swanson, 2005; Lawler & King, 2000; Smylie, 1995).

Clinical Practice in Teacher Education

In teaching, clinical practice has traditionally been relegated to opportunities for participant observation that might or might not accompany a course and to something referred to as student teaching, which varies across institutions in terms of length, responsibilities, supervision and location. While many educators argue that the prospective teachers may benefit from experience in the field (Castle, Fox, & Souder, 2005; Clift & Brady, 2005; Latham & Vogt, 2007; Paese, 2003; Ridley et al., 2005; Ronfeldt, 2012), some argue that they do not unless carefully supported and aligned with the methods courses (e.g., Britzman, 1991; Perry & Power, 2004).

We argue that time in the field is potentially meaningless unless the prospective teacher is engaged in *focused* clinical practice in which practitioners are actively studying their own actions and impact alongside other practitioners in ways similar to those described in medicine, nursing, law and social work. Such practice must be threaded through teacher preparation, not merely embedded in a methods course or two. Nor is it enough to move teacher education into a school context. As Lunenberg and Korthagen (2009) point out: "Although student teachers spend more time in schools than 10 years ago, this has not automatically affected the way teacher educators in teacher education institutions teach nor what pre-service teachers learn about teaching" (p. 229).

In the next section, we provide several examples of the ways in which context and practice can be intertwined in teacher preparation.

Focusing Clinical Practice in Initial and Continuing Teacher Preparation

To create sustainable programs that promote the development of skilled practitioners—who are all oriented toward enhancing a variety of forms of learning—we need to attend carefully to the contexts for that preparation. Determining appropriate settings in which to gain clinical knowledge is a major factor in professional education. One way to look at and appraise context for its appropriateness is to think about what the learner should be able to gain in that setting and what the outcome of that learning might imply for receivers of the practice.

Microteaching (MacLeod, 1987), once a popular technique for teacher preparation, involved videotaping a lesson that was taught to fellow students. The lesson was to be a demonstration of specific techniques such as asking questions, waiting for answers, practicing eye contact, etc. The instructor would then debrief the lesson and the successful execution of the target behaviors. Often, microteaching represented just one aspect of the clinical practice framework that Grossman et al. (2009) describe—that is, *approximation of practice*—and, like so many efforts before and since to standardize teaching, focusing solely on isolated teaching techniques has never led to the highly integrated, deeply contextualized, fluid practice that is the hallmark of well-prepared teachers. As Cochran-Smith and Powers (2010) noted:

> A century ago, teacher-preparation programs concentrated on training teachers to display certain behaviors in the classroom. It was eventually concluded, however, that although teachers could be trained to produce almost any classroom behavior, these were "empty techniques" because they failed to account for the many decisions teachers had to make and the knowledge they needed to decide wisely.
>
> (p. 12)

Practice that is decontextualized makes no sense. What does make sense is thinking about educator preparation as the enhancement and support of skillful practitioners. It involves situated knowing—that is, knowing the context, knowing what is appropriate in the given setting and being able to draw deeply from a well of good information to shape the appropriate action. This is precisely what Durning et al. (2010) define as context in medical settings—that is,

> . . . "the weaving together" of the participants and the setting in the clinical encounter. This weaving together, or interaction, creates meaning that evolves during the encounter. Thus, context is more than the individual participants in the clinical encounter or the setting where the encounter occurs—it entails the physician, the patient, the setting, and the interactions of all three.
>
> (p. 66)

There is a recognition here that beginners must have basic, fundamental knowledge and knowledge of practice, that there is a fluency to practice—a knowing when to do what, that such knowledge is gained over time with support and that context has an enormous shaping effect.

Developing powerful environments in which future teachers can bring theory and practice together as doctors do in clinical internships is essential in teacher education. Grossman et al. (2009), following their study of the professional education of clergy, clinical psychologists and teachers, claimed that the context for professional education must be one in which there is a purposeful and focused effort to enable beginners to see and engage in representations, decomposition and approximations of practice:

> Representations of practice comprise the different ways that practice is represented in professional education and what these various representations make visible to novices. Decomposition of practice involves breaking down practice into its constituent parts for the purposes of teaching and learning. Approximations of practice refer to opportunities for novices to engage in practices that are more or less proximal to the practices of a profession.
>
> (Grossman et al., 2009, p. 2060)

The context for such preparatory work requires both opportunity for reflection and for enactment.

Recently, Zeichner (2010) has argued that campuses cannot be connected to schools and communities without creating a space for professional dialogue that is neither one; it must be a space that is jointly constructed and that serves as a safe and welcoming space for educators to come together. Oldenburg (1989) described such space as a third space. Gorodetsky and Barak (2008), drawing from ecology, described such a space by using the ecological analogy of an edge environment.

In the social setting of a school–university partnership, an edge environment is a space that is developed out of the partnership between two or more social organizations—of them but not either; easily affected by change in the original environments from which they draw their liveliness; requiring flexibility from leadership both within and outside the edge environment (see also Wenger, 1998; Wenger & Snyder, 2000). Like their ecological counterparts, edge environments are places where strong, new, creative communities can emerge and flourish, supporting the original communities from which they emerged and providing a place for the testing of new ideas and new forms of organization and relationship.

Such settings are increasingly being developed as partnerships between universities, schools and school systems as a means of enabling novice teachers to bring theory into practice and as a way of supporting substantive change in the professional learning environment for both new and experienced teachers and teacher educators. Focused clinical practice in this type of space should benefit students and experienced teachers. As Gorodetsky and Barak's (2008) work makes clear, it is extremely difficult to create settings in which there is such mutual benefit. In the first place, such settings require accommodation from all partners for the development of a new entity that is focused on supporting novices to become part of the professional community:

> Carrying over these implications from the edge metaphor to educational partnerships suggests that for a partnership to flourish, the collaborating partners, e.g., the school and the college or university, should establish a new, participative community. This community should be peripheral to both; however, it should maintain permeable borders with the core institutions to enable multidirectional flows of knowledge. This should be a real (concrete) community that will provide conditions encouraging the growth of new, culturally distinguished features.
>
> These are often uncomfortable settings because being in the edge, or peripherality, is the means for new growth and not a space for enculturation to existing core communities. A very basic feature of edges is their increased resilience towards change that can be transmitted to the communities associated with it.
>
> (Gorodetsky and Barak, 2008, pp. 1908–1909)

Thus, these settings, like their ecological counterparts, are fragile and not easily replicated. So, while such settings enable the growth of professional practice among all participants, it is the mutual commitment on the part of the various partners to engagement in the study and nurture of professional practice and their openness to experimentation that sets them apart as successful professional communities.

We illustrate some of these in the next part of this chapter, where we discuss four current teacher education programs that are attempting to situate the discussion of learning from coursework, clinical practice and assessment within the complex and dynamic *system* that comprises learning to teach and to teach well. Viewing clinical practice as a beneficial learning environment for all participants has the potential to enhance learning about teaching and to allow participants to engage with an increasingly diverse and technologically sophisticated student population.

Selected Teacher Preparation Programs Working at the Edge

We discuss four university-based programs in this section: They are situated at the University of Arizona, the University of Florida, the University of Pennsylvania, and Black Hills State University. These programs are in various stages of construction but, across all, two major factors guide program development and implementation: a deliberate attempt to focus clinical experiences on interactions that promote students' learning and a continuous inquiry into making clinical practice beneficial for *all* participants, not just the university-based preservice teachers but also the field-based partners.

The University of Arizona

Two teacher education programs at the University of Arizona provide examples of ways in which clinical practice can be integrated into the entire framework of a teacher education program. The first of these is the *Communities as Resources in Early Childhood Teacher Education (CREATE)* program that constitutes a redesign of early childhood teacher preparation at the university based on the understanding that "early childhood teacher preparation is shifting from a focus on learning *about* to promoting learning *with and from* family members, children, university students, and early childhood caregivers" (createarizona.org). This 2-year program immerses prospective teachers in 1 year of working in a birth-through-preschool early learning center and another full year of working in a K–3 classroom. In addition, prospective teachers engage with families in their homes and at school-based and community-based family events. These engagements are coordinated with partner schools in three districts that partner with the College of Education: Tucson Unified School District, Flowing Wells Unified School District and Sunnyside Unified School District.

The program is organized around four guiding principles that are enacted throughout the program (Clift, Iddings, Jurich, Reyes, & Short, 2011):

Principle 1: Promoting early childhood educators' understanding of the cultural knowledge and skills ("funds of knowledge") within diverse cultural communities. The first principle is derived from the concept of *Funds of Knowledge* (Moll, Amanti, Neff, & González, 1992) and is basic to the project. Moll et al. (1992) argued that large stores of cultural, familial and personal knowledge about farming or gardening, caring for and working with animals, trades, finance, etc. are embedded within families and are essential for family operations. Students are assigned to visit with families and learn about what they know and do so that they can incorporate their learning into their research projects and into lessons and in- and out-of-class activities. González is both a consultant to the project and a course instructor.

Principle 2: Using literature as a base for children's understanding of themselves and others. Drawing on the proposition that knowledge—particularly local knowledge—is often shared through stories, students learn about family stories and children's stories through family visits and three other activities that are essential to the prospective teachers' learning: family story backpacks, cultural community story boxes and *canastas*. The family story backpacks are organized thematically around a familiar theme such as birthdays or bedtime rituals. Children check out backpacks, which contain three books, an artifact, a journal and often a digital recorder. Families interact with the backpack and, if they choose to do so, write in the journal about working with the backpack or adding thematically related stories of their own. The story boxes are for classroom use. They, too, contain books and artifacts, which are organized around a local or an international cultural group. Early childhood teachers and prospective teachers design engagements in which the children interact with the story boxes in a variety of ways to build vocabulary, enhance social and cultural knowledge and develop complex literacy skills. The canastas are baskets that contain books and artifacts related to the cultures, activities and landscapes that can be found in southern Arizona. These canastas are placed in schools' family centers and in classrooms. Families add their stories to the canastas in writing, video, audio, etc. After a canasta has been in one school for several months, it is passed on to another school, and families can add to the layers of meaning as they engage with the stories from other schools within the community. Detailed descriptions of each can be found on the website (createarizona. org). Principle 2 helps make Principle 1 more concrete.

Principle 3: Involving families in literacy education for children—and for teachers. In addition to the six home visits each prospective teacher makes during coursework, faculty, staff, prospective teachers and mentor teachers in CREATE develop and implement school-wide afternoon or evening literacy events for families and their children at the school. These range from *cafecitos* in which families come together with teachers and prospective teachers to share stories and engage in informal discussions to family literacy nights for children, their families, teachers and prospective teachers to showcase literacy practices. Principle 3 builds on the first two principles and provides prospective teachers, teacher educators and mentor teachers opportunities to engage with families and the Tucson community, thereby blurring boundaries and positioning all as educators and learners.

Principle 4: Providing prospective and practicing teachers and teacher educators with opportunities to work and reflect together in community and school settings. Putting Principle 4 in place is an ongoing process that began with having district administrators serve on the advisory board and then adding teachers and family members in Year 2. The early childhood program coordinator and her staff meet regularly with all mentor teachers as they work to bridge the schools' curricula with the teacher preparation curricula. This is aided by a university site coordinator who arranges all early childhood (Year 1) and elementary (Year 2) teacher education classes taught at the school sites and monitors prospective teachers' work at the school sites. All instructors meet bi-weekly to review curricula, assessments and student progress and talk frequently with teachers and families. Each summer, teachers, instructors and guests meet in a 2-day summer institute to engage in and critique program activities.

Beyond Bridging is the second University of Arizona program that we consider in this chapter. While CREATE involves the entire cohort of early childhood students, Beyond Bridging is a math- and science-intensive research and development project that involves only one cohort of the Elementary Education Program at the University of Arizona. It was deliberately designed to explore the potential of a hybrid space in which to engage university teacher educators, school-based mentor teachers and preservice teachers in collective study of ways to bring theory and practice together in teacher education and teacher professional development. Partner schools agree to house methods classes and to participate in jointly selected activities in which prospective teachers, mentors and university-based educators examine prospective teachers' impact on children's learning.

One example is a mathematics task in which prospective teachers, mentor teachers and teacher educators conducted and analyzed interviews with elementary children around task-based problem-solving interviews (Wood & Turner, 2014) of elementary children. The mentors were able to help prospective teachers and teacher educators locate children's responses within the context of classroom history and prior interactions, thus enhancing both knowledge of students and creating plausible alternative understandings of children's behavior and thought processes. These conversations also enabled mentors, teacher educators and prospective teachers to discuss differing perspectives on instruction and reasoning.

Another example—this time in science (Gunckel, 2013)—enabled prospective teachers and their mentors to engage in a curriculum materials analysis. Once again, all instruction in the methods class took place at a partner elementary school and involved collaboration between the science methods instructor and mentor teachers to plan time and space for co-teaching and then reflection on selected lessons. Then, in a special class session, small groups of mentors and prospective teachers used a set of guiding questions to analyze a curriculum task for a hypothetical third-grade class; this inquiry was followed by a task using the same guiding questions to analyze the curriculum materials that the preservice teachers were using to plan and teach science lessons in their mentors' classrooms.

The interactions within these small groups provided opportunities to connect inquiry science teaching advocated in the methods course with their mentors' classrooms. As with the mathematics discussions, mentors were able to help prospective teachers contextualize their plans. The discussions also allowed teacher educators, mentors and prospective teachers time to engage in tough conversations around competing beliefs about students and learning. As conversations continued, mentors sometimes shifted into learner mode, and prospective teachers sometimes shifted into teacher mode. In all cases, the divisions between teacher education discourse and classroom teacher discourse were bridged, and constructs were shared and viewed in practical terms.

In both CREATE and Beyond Bridging, the clinical classroom and the possibility for representation, decomposition and approximation of practice begins with moving university instructors off campus and into schools and communities and, in doing so, an edge community has begun to take shape that is focused on clinical practice of preservice and experienced teachers and informed by research that is grounded in practice. This was made possible because all stakeholders—direct and indirect—encouraged and supported this move. The university-based stakeholders then began revising curricula based on principles and research, but as they began to enact curricula, they engaged mentors and prospective teachers in reviewing and critiquing the curricula. Such review is ongoing, and corrections can be made mid-course and at the end of a course. In both projects, there is time for engaging in reflective conversation, and the result is a better understanding of rationales for teaching and the constraints that impact practice. These conversations, in turn, impact school curricula and teacher preparation curricula (Clift, Reinhardt, & Robbins, 2012; Wood & Turner, 2014).

The University of Florida's Leadership Development Program

Focusing on the unique needs of practicing teachers located in high-needs, high-poverty schools, the faculty at the University of Florida (UF) works in collaboration with Florida teachers and administrators (Ross et al., 2011). The faculty has developed a teacher education program designed to help practicing teachers develop as leaders, learners, change agents and advocates for all children and the teaching profession within their school building and larger community. The program assists school reform efforts in these partner schools by shifting the culture toward academic success for all students within each school.

Titled *Teacher Leadership for School Improvement (TLSI)*, the program is job-embedded. The students are practicing professionals from the UF university partner schools and districts; they move through the program in school-based cohorts. Coursework and experiences are designed to relate to these teachers' everyday work and require that they continually link theory to practice. So as to extend the physical reach of the program, some TLSI students take online courses with university instructors but experience this coursework in a blended (or hybrid) format, meaning that face-to-face course meetings supplement the online content. Blended course experiences are facilitated by Professors-in-Residence (PiRs) on site at TLSI students' schools and/or districts as part of whole-school reform initiatives in partner schools that focus on the retention, recruitment and development of highly qualified teachers. As of fall 2012, over 600 students had enrolled in the program (460 master's-degree students and 150 specialists), with a total of 260 graduates since the program began in 2005. Approximately 50 new students are admitted each year.

Developing the skills and knowledge to be a teacher researcher, master teacher and teacher leader are the essential goals for students in the program. They pursue these goals by progressing through a series of six TLSI core courses (Teacher Inquiry, Transforming the Curriculum, Data-Driven Decision Making, Differentiating Instruction, Culturally Responsive Classroom Management and Teacher Leadership); selecting an area of specialization (choices include Reading Endorsement with all state requirements, Educational Technology, Media Literacy, Early Learning or Interdisciplinary); and creating a culminating portfolio that represents their learning and growth in relationship to each TLSI goal, as well as their implementation of their learning in their teaching. A three-credit practicum helps students translate what they are learning in core and specialization courses into their practice and assists them in developing the portfolio.

As a correlate of the TLSI's effort to support school change, the UF faculty began to work with its partner schools to create sites for internship placements for ProTeach students—a 5-year program for preservice teachers that culminates in a master's degree. The TLSI teachers and graduates seemed like ideal mentor teachers for the ProTeach students during their residency year, and the PiRs were already in place to supervise. They began with a pilot for one semester in fall 2011 and have now moved to a full-year internship model. The interns are placed in classrooms with a TLSI graduate or current TLSI student and take online courses to complete their master's year. The TLSI teachers, having cultivated an inquiry stance and improved their skills as master teachers and teacher leaders, are now taking on the role of teacher educator with enthusiasm. The two programs (TLSI and ProTeach) were designed with the same underlying assumption that consistency and coherence support learning of educators at all levels. Additionally, the programs help socialize new teachers into collaboration and inquiry as part of the way teachers work and as strategies to promote ongoing teacher learning throughout their careers.

The University of Pennsylvania's Inquiry Orientation

The elementary and secondary teacher education programs of the University of Pennsylvania are, like those of UF, focused on preparing teachers for urban schools. The programs are committed to social justice and designed to "prepare ethical, reflective, collaborative, visionary teacher-leaders" (http://tep.gse.upenn. edu/). The curriculum of the programs is unified and built around inquiry with assessment events that are specifically designed to enable students to use community assets to shape and strengthen classroom teaching practices within a continuously evolving process of inquiry, critical reflection and revision. The first of these assessments—neighborhood studies (elementary) or ethnographies of the neighborhoods in which the students will teach (secondary)—is completed in the program's 6-week summer semester by small groups of students who will be placed as cohorts in schools in the areas that they study. Kumar, Dean, and Bergey (2012)— all teacher education faculty—describe this first assessment as an artifact of

> the program's design (that) draws on sociocultural theories of learning that emphasize the appropriation of mediational tools through experiences of legitimate peripheral participation (LPP) and boundary crossing (Lave & Wenger, 1991; Tsui & Law, 2007; Tsui, Edwards, Lopez-Real, & Kwan, 2009; Wenger, 1998). This framework suggests that individuals learn by being involved with people who think in different ways and by having experiences that challenge them to rethink prior assumptions.
>
> (pp. 1–2)

Both the elementary (in the fall) and secondary (in the summer) programs use the framework of Carini's *Descriptive Review* (see Himley & Carini, 2000) to guide their observations and analyze their interactions with a learner. Later in the fall, both groups begin deep analysis of lesson plans relative to their implementation in their classrooms. In the spring, they create curriculum that is grounded in knowledge of content, focused on big ideas (Wiggins & McTighe, 2006) and supported by both formative and summative assessment. The final assessment for both groups is a digital portfolio that grows out of individual inquiry conducted over the course of the 10-month program. These inquiry portfolios are scaffolded by the earlier assessments so as to enable students to describe their personal journeys into teaching and to provide evidence of their own professional development and understanding of the complex setting that is education in urban schools serving children of poverty.

Rust and Bergey (2012) studied the inquiry portfolios and found that the clinical practices associated with each of these assessments—the development of observation skills, including interviews, developing time samples, using classroom maps and analyzing student work; the shaping and assessment of lessons designed specifically for a single child or small group; the design, implementation and assessment of a curriculum unit; the use of video to document teaching; reflective journals framed around teaching and interaction with learners and other adults—seem to have resulted in the development of what Cochran-Smith (2001) describes as "an inquiry stance" on the part of program students. Rust and Bergey (2012) stated that the student teachers tended to think of themselves as teacher researchers. They reflected in and on action. They were able to assess and adapt lessons and interactions to their school and classroom contexts.

Most important to the program designers is the ongoing analysis and re-analysis by the students of the meaning of *urban* and the implications this has for who they become as teachers. They do not write about this per se; rather, it appears in the descriptions of what they do, what aspects of the program they draw on and how they shape their practice over time. Rust and Bergey (2012) give the example of Janet:

> She arrived with preconceptions about urban schools that she candidly describes: "I had expected it to be . . . dilapidated and run-down . . . judgments formed due to other people's perceptions." What she initially discovers is an unexpected vibrancy in the community and a diversity of architecture to which her undergraduate experience made her especially sensitive. We can watch her understanding of the breadth and depth of the community's assets grow such that, when she could move to a more affluent and better resourced setting (as about a third of her colleagues do), she chooses not to. Hers is not a romantic vision. Rather, she seems to have interpreted her summer readings of Moll et al. (1992), Murrell (2001), Sugrue (1993), Yosso (2005), and others as a mandate for action. So, she situates herself solidly in the community and takes up the challenge of teaching her students about their community—both the neighborhood and the city with the children learning to draw maps of their neighborhood, learning to identify the assets of the neighborhood, learning to use English along with their architectural drawings as a means of expression and communication.
>
> (p. 15)

What Rust and Bergey (2012) saw in these portfolios was a powerful indication of the impact of efforts made across the program to help students encounter excellent *representations* of practice, engage in *decomposing* practices and—especially in their planning and implementation of instruction—*approximate* the work of their more skillful and experienced instructors and classroom mentors (see Grossman et al., 2009). The net result seems to be that these new teachers are committed to situating themselves in communities of practice that are similarly focused on urban schools.

Clinical Practice at the Teacher Learning Center

Hovland and Chandler (2008) described a partnership between the South Dakota Department of Education, Black Hills State University and the Spearfish School District to provide a professional development environment in which preservice, new and experienced teachers could come together to study practice. Along with the school principal, Hovland and Chandler—both university faculty with positions in the local school—developed and studied a professional development environment in which preservice and practicing teachers could comfortably view two live classrooms:

> Inspired by the *behind the glass* observation system used in the Reading Recovery program (Clay, 1993), two one-way, ten-foot-wide mirrors were built on each side of a middle classroom, allowing observers a clear view of teacher/student interactions in the adjacent first- and second-grade classrooms. The middle classroom was designed to support teacher development by providing opportunities for observation of "live" elementary classrooms as well as a place for reflective conversations regarding teacher decision-making, instructional techniques, classroom environment, and classroom management.
>
> (Hovland and Chandler, 2008, p. 27)

Following discussions that emerged from these observations, cognitive coaching by designated mentors from among the teaching staff was used to help the teachers-in-residence reflect on their practice. Hovland and Chandler (2008) wrote:

> The mentors became proficient in using three conversations aimed at supporting reflective practice: (1) the planning conversation, (2) the reflective conversation, and (3) the problem-resolving conversation. These support tools enabled the mentors to provide new teachers opportunities to think through lessons before teaching and to reflect on teaching.
>
> (p. 30)

Drawing on their experience of intense support for new teachers through interaction with the schools, Hovland and Chandler (2008) concluded:

> The Teacher Learning Center project strengthens the teacher preparation program at Black Hills State University by providing opportunities for education students to experience several important elements of clinical practice including, but not limited to, opportunities to observe authentic instruction, to reflect, and to discuss what they see happening behind the glass.
>
> (p. 31)

These are the critical skills that Grossman et al. (2009) found essential in professional preparation, and they are accomplished in a setting that requires collaboration and negotiation and supports inquiry among experienced and novice teachers.

Focused Clinical Practice and the Education of Teachers

Moving from edge environments, we offer descriptions of two long-standing programs—Montessori initial teacher preparation and Reading Recovery—as examples of what we mean by focused clinical practice designed to enable representations, decomposition and approximations of practice that is described by Grossman et al. (2009) as essential to professional preparation.

Montessori

Preparation for teaching in a Montessori school provides a powerful example of a focused clinical preparation program for teachers. Typically, such preparation adheres closely to Maria Montessori's vision of a child-centered education guided by careful observation of children working in a "prepared" environment, as described in *Dr. Montessori's Own Handbook* (1965), *The Montessori Method* (2008) and *Spontaneous Activity in Education* (1917/2008). Children in a Montessori school are generally free to "work" alone or in small groups in areas and with didactic materials of their choosing. The curriculum and structure of the school day are highly individualized. Hence, preparation for teaching in a Montessori setting requires that teachers become adept with the didactic materials that Maria Montessori developed (representation) by learning to work with them (approximation) in the prescribed ways that she defined (decomposition) so as to have the freedom to choose to introduce and work with those materials that most appropriately meet each child's interests and needs.

Maria Montessori described the classroom environment as a second teacher, so prospective Montessori teachers must learn to design child-centered environments in which the furniture and surroundings are expressly child-appropriate and every didactic material that is displayed has a place, is available to the child and can be returned to that place by the child. This is the "ordered" environment that Montessori saw as essential to enabling children to develop a sense of organization and, hence, self-discipline and to move toward independence. In such environments, observation by the teacher is critical so as to determine which children may need help, which aspects of the environment are working well and when to introduce a new piece of equipment or to demonstrate a new way of working with the equipment (Montessori, 1965, 1917/2008, 2008).

Preparation of teachers for Montessori environments is now typically situated in a higher-education institution as part of a larger early childhood education program and is accredited either by the American Montessori Society (AMS) or the International Montessori Association (AMI). The elements that guided the first Montessori schools—observation (representation), deep knowledge of the didactic materials (decomposition) and design of the environment (approximation)—remain essential to Montessori programs and are accomplished through coursework and guided internships. Both coursework and internships are designed to offer supervised practice with equipment with an instructional approach that includes learning to use specific, targeted language in a normal voice (not a childish voice), minimal gestures and implementation of the *three-period lesson*—presentation, practice until one is sure that the child has developed the necessary knowledge and understanding, and assessment that confirms the child's achievement.

Often, preservice students are required to develop their own versions of *The Montessori Handbook* (decomposition and approximation). To do so means that they are able to describe each piece of equipment, ranging from the practical life and sensory equipment to the mathematical, note each step of use and include in their description points of interest relative to each piece and the intended learning for children of different ages. They begin such work by reading about the piece of equipment, observing a skilled instructor model its use (representation), practicing with the instructor (decomposition and approximation), continuing practice on their own and with other interns (decomposition and approximation), writing and submitting a lesson plan for its use (decomposition) and, finally, moving into supervised use with children (approximation). Gradually, interns' reflections on practice become part of their own manuals and are commented on by their mentor or program instructor. Although some Montessori training programs have gone online, these steps—with this attention to the detail of use—continue to be essential elements of the professional preparation of Montessori teachers.

Reading Recovery

Reading Recovery (Clay, 1985, 1993) is another powerful example of a program designed to guide teaching practice by specifying the nature of the practice (representation) and the ways in which the practice may be enacted (decomposition) but leaving the actual teaching to the teacher, who adapts his or her instruction to the individual child. The underlying premise of Reading Recovery is that as different children learn to read, they have different patterns in terms of reading behavior. Hence, the purpose of individualized instruction is

- to observe precisely what children are saying and doing
- to use tasks that are close to the learning tasks of the classroom (rather than standardized tests of reading)
- to observe what children have been able to learn (not what they have been unable to do)
- to discover what reading behaviours they should now be taught from an analysis of performance in reading texts, not from pictorial or puzzle material, or from normative scores

- to shift the child's reading behaviour from less adequate to more adequate responding, by training on reading tasks rather than training visual perception or auditory discrimination as separate activities.

(Clay, 1985, p. 13)

Becoming a Reading Recovery instructor begins with an intensive week of learning how to observe and assess a child's early literacy status (representation and decomposition), followed by weekly classes in which teachers report on their daily experiences teaching four students for 30 minutes a day (decomposition and approximation). In the United States, a teacher leader also observes each teacher's teaching four times a year and consults on the teacher's work with the children and program implementation. Throughout the intensive first year of professional development, Reading Recovery teachers learn to:

- systematically and regularly assess each child's current understandings
- closely observe and record behaviors for evidence of progress
- use teaching procedures competently and appropriately
- put their observations and analyses into words and articulate their questions and challenges
- self-analyze teaching decisions to determine the effect on each child's learning
- tailor interactions to extend each child's understandings
- communicate about Reading Recovery within the school
- communicate regularly with the classroom teacher about each child's progress in both settings.

(Reading Recovery Council of North America, 2012, http://readingrecovery.org/reading-recovery/training/for-teachers)

In other words, teachers are educated to be faithful to the instructional practice, but they are expected (and monitored) to implement the practice in ways that meet the needs of individual students.

Initial training is only the beginning of becoming a Reading Recovery teacher. Reading Recovery teachers engage in six or more ongoing professional development sessions with teacher leaders and colleagues, two-thirds of which involve observing others teaching and discussing the child's reading and the teacher's teaching (representation and decomposition). As Shanahan and Barr (1995) noted, "the careful selection of highly skilled and motivated teachers and the approach to professional development seem to significantly enhance the outcomes of the program, as does its tutorial format" (p. 978).

In the clinical training for professional practice required by both Montessori and Reading Recovery, teacher education is respectful of the teacher who is learning and, most importantly, ever-mindful of the students' responses throughout all instructional interactions. The benefit to the students is ever-present—and this is examined by more experienced teachers observing and commenting along with the teachers who are learning to practice.

Across These Programs

Common to all of these programs is the interpretation of clinical practice as grounded in research and theory—powerfully connected to practice, demanding of reflection and conducted within a community of practice. Context is critical to the success of these examples of practice. Choices have been made about where and with whom the learner will work. Choices have been made about what it is that the learner should learn and about how to scaffold that learning.

There is, in these examples, a tacit understanding that learning to reason toward effective practice in teaching is fundamentally the same as learning the ropes in any other field. It involves situated knowing—that is, knowing the context, knowing what is appropriate in the given setting and being able to draw deeply from a well of good information and powerful representations of practice to shape the appropriate action. There is, in these efforts to reshape teacher education with and around robust models of clinical practice, a commitment to sustained symbiotic, interpersonal, interinstitutional and interdependent social and structural arrangements in which adult professionals working together learn from one another (Boyd et al., 2009; Castle et al., 2005; Ingersoll, 2001; Johnson & Birkeland, 2003).

Moving to Action

In their study of Chicago reform in the 1990s, Bryk, Sebring, Allensworth, Luppescu, and Easton (2010) identified five qualities that are essential to a high-functioning public school: effective leadership, collaborative teachers, involved families, a supportive environment and ambitious instruction. Bryk et al. (2010) believe that all five qualities must be present in any successful school reform, but they are not prescriptive about the proportion. If we look carefully at the research examined in this chapter regarding teacher education, we could easily begin to make a similar list. We could, for example, claim that clinical practice conducted in an environment that is respectful and enabling of the merging of theory and practice is essential. We could also claim that experienced teachers must have a much more powerful role in the preparation of new teachers so as to enable the representation, decomposition and approximation of practice that is now understood as essential to the growth of professional expertise. We could claim that scale is an important factor: Programs in which the individual is known and carefully mentored and, simultaneously, has the support of a collaborative community (a small cohort, a peer group, a professional learning community) enable the formation of the individual teacher's skills. And we could claim that there must be room for a variety of models in a variety of settings to emerge since there is no best system that can account for and respond to the diversity inherent in this complex educational landscape. But none of these—alone or together—is enough.

There is no question that new models of teacher education are emerging. The ones that we have referred to herein are all, in one way or another, edge environments working as incubators for ideas about teacher growth and development; about healthy, successful school environments; about the role of education for all in a democracy that is struggling to determine how best to engage its entire populace. These experiments are too new to tell us how, in the long run, they will affect student learning in classrooms, the retention of teachers, a sustained high level of practice among teachers or the quality of schools in urban and rural settings. They should be studied carefully and over time so that we are able to say with certainty what the critical qualities of really good teacher education are.

From the aforementioned examples and others in this volume, it is clear that such study has begun. Further, it is clear that designing, implementing and sustaining focused clinical experiences that are beneficial for both educators and students is a systemic, multi-directional task that must move beyond individual arrangements and cooperative, convenient agreements to provide prospective teachers with a place to try out selected pedagogies or to observe more experienced teachers. What is needed is thinking broadly about what we already know about successful, comprehensive organizational change—which is what is really at stake here—and, drawing on that information, being willing to try a number of approaches simultaneously.

If undertaking this task were easy, there would be no need for the chapters in this volume. Furthermore, if this task were easy and the benefits of systemic efforts to create focused clinical practice were obvious, we would likely see fewer attempts to bypass university-based teacher education completely. Overall, the university systems of this country have a powerful role to play here as the acknowledged intellectual centers of their communities and as providers of research and expertise.

While we can be sure that there will never be one best way to prepare teachers, we can now claim with certainty that focused clinical practice is critical, that it must be guided and that we have already learned a lot about how to do this work. The movement toward action is beginning; the movement toward studying the impact of action is also beginning, albeit more slowly. The important tasks are to maintain momentum, to understand who benefits and why, to interrogate the value of those benefits and to create lasting, interdependent arrangements that promote dynamic professional education for adults and learning resources for children and adolescents.

References

Adams, A., Bondy, E., & Kuhel, K. (2005). Pre-service teacher learning in an unfamiliar setting. *Teacher Education Quarterly, 32*(2), 41–62.

Benner, P., Sutphen, M., Leonard, V., & Day, L. (2010). *Educating nurses: A call for radical transformation*. San Francisco, CA: Jossey-Bass.

Boyd, D., Grossman, P., Hammerness, K., Lankford, H., Loeb, S., Ronfeldt, M., & Wyckoff, J. (2009). The influence of school administrators on teacher retention decisions. Retrieved from http://www.teacherpolicyresearch.org/portals/1/pdfs/NYC%20 Math%20Immersion.pdf

Bransford, J.D., Brown, A.L., & Cocking, R.R. (1999). *How people learn: Brain, mind, experience, and school*. Washington, DC: National Academy Press.

Britzman, D.P. (1991). *Practice makes practice: A critical study of learning to teach*. Albany, NY: SUNY Press.

Bryk, A.S., Sebring, P.B., Allensworth, E., Luppescu, S., & Easton, J.Q. (2010). *Organizing schools for improvement: Lessons from Chicago*. Chicago, IL: University of Chicago Press.

Castle, S., Fox, R.K., & Souder, K.O. (2005). Do professional development schools (PDSs) make a difference? A comparative study of PDS and non-PDS teacher candidates. *Journal of Teacher Education, 57*, 65–80.

Clay, M.M. (1985). *The early detection of reading difficulties* (3rd ed.). Auckland, New Zealand: Heinemann.

Clay, M.M. (1993). *Reading Recovery: A guidebook for teachers in training*. Portsmouth, NH: Heinemann.

Clift, R., Iddings, A., Jurich, D., Reyes, I., & Short, K.G. (November 30, 2011). Enacting a New Vision of Early Childhood Literacy Education. Research Symposium. Annual Conference of the Literacy Research Association, Jacksonville, FL.

Clift, R.T., & Brady, P. (2005). Research on methods courses and field experiences. In M. Cochran-Smith & K. Zeichner (Eds.), *Studying teacher education: The report of the AERA Panel on Research and Teacher Education* (pp. 309–424). Mahwah, NJ: Lawrence Erlbaum.

Clift, R.T., Reinhardt, K.S., & Robbins, S. (December 2012). Creating CREATE Year Two: Funds of Knowledge and Story as Bases for Transforming Teacher Preparation. Literacy Research Association (LRA), San Diego, CA.

Clift, R.T., & Say, M. (1988). Public schools and pre-service teacher education: Collaboration or conflict? *Journal of Teacher Education, 39*(3), 2–7.

Cochran-Smith, M. (2001). Constructing outcomes in teacher education. *Educational Policy Analysis Archives, 9*(11). Retrieved from http://epaa.asu.edu/ojs/article/view/340/466

Cochran-Smith, M., & Powers, C. (2010). The key to changing the teaching profession: 6 new directions for teacher preparation. *Educational Leadership, 67*(8), 6–13.

Daley, B.J. (2001). Learning and professional practice: A study of four professions. *Adult Education Quarterly, 52*(1), 39–54.

Drago-Severson, E. (2011). How adults learn. *Journal of Staff Development, 32*(5), 10–12.

Durning, S., Artino, A., Boulet, J., Van Der Vleuten, C., La Rochelle, J., Arze, B., & Schuwirth, L. (2010). Making use of contrasting participant views of the same encounter. *Medical Education, 44*(10), 953–961.

Dyess, S.M., & Sherman, R.O. (2009). The first year of practice: New graduate nurses' transition and learning needs. *The Journal of Continuing Education in Nursing, 40*(9), 403–410.

Gorodetsky, M., & Barak, J. (2008). The educational-cultural ecological edge: A participative learning environment for co-emergence of personal and institutional growth. *Teaching and Teacher Education, 24*, 1907–1918.

Grande, M., Burns, B., Schmidt, R., & Marable, A. (2009). Impact of a paid urban field experience on teacher candidates' willingness to work in urban schools. *Teacher Educator, 44*(3), 188–203.

Grossman, P., Compton, C., Igra, D., Ronfeldt, M., Shahan, E., & Williamson, P. (2009). Teaching practice: A cross-professional perspective. *Teachers College Record, 111*(9), 2055–2100.

Gunckel, K.G. (2013). Fulfilling multiple obligations: Pre-service elementary teachers' use of an instructional model while learning to teach and plan science. *Science Education, 97*(1), 139–162.

Guyton, E., & McIntyre, J. (1990). Student teaching and school experiences. In W. Houston (Ed.), *Handbook of research on teacher education* (pp. 514–534). New York, NY: Macmillan.

Himley, M., & Carini, P. (2000). *From another angle: Children's strengths and school standards.* New York, NY: Teachers College Press.

Hinchey, P.H., & Cadiero-Kaplan, K. (2005). The future of teacher education and teaching: Another piece of the privatization puzzle. *Journal for Critical Education Policy Studies, 3*(2). Retrieved from http://www.jceps.com/index.php?pageID=article&articleID=48

Holmes Group (1986). *Tomorrow's teachers.* East Lansing, MI: Author.

Holmes Group (1990). *Tomorrow's schools: Principles for the design of professional development schools.* East Lansing, MI: Author.

Holmes Group (1995). *Tomorrow's schools of education: A report of the Holmes Group.* East Lansing, MI: Author.

Hovland, M., & Chandler, C. (2008). Enhanced teacher preparation coming to you live from the Teacher Learner Center! *Kappa Delta Pi Record, 45*(1), 26–31.

Ingersoll, R.M. (2001). Teacher turnover and teacher shortages: An organizational analysis. *American Education Research Journal, 38*(3), 499–534.

Johnson, S.M., & Birkeland, S.E. (2003). Pursuing a "sense of success": New teachers explain their career decisions. *American Education Research Journal, 40*, 581–617.

Joyce, B.R., & Clift, R.T. (1984). The Phoenix agenda: Essential reform in teacher education. *Educational Researcher, 13*, 5–8.

Knowles, M.S., Holton, E.F., & Swanson, R.A. (2005). *The adult learner: The definitive classic in adult education and human resource development* (6th ed.). Burlington, MA: Elsevier.

Kumar, R., Dean, C.P., & Bergey, R.N. (2012). Knowledge of community and technology as parallel tools of agency in teacher preparation. In R. Flessner, G.R. Miller, K.M. Patrizio, and J.R. Horwitz (Eds.), *Agency through teacher education* (pp. 85–96). Lanham, MD: Rowman & Littlefield.

Labaree, D. (2004). *The trouble with ed schools.* New Haven, CT: Yale University Press.

Latham, N.I., & Vogt, W.P. (2007). Do professional development schools reduce teacher attrition? Evidence from a longitudinal study of 1,000 graduates. *Journal of Teacher Education, 58*, 153–167.

Lave, J., & Wenger, E. (1991). *Situated learning: Legitimate peripheral participation.* New York, NY: Cambridge University Press.

Lawler, P.A., & King, K.P. (2000). *Planning for effective faculty development: Using adult learning strategies.* Malabar, FL: Krieger.

Lunenberg, M., & Korthagen, F. (2009). Experience, theory, and practical wisdom in teaching and teacher education. *Teachers and Teaching: Theory and Practice, 15*(2), 225–240.

MacLeod, G.R. (1987). Microteaching modeling. In M.J. Dunkin (Ed.), *The international encyclopedia of teaching and teacher education* (pp. 720–722). Oxford, United Kingdom: Pergamon.

Moll, L., Amanti, C., Neff, D., & González, N. (1992). Funds of knowledge for teaching: Using a qualitative approach to connect homes and classrooms. *Theory into Practice, 31*(2), 132–141.

Montessori, M. (1917/2008). *Spontaneous activity in education.* Oxford, United Kingdom: Benediction Classics.

Montessori, M. (1965). *Dr. Montessori's own handbook.* New York, NY: Schocken Books.

Montessori, M. (2008). *The Montessori Method.* Radford, VA: Wilder.

Murrell, P.C. (2001). *The community teacher: A new framework for effective urban teaching.* New York, NY: Teachers College Press.

National Council for the Accreditation of Teacher Education (NCATE) (2010). *Transforming teacher education through clinical practice: A national strategy to prepare effective teachers.* Retrieved from http://www.ncate.org/Public/Publications/TransformingTeacher Education/tabid/737/Default.aspx

Nursing Executive Center (2005). *Bridging the preparation-practice gap.* Washington, DC: Author.

Oldenburg, R. (1989). *The great good place: Cafés, coffee shops, bookstores, bars, hair salons, and other hangouts at the heart of a community.* New York, NY: Marlowe & Co.

Paese, P.C. (2003). Impact of professional development schools pre-service through induction. *Action in Teacher Education, 25*(1), 83–88.

Patterson, A.D., McGoech, D.M., & Olsen, H.C. (1990). *A brief history of the Association of Teacher Educators* (2nd ed.). Reston, VA: Association of Teacher Educators.

Perry, C.M., & Power, B.M. (2004). Finding the truths in teacher preparation field experiences. *Teacher Education Quarterly, 31*(2), 125–136.

Reading Recovery Council of North America. (2012). Training for Reading Recovery teachers is a yearlong period of change as teachers learn to make decisions based on a child's responses during individual teaching sessions. Retrieved from http://readingrecovery.org/reading-recovery/training/for-teachers

Ridley, D.S., Hurwitz, S., Davis Hackett, M.R., & Knutson Miller, K. (2005). Comparing PDS and campus-based pre-service teacher preparation: Is PDS-based preparation really better? *Journal of Teacher Education, 56*(1), 46–56.

Ronfeldt, M. (2012). Where should student teachers learn to teach? Effects of field placement school characteristics on teacher retention and effectiveness. *Educational Evaluation and Policy Analysis, 34*(1), 3–26.

Ross, D., Adams, A., Bondy, E., Dana, N.F., Dodman, S., & Swain, C. (2011). Impact of a cohort-based, job-embedded, blended teacher leadership program. *Teaching and Teacher Education, 27*, 1213–1222.

Rust, F. O., & Bergey, N. L. (April 2012). Developing action-oriented knowledge among pre-service teachers. Paper presented at the Annual Meeting of the American Education Research Association, Vancouver, BC, Canada.

Shanahan, T., & Barr, R. (1995). Reading Recovery: An independent evaluation of the effects of an early instructional intervention for at-risk learners. *Reading Research Quarterly, 30*, 958–996.

Smylie, M.A. (1995). Teacher learning in the workplace: Implications for school reform. In T.R. Guskey and M. Huberman (Eds.), *Professional development in education: New paradigms and practices* (pp. 92–113). New York, NY: Teachers College Press.

Sugrue, T. J. (1993). The structures of urban poverty: The reorganization of space and work in three periods of American history. In M. Katz (Ed.), *The underclass debate: Views from history* (pp. 85–118). Princeton, NJ: Princeton University Press.

Sullivan, W. M., Colby, A., Wegner, J. W., Bond, L., & Shulman, L. S. (2007). *Educating lawyers: Preparation for the profession of law* (Vol. 2). New York, NY: John Wiley & Sons.

Tsui, A., Edwards, G., Lopez-Real, F. J., & Kwan, T. (2009). *Learning in school-university partnership: Sociocultural perspectives.* New York, NY: Routledge.

Tsui, A.B.M., & Law, D.Y.K. (2007). Learning as boundary-crossing in school-university partnership. *Teaching and Teacher Education, 23*(8), 1289–1301.

Wenger, E. (1998). *Communities of practice.* New York, NY: Cambridge University Press.

Wenger, E.C., & Snyder, W.M. (2000). Communities of practice: The organizational frontier. *Harvard Business Review.* Retrieved from http://www.nff.wildapricot.org/Resources/Documents/communities_practice_wenger_snyder.pdf/3

Wiggins, G., & McTighe, J. (2006). *Understanding by design* (2nd ed.). New York, NY: Prentice Hall.

Wood, M.B., & Turner, E.T. (2014). Bringing the teacher into teacher preparation: Mentor teachers and prospective teachers in joint methods activities. *Journal of Mathematics Teacher Education.* Retrieved from http://link.springer.com/article/10.1007/s10857-014-9269-4#page-1

Yosso, T.J. (2005). Whose culture has capital? A critical race theory discussion of cultural wealth. *Race Ethnicity and Education, 8*(1), 69–91.

Zeichner, K. (2010). Rethinking the connection between campus courses and field experiences in college- and university-based teacher education. *Journal of Teacher Education, 61*(1–2), 89–99.

4

CLINICAL PROTOTYPES

Nontraditional Teacher Preparation Programs

Michelle Haj-Broussard, Jennifer L. Husbands, Belinda Dunnick Karge, Kimberly Walker McAlister, Marjorie McCabe, John A. Omelan, Phyllis Payne, Vickie V. Person, Karen Peterson and Cyndy Stephens

Nontraditional educator preparation programs have given individuals the opportunity to earn teacher certification in a structured program while concurrently teaching in a classroom with support and supervision. Nontraditional programs capitalize on the participants' prior work and life experiences. As with traditional educator preparation programs, nontraditional preparation programs cannot be described by a specific model; they vary significantly from state to state, within states and within institutions. This chapter was authored by members of the National Association for Alternative Certification (NAAC), a professional organization that advocates for standards-based and research-driven best practices and policy related to nontraditional routes for educator recruitment, selection, preparation and support. The organization focuses on effective staffing of educators who enter—and are retained in—PK–12 schools via nontraditional routes. This chapter will describe the clinical practices of five nontraditional programs for obtaining certification in five different states along with how the training and/or coursework align with those clinical experiences.

Studies have shown that graduates of intensive nontraditional programs remain in the field as long as—or longer than—traditionally trained teachers (Gimbert & Stevens, 2006; Haberman, 1999; Ingersoll & Smith, 2003; Karge, Gleaser, Sylva, Levine, & Lyons, 2006; Paccione, McWhorter, & Richburg, 2000), they tend to be older and more diverse than persons graduating from traditional programs (Guyton, Fox, & Sisk, 1991; Haberman, 1994; Karge, Lasky, McCabe, & Robb, 1995; Rosenberg & Sindelar, 2005; Shen, 1998; Tyler, Yzquierdo, Lopez-Reyna, & Flippin, 2004; Zeichner & Schulte, 2001) and evaluations of their pedagogical content knowledge and practice using performance-based evidence are equivalent to those of traditionally prepared teachers (Harvey & Gimbert, 2007; Noell, Burns, & Gansle, 2009; Sandlin, Young, & Karge, 1994). Furthermore, all nontraditional or alternative certification programs that are housed in institutions accredited by the Council for the Accreditation of Educator Preparation (formerly the National Council for Accreditation of Teacher Education [NCATE]) adhere to the same professional and accreditation standards as traditional programs and are evidence-based (NCATE, 2010–2012; Sears, Burstein, Ashton, & Murawski, 2009).

The U.S. Secretary of Education's Third Annual Report on Teacher Quality (U.S. Department of Education, 2004) advocates for alternative certification. Moreover, testimony given to the U.S. House Education and the Workforce Committee (Hunter, 2012) argues that alternatively certified teachers are equally as effective—if not more so—than traditionally certified educators. Although in a previous chapter, Zeichner and Bier (2015) discuss that "there is some evidence of a 'learning loss' by pupils as underprepared beginning teachers of record are catching up with teachers who completed all of their preparation for an initial teaching license prior to becoming responsible for classrooms" (Zeichner & Conklin, 2005, cited in Zeichner & Bier, 2015, p. 30), a recent Institute for Education Sciences (IES) report (Clark et al., 2013) found that there is no statistical difference between the student outcomes of traditionally versus alternatively certified teachers. Moreover, it found that for Teach for America (TFA) in particular, the novice TFA teachers' students make significant gains in mathematics as compared with the students of experienced teachers who have matriculated from traditional programs. Additionally, the IES study found that students of mathematics teachers from the New Teacher Project—another program specifically cited in Zeichner and Bier (2015)—performed as well as—and often better than—students of traditionally prepared peers with the same level of experience. The classification of the type of program—i.e., *early entry, hybrid* or *college-recommending*—is not as important as the characteristics of each specific program. More than 20% of teacher preparation program completers came through an alternate-route program in 2008–2009 (U.S. Department of Education, 2011), as shown in Figure 4.1. Humphrey, Wechsler and Hough (2008) indicated many strong characteristics of effective alternative teacher certification programs, including carefully selecting school contexts, carefully constructing coursework that meets candidates' needs at their school and providing a trained mentor to support the candidates during their clinical practices.

The Position of Clinical Experiences in Alternative Certification Programs

In her book, *Powerful Teacher Education: Lessons from Exemplary Programs*, Darling-Hammond (2006) highlights construction of the clinical experience as the glue for powerful preparation. She expresses the importance of a combination

2008–2009 Preparation Program Completers
Source: U.S. Department of Education, Title II reports, accessed at https://title2.ed.gov

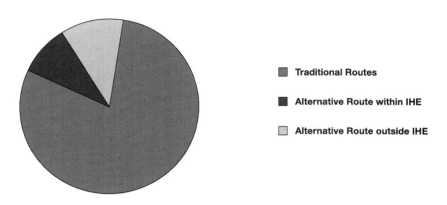

Traditional Routes

Alternative Route within IHE

Alternative Route outside IHE

FIGURE 4.1 2008–2009 preparation program completers

of theory and practice and a gradual introduction to the art of teaching while participating in the clinical experience. Haberman (2010) discusses how the transition from preparation to clinical experience is anything but gradual or gentle. He discusses how the *basic knowledge* learned in preparation is often brutally asphyxiated by the entrenched rituals, practices and policies in the real world. His solution is "on-the-job mentoring by outstanding teachers and coaches" that help the candidate in "replicating the behaviors of effective teachers" (Haberman, 2010, p. 141). The programs discussed in this chapter provide the *glue* that Darling-Hammond (2006) discussed between preparation and practice. The programs go further to help candidates negotiate the system by collaborating with school systems, by supporting and encouraging candidates' use of exemplary practices and by providing ongoing mentoring while candidates work in the classroom. Furthermore, these programs all answer Haberman's (2010) call for accountability in teacher preparation by examining their outcomes.

The image in Figure 4.2 is a conceptual representation of clinical experiences in alternative certification. The circles represent what the candidates negotiate as they develop during their clinical experiences. As you can see by examining the innermost circle, the candidates are provided with instruction and mentoring as they begin teaching. Later, the instruction is reduced, but the mentoring remains to support their teaching. Finally, the candidate is mentored as they teach with no more formal instruction and then, when the program deems them capable, they are recommended for their teaching certificate. Thus, the reconceptualization of teaching and learning teaching put forth in Chapter 1 of this book is not always clearly delineated, and there are some areas that overlap within alternative certification programs.

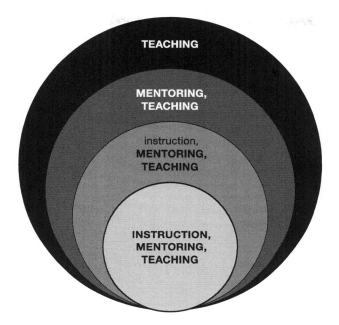

FIGURE 4.2 NAAC conceptual framework for clinical practice

Governors State University Alternative Certification Program

Program Overview

The Governors State University (GSU) Alternative Certification Program serves the Southland region of the Chicago area, the suburbs directly south of the city. In the last decade, with the gentrification of the city, this region has had a huge influx of students of low socioeconomic status (SES), with many districts now having a higher percentage of low SES students than Chicago. The program began as an internship program; after being awarded a $7.1 million Teacher Quality Partnership (TQP) grant, the program transitioned to a residency model. It received national recognition in 2006 when it was one of six national finalists for the Christa McAullife Award for Excellence in Teacher Preparation, the first alternative certification program to be so honored. The program was initially an elementary program but expanded to secondary mathematics and science with the TQP grant. The GSU Alternative Certification Program is grounded in the following framework, which has evolved from ongoing partnerships with high-needs schools in the region over the last 20 years. The framework highlights the complexity of teaching and provides a rationale for rigor and strong partnerships in teacher preparation, particularly the clinical fieldwork component.

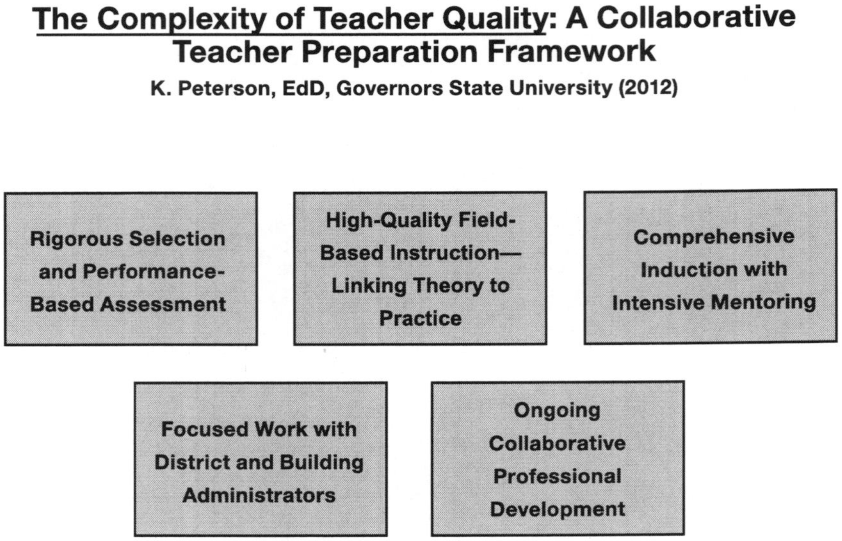

The Complexity of Teacher Quality: A Collaborative Teacher Preparation Framework
K. Peterson, EdD, Governors State University (2012)

Rigorous Selection and Performance-Based Assessment	High-Quality Field-Based Instruction— Linking Theory to Practice	Comprehensive Induction with Intensive Mentoring
Focused Work with District and Building Administrators	Ongoing Collaborative Professional Development	

FIGURE 4.3 Teacher preparation framework, Governors State University

The program partners with approximately 15 districts, some among the poorest in the country. The program was approved under legislation specifically designed to recruit career changers, requiring at least 5 years of work experience following the achievement of a bachelor's degree. The annual cohort contains approximately 30 candidates coming from a wide range of careers, including attorneys, accountants and social workers, who bring rich experience to the high-needs schools in the region. Candidates who are interns are the teachers of record and receive a first-year-teacher salary. Candidates who are TQP residents receive a $30,000 stipend through the grant during the residency year, and candidates who are non–TQP residents are paid a $12,000 stipend by the districts.

Clinical Component

The success of the GSU Alternative Certification Program is very strongly grounded in the scaffolded clinical components of the program. The 18-month program is divided into four cores, with candidates having 16 hours of professional education coursework before beginning the internship/residency. While this coursework is not completed during their internship/residency, it is still done within a classroom setting in the Core I and Core II components of the program.

During Core I (March–June), candidates complete 3 days of observations, two with program completers in partner schools and one with a National Board Certified teacher in the Chicago metropolitan region. Since this experience primarily entails observation, it could be considered a learning experience according to the text framework.

During Core II (the first summer), candidates take a 2-hour credit field experience course, teaching with a cooperating teacher(s) for 13 half-day sessions. Because of summer school schedules, they may have one or two placement sites during the 6 weeks. Since this experience has the candidate observing, teaching and receiving feedback on their teaching, this would be a learning teaching experience.

Core III is the year-long internship or residency. Both the internship and residency options have a very strong mentor component administered through the university in collaboration with its partner districts. Mentors complete the university's 2-day foundational mentor training and then participate in a year-long mentor learning community. Mentors meet with the mentor coordinator at the university bi-weekly for 3-hour sessions, which address ongoing mentor professional development, problem solving and networking in support of the candidates. For the residency, there is a strong emphasis on co-teaching: The program leaders work closely with the mentors to optimize having two teachers in the classroom. Mentors and protégés have specific protocols or anchor assignments they must complete together that will assess the protégés' readiness, such as analysis of student work, formative assessment utilizing the Danielson Framework and setting action plan goals. In addition, the program provides a lead mentor who visits classrooms regularly to keep a pulse on the performance of the candidates and identify any needs to be addressed. A strong support component of both the internship and residency is the 12-hour Instructional Enhancement Contracts. A cadre of trained, retired mentors provides focused assistance beyond mere remediation to the candidates, as requested by principals, mentors, the lead mentor or the candidates themselves. This residency blends the acts of learning teaching and teaching.

During Core IV (the second summer), candidates take a culminating course based on research-based strategies, such as *Understanding by Design* (McTighe & Wiggins, 2005) and *Classroom Instruction That Works* (Marzano, Pickering, & Pollock, 2001). They apply the research based on their rich teaching experiences over the past year. This experience circles back to the learning and allows the candidates to better reflect on what they do in the classroom and how what they are learning in their residency relates (or not) to the research that is prevalent in the field.

As part of the TQP grant, the university has developed a Master of Arts in Teaching (MAT) program that takes this strong mentoring component to the next level. Residency mentors (lead teacher mentors) are selected by a joint committee of university and district personnel through a very rigorous process. They are university instructors who teach a 1-hour seminar course one on one with their residents with focused work time to complete the program protocols.

Another important component of this program is close collaboration with partner districts on their induction/mentoring programs to ensure that the teachers receive ongoing support. For each partner district, GSU provides professional development for induction/mentoring and alternative certification at a district administrative team meeting. In addition, the university provides program development and networking sessions for induction leaders in the districts.

The TQP grant has provided the opportunity to focus even more directly on the final two components of the framework: focused work with district administrators and collaborative professional development with the partner schools. Johnson, Kraft, and Papay (2012) highlight the importance of the school context for new teachers regarding both teacher satisfaction and student outcomes. This research emphasizes the need for ongoing work with districts, with a particular focus on working with school leaders. As part of the TQP grant, Dr. Joseph Murphy from Vanderbilt University has been working with the university and partner districts on leadership initiatives. A team of university and district leaders developed a performance-based evaluation system for principals. Professional learning communities on principal evaluation and Dr. Murphy's work on closing the achievement gaps, as well as other professional development opportunities, are ongoing.

Program Outcomes

Through the first nine cohorts of the program, 93% of candidates who were recommended for certification were still teaching or had gone on to administration. In this performance-based assessment model, it is not unusual for there to be one or two candidates who are counseled out of the program or not recommended for certification. It has been more difficult to track retention in Cohorts 10 through 13 because many of the partner districts have had financial hardships and made substantial cuts, some experiencing a reduction in force for all non-tenured teachers. In most cohorts, there were more than 60% teachers of color and 40% male participants for this elementary program. For the first cohort of the TQP grant, all 15 teachers are still teaching, although some are in different districts because of budgetary cutbacks.

The candidates' readiness is assessed in the clinical component based on a rubric adapted from the Danielson Framework and aligned with the Illinois Professional Teaching Standards. Candidates consistently show improvement from the summative assessment from Semester 1 to Semester 2. For example, in instructional delivery, the cohort average improved from 2.52 to 3.24 (on a 4-point scale). The number of candidates who were proficient or distinguished (the two highest rankings) grew from 47.9% to 82.8%. In lesson design, the increase was from 2.82

to 3.30, and the percentage of candidates rated proficient and distinguished grew from 50% to 85.2%. During the internship/residency, on an assignment determining impact on student learning, candidates work closely with an individual student on writing. In the most recent year, candidates' student scores increased from 66% to 86%. As part of the TQP grant, the external evaluator—OER Associates—conducted site visits of the residents' classrooms and interviewed all candidates, mentors and administrators.

Rasher and Goold (2011) did an external review of the program and found some equally important outcomes. They found that of the principals interviewed, "half believed that the residents are superior to their non-TQP counterparts; the remaining half believed that the residents are as effective as their non-TQP counterparts. All principals would like to continue to have their schools participate in the TQP program" (Rasher & Goold, 2011, p. 10). The researchers felt that the GSU TQP has successfully selected and prepared high-quality mentors and developed a mentor learning community. They noted that the mentors exhibit strong skills in curriculum and instruction, interaction, classroom management, assessment and the implementation of co-teaching strategies. Overall, the mentors are exemplary teachers who serve as high-quality role models to their resident protégés. Furthermore, they stated that "all mentors and residents use technology and data analysis to improve teaching and learning. Most worked together to collect, manage and analyze data to improve teaching and learning" (Rasher & Goold, 2011, p. 11). In discussing the outcomes of the residents on the Classroom Observation Protocol, the researchers stated, "TQP residents far exceeded expectations on four of the five dimensions as measured by the Classroom Observation Protocol. The average (mean) rating on a five point scale is 4.3 on Curriculum & Instruction, 4.5 on Interaction, 4.5 on Classroom Management, and 4.5 on Assessment. Use of Technology was rated low, with an average rating of 2.2" (Rasher & Goold, 2011, p. 14). (Note: Some of the districts do not yet have sufficient technology resources. The grant is working on strengthening this area, not only with the candidates but with the districts overall.)

Regarding the Principal Performance-Based Evaluation system, the external evaluators reported that the large majority of participants believe that the GSU system is more objective, fair or comprehensive than the previous principal evaluation system used in their districts. Principals also noted that a key strength of the evaluation system is helping them become better instructional leaders (Rasher & Goold, 2013).

The program is now focusing its work with its external evaluator to examine the impact of the teachers on student learning. This includes looking at state and local assessments and course assignments with an impact on student learning and utilizes data coordinators to assist with this process in each district.

Georgia Teacher Academy for Preparation and Pedagogy (GaTAPP)

Program Overview

GaTAPP began in 2000 as one statewide solution to the shortage of teachers in Georgia. Since 2005, an average 22% of all Georgia new hires are completers of nontraditional educator preparation programs (Stephens, Nweke, Afolabi, & Eads, 2006; Georgia Professional Standards Commission & Georgia Department of Education, 2011). The current Educator Preparation Rule (505-3-.05) for GaTAPP was approved by the Georgia Professional Standards Commission (GaPSC) for all preparation programs in spring 2008. At that time, Georgia's nontraditional preparation program was renamed Georgia Teacher Academy for Preparation and Pedagogy (GaTAPP). The current standards-based rule is the most prescriptive and rigorous rule in Georgia Educator Preparation history. All GaPSC-approved "providers" are approved on standards and review processes that apply to all approved traditional and nontraditional educator preparation programs in Georgia and, subsequently, all providers must adhere to requirements in the statewide rule.

The goal of the GaTAPP program is to prepare exemplary teachers with verified rich content knowledge who enter classrooms via nontraditional preparation programs to perform at high levels and retain their knowledge, skills and dispositions over time in PK–12 schools. Program objectives are to model and deliver a consistent and rigorous preparation curriculum for planning, instruction and assessment strategies and equip teacher candidates with skills to positively impact student learning. Providers incorporate research-based pedagogical skills and practices that are necessary for successful teaching. GaTAPP is a collaborative partnership between the GaPSC, other approved educator preparation providers, PK–12 schools and school districts, the PK–16 education community and the educator candidates themselves. In addition to curriculum, instructional and pedagogic preparation, the job-embedded program includes an intensive induction and team-based coaching component. The candidates, who are issued an Induction Teaching Pathway 4 (INT4) Certificate upon acceptance into the GaTAPP program, are in a job-embedded, 1- to 3-year residency, which includes consistent monitoring using both formative and summative assessments on pedagogical skills and content knowledge by a Candidate Support Team (CST) for the program's duration as they progress toward program completion verification leading to Induction Teaching Pathway 1 (INT1). All new teachers in Georgia are in induction for 3 years and must meet all requirements to move to the Professional Certification in Georgia's tiered certification. The approval process for Georgia Professional Standards Approval for the Educator Preparation Provider for nontraditional programs mirrors those applied in NCATE accreditation (transitioning to the Council for the Accreditation of Educator Preparation [CAEP] by fall 2016), which is the same process and standards for traditional educator preparation programs. As a matter of ensuring rigor and program breadth, GaTAPP programs must also meet additional Georgia requirements in GaPSC Rule 505-3-.05 (Georgia Professional Standards Commission, 2009).

Clinical Component

GaTAPP clinical practice is job-embedded for not less than 1 academic school year and no more than 3 years. Program success is due in large part to two critical components: 1) activities of the CST and 2) formative performance-based assessments of candidate impact on student learning. These components are essential in determining a candidate's individualized instruction and support needs. On entry to the GaTAPP program, candidates are assigned a CST that is comprised of a School-Based Administrator, School-Based Mentor, Provider Supervisor and Content Specialist. The CST meets a minimum of twice a year and more often as needed based on candidate performance assessments. All mentors and supervisors who coach candidates are trained in program expectations and coaching skills that meet standards and requirements for coaches, as delineated in GaPSC Educator Preparation Rule 505-3-.86, Coaching Endorsement Program. Candidates must participate in GaTAPP coaching and induction experiences for a minimum of 1 academic year and continue in these activities until they successfully complete all requirements of the GaTAPP program.

GaTAPP requires a comprehensive 80+-hour Essentials of Effective Teaching (Essentials) course to assess readiness prior to a candidate's eligibility to enter a classroom as a teacher of record. This course would best be termed a learning experience, and becoming the teacher of record would, of course, be termed teaching. Some exceptions to this learning experience are possible in cases of emergency hires when a candidate begins teaching and simultaneously participates under close supervision in the Essentials course and classroom. Most courses are offered during summer sessions and in year-round seminars that are based on candidates' assessed needs evidenced throughout the program. GaTAPP requires that completers meet 24 competencies from Charlotte Danielson's *Enhancing Professional Practice: A Framework for Teaching* (2007). During the first year in GaTAPP and in addition to 180 classroom days as a teacher of record, the candidates are required to participate in approximately 380 hours of field experiences outside their classroom, seminars, mentor and coaching sessions and meetings with the CST. Candidates must score at the proficient level on all competencies and on 12 dispositions, earn a passing score on the state-required content assessment (Georgia Assessment for Certification of Educators), complete an Individual Induction Plan (IIP) and meet all Georgia special requirements to achieve a Professional Georgia Teacher certificate.

Statewide common assessments results plus provider-specific assessments are collected and stored in a Web-based system for organization, aggregation and analysis. While participating in the GaTAPP program, candidates continually provide their coaching teams with evidence of student achievement and progress for team review and discussion. In addition to the previous description regarding job-embedded, performance-based instruction and assessments, candidates have bi-monthly or monthly seminars focused on assessed needs and/or enhancement of verified content pedagogy. For example, the seminar may include additional instruction and practice on differentiated instruction. Candidates use data gathered for specific learning experiences during field experiences in classrooms culturally and socioeconomically different from their own classrooms to develop lesson plans. The lesson plans are taught in simulated classrooms, and candidates are given feedback/coaching from peers and the instructor. A cohort group of high school math teachers may develop a lesson plan collaboratively using the Common Core Georgia Performance Standards for math, teach the lesson in their own classrooms and share experiences and reflection on practices in the next seminar, where they will receive peer and instructor coaching. These anchor assessments and other results are shared with candidates, GaTAPP faculty and other stakeholders to inform decisions about candidate performance, program effectiveness and unit operations. This recursive, collaborative process is an example of how the candidates learn teaching.

Provider faculty is assessed for proficiency on the same measures as candidates. During program instruction and coaching, faculty is expected to model effective teaching practices that foster candidate proficiencies. In addition, providers survey the school administrators of GaTAPP graduates and also survey program completers. Each group is asked to comment on the continued use of and proficiency in content delivery, instructional strategies and classroom and school practices addressed in the GaTAPP program and impact on student achievement. Each group responds to inquiries regarding the performance level of GaTAPP completers. Completer data inform decisions for program refinement and provider modifications.

GaTAPP, like all traditional programs in the state, identifies the transition points (benchmarks) at which decisions are made regarding the progress of the candidate. Key assessments and the data from assessment results are used at the identified points by the CST and the candidate to determine 1) progress toward completion of the program, 2) recommended interventions and/or 3) continuation or termination. GaTAPP has common key assessments statewide, and data are collected locally and at the state level.

The statewide common assessments for GaTAPP are based on the rubrics for each of the four domains and all elements of Charlotte Danielson's *Enhancing Professional Practice: A Framework for Teaching* (2007). The candidates must score at the proficient level (3) on all indicators of each element in all four domains as one requirement for recommendation for the Professional Georgia Teacher certificate.

GaTAPP has recently developed *Essentials of Effective Teaching (eModules)* instruction and reinforcement tools in a blended model that provides both face-to-face and online learning and practice. The instruction models a flipped classroom, providing multiple resources for curriculum, performance-based instruction and assessment focused on the pedagogical knowledge and skills necessary for a candidate to effectively teach in his or her validated academic content area (Georgia Professional Standards Commission, 2012). The eModules are easily accessed by providers for individualized instruction and coaching based on the needs of each candidate respective to content knowledge, pedagogical skills, learning modalities, learning styles, interests and other confirmations of a candidate's assessed readiness to teach. Such evidence is provided by but not limited to candidates' transcripts and observations of classroom performance, as these convey proficiency in the required 24 competencies and the anchor assignments for this program rather than the number of coursework hours and seat time (Revised GaTAPP Rule 505-3-.05, 2010). These eModules are a combination of learning and learning teaching. GaTAPP candidates seeking Georgia Clear Renewable Certification in Special Education and Early Childhood Education must participate in additional instructional and practice experiences because undergraduate content degrees do not fully provide method and pedagogy for content delivery and assessment with special-needs children and youth. Again, this experience is a blend of learning and learning teaching.

Program Outcomes

Statewide school personnel data show high statewide rates of retention for non-traditionally prepared teachers. GaTAPP candidates and completers include a higher rate of males, teachers of color and disabled individuals than is found in traditional educator preparation programs. Though formal studies are just beginning to provide a wide-ranging view of achievement for high school students taught by nontraditionally prepared teachers, the current data show that achievement is comparable to that of students in classes with traditionally prepared teachers. School, District and State Teachers of the Year are increasingly reflected in the nontraditional teacher population. Educators who complete the GaTAPP program are also found in the ranks of designated teacher leaders, superintendents, state education commission or board members, principals and assistant principals and instructional coordinators in schools statewide. Annual statewide teacher retention rates in the GaTAPP program average 89–90%, while teachers of record in the 2009–2014 FOCUS Transition to Teaching program average approximately 89% retention over a 3-year period (FOCUS Transition to Teaching Program, 2008, 2009) and 86% retention over a 4-year period in the 2006–2011 Georgia Teaching Force Program (Georgia Teaching Force Program, 2006–2012). It is important to note that these retention averages were appreciably higher prior to the current economic downturn in which large numbers of high-performing nontraditional teachers were subject to last-hired and tenure policies for the reduction in force (Georgia Professional Standards Commission, 2008, 2009, 2010, 2011). The overall high retention rates are significant when compared with the retention of all Georgia teachers, since nontraditional teachers are more likely to be hired into high-needs, hard-to-staff schools and content areas.

California State University, San Bernardino, Special Education Intern Program

Program Overview

The California State University, San Bernardino (CSUSB), Special Education Intern Program is housed in San Bernardino, CA, at one of the 23 state university campuses. Candidates who complete the intern program earn an Education Specialist preliminary credential in one of the following specialization areas: Mild/Moderate Disabilities, Moderate/Severe Disabilities or Early Childhood Special Education. Most of the coursework for the intern credential is applicable to the master of arts degree in education with a special education concentration. Candidates in the intern program teach full-time in a partnership district in a special education setting while working on their California intern credential and completing required credential coursework. Interns attend classes one or two nights a week in a cohort format. This is the learning portion of their experience. The course sequence includes preservice coursework before entering a teaching setting, all of the same academic coursework as traditional (non-intern) student teaching candidates and continuous fieldwork supervision for the entire 2-year program. The coursework is done while candidates are teaching in the field and being mentored and supervised. Thus, the field experiences associated with the courses are integrated in the internship, providing a learning teaching experience for the candidates. Candidates in the intern program come from many different backgrounds. Many candidates enter the program to take advantage of the opportunity to be employed full-time while earning a special education credential. There are also significant numbers of candidates who have been paraeducators (aides) in special education settings. In recent years, many general educators who have been laid off have elected to enter special education intern credential programs. The program has partnerships with approximately 60 school districts in urban, suburban and rural school districts.

Clinical Component

Intern candidates complete 140 hours of preservice coursework that includes classroom experience—this occurs before the intern becomes the instructor of record. This is their learning experience. After the intern becomes the instructor of record with all rights and responsibilities, he or she is enrolled continuously in the intern supervision course for the entire 2-year program. Supervision includes the assignment of a university supervisor who observes or meets with the intern candidate every 2 weeks for the entire program. The main purpose of this intensive supervision experience is support that helps the intern in every way to learn teaching. The university supervisor observes and models lessons, helps the intern set up his or her classroom, participates in individualized education program (IEP) meetings, assists with paraeducator and family collaboration and sets goals individualized for the intern. The intern candidates earn eight quarter units of credit for every quarter of the intern program (2 years). Interns' learning is continuous; they also participate in professional development opportunities each quarter and communicate regularly with the program coordinator and program assistant. Teaching learning is also continuous, with frequent communication and collaboration occurring between the university supervisors and the program coordinator and program assistant. In addition to the university supervision component of the intern program, all interns are assigned a district support provider to help with all district-specific issues/needs for the duration of the program. Candidates often report that the support from the intern program was the sort they would have expected from a small, private university, not a large state school. It is a program goal to make sure that every intern has interactions that are attentive, timely and—most of all—supportive of the development of their professional practice.

Program Outcomes

The CSUSB Special Education Intern Program has a retention rate of approximately 95%. This metric includes completion of the program and staying in the district of employment while in the program. A very small percentage of candidates change districts after earning the credential but stay in the field of special education. A very important aspect of the intern program is that former interns make up approximately 30% of the district support providers for current interns. In other words, graduates of the intern program choose to stay involved and mentor new intern candidates. The practice of past interns supporting current interns is a strong indicator of the success of the program and significantly assists with recruitment efforts. Former interns often recommend the program to prospective candidates.

Region 4 Education Service Center Alternative Certification Program
Program Overview

The Region 4 Alternative Certification Program (ACP) is located in Houston, TX. Region 4 is one of 20 Education Service Centers (ESCs) in the state that are dedicated to providing products and services to districts, teachers and students.

With over one million students, 53 districts and more than 100 charter schools, the Region 4 ESC is the largest service center in the state. The Region 4 ACP was created in the fall of 1990 to meet the needs of local districts in staffing special education and bilingual candidates. Since that time, the Region 4 ACP has added over 50 additional certification areas and has developed into the largest ESC-based alternative certification program in the state. Over 14,000 teachers, principals and superintendents have been certified since the inception of the program. In addition to the acclaimed teacher preparation program, the Region 4 ACP has an active school leadership department. Both the principal and superintendent programs are active in recruiting and preparing Texas school leaders. Each year, over 90 principal candidates and 25 superintendent candidates receive their state certification through the Region 4 ACP in administration. The Region 4 ACP continues to meet the needs of local districts, as evidenced by the recent addition of a school counselor program in 2012.

While the Region 4 ACP primarily serves the greater Houston area and seven surrounding counties, the online delivery of content allows instruction to occur across the entire state. The Region 4 ACP currently partners with four Texas service centers to support and deliver teacher training and six service centers to provide principal training and support. These partnerships have been beneficial for smaller, more rural school districts that may not have had access to high-quality teacher certification with service center support.

The Region 4 ACP follows all state guidelines in regard to admissions, preparation, training and teaching. All candidates are screened for criminal history as required by state regulations. Each candidate must meet minimum entrance requirements, which include basic skills competency, an interview, a minimum grade point average and subject matter content hours from an accredited university or college. Those students seeking certification in a foreign language or as a bilingual teacher must also pass an interview in the language of instruction. Candidates applying for the principal, superintendent or counselor program must have a master's degree. Once enrolled, candidates have the option to complete the training via Blackboard or in a face-to-face setting at Region 4. Blackboard is an online delivery system that allows users and instructors to interact in a variety of ways. The coursework for both the online and face-to-face instruction is rigorous. The Region 4 program is not a self-paced, self-guided or correspondence course. Although candidates are not required to meet at a specific time during the course, they are required to log in a minimum of 5 days a week. Coursework is interactive, with trained instructors who are current educational practitioners leading the discussions. Coursework lasts approximately 20 weeks and provides 250 hours of credit toward the state-required 300 hours. Special education, bilingual, English as a second language (ESL) and EC-6 Generalist certification areas require additional content-specific coursework. All coursework is pedagogically based and focused. In addition to the aforementioned coursework, all candidates are required to conduct a book study and complete 30 hours of field experience, as required by state guidelines. Upon completion of the preservice coursework and field experience, candidates become eligible to take the Texas Examination of Educator Standards (TExES) content exams. These exams, which are administered by the Educational Testing Service, are required by Region 4 to begin an internship or clinical teaching assignment. The coursework, field experiences and content exams are all tools to assess candidates' readiness. Candidates may not begin the practicum portion of their program without having passed the appropriate TExES exam and all required coursework.

Clinical Component

Candidates who have completed all requirements may choose between two practicum options to complete their certification: an internship or clinical teaching. An internship is a paid 10-month (or full school year) assignment that may begin anytime during the school year. The candidate is responsible for searching for—and attaining—his or her own internship in an accredited public, private or charter school. Once hired, the candidate becomes an intern and is assigned a mentor by the school district and a field supervisor from Region 4. Field supervision for the Region 4 ACP is conducted by retired school district personnel. Region 4 requires that all field supervisors have supervisory experience and credentials. Many of the 60 field supervisors employed by Region 4 are former principals or superintendents. Field supervisors, mentors and campus administrators work collaboratively during the school year to ensure that the intern receives support and is provided ongoing, meaningful professional development. Interns are recommended for standard certification only upon successful completion of the 1) internship year, 2) ongoing training as required by state guidelines, 3) 56 hours of professional development, which includes 6 hours of test preparation, 4) the Pedagogy and Professional Responsibilities (PPR) exam and 5) a recommendation from the program and the principal. These could be considered anchor activities but not assignments.

Instead of the internship, candidates may opt for a more traditional practicum experience referred to as *clinical teaching*, which is the alternative certification equivalent to student teaching. Twice a year, once in the fall and once in the spring, the Region 4 ACP collaborates with districts to place candidates in schools for clinical teaching. The clinical teaching assignments are 12 weeks in length. As with student teaching, the clinical teacher is required to participate in a full-day assignment and gradually assume responsibility of the classroom with assistance from the cooperating teacher. As with the internship, a field supervisor is assigned to observe and support the clinical and cooperating teacher throughout the assignment. Both the clinical teaching and internship experiences are a mix of learning teaching and teaching. The clinical teacher is required to meet the same exit requirements as the intern, with the exception that the recommendation for certification is made primarily in collaboration between the field supervisor and the cooperating teacher.

Program Outcomes

Region 4 has produced two National Bilingual Teachers of the Year and numerous district/campus teachers of the year. In terms of the leadership program, 10 current superintendents in the Region 4 area have received their certification through the Region 4 program. Moreover, Region 4 has received awards and recognition from programs with whom they collaborate. Cypress Ridge High School—a school in the region—and Katy Independent School District in Region 4 have both given awards to the Region 4 ACP for their collaboration with the program and the enhanced academic performance of their students.

Northwestern State University, Louisiana

Program Overview

In 1884, Northwestern State University began as the Louisiana State Normal School in Natchitoches, Louisiana, and the institution's rich legacy of teaching and learning continues more than 130 years later. Recognizing the power of technology to bring educational opportunity to all students, Northwestern State University now delivers 29 accredited online degree programs, including several in education. The Master of Arts in Teaching (MAT) degree is offered online in the areas of early childhood education (PK–Grade 3), elementary education (Grades 1–5), middle grade education (Grades 4–8 in content areas), secondary education (Grades 6–12 in specific content areas) and special education (by grade band). These online MAT programs range from 33 to 39 graduate course hours, including a two-semester internship. Admission to the MAT program requires an undergraduate degree from a regionally accredited institution, a minimum grade point average, acceptable PRAXIS I and II content test scores and acceptable GRE scores for full admission to the Northwestern Graduate School and the College of Education and Human Development. Candidates enrolled in MAT programs may continue to work, whether in a school or other setting, until the internship. To begin the internship, they must secure a teaching position within their content area at an approved Louisiana school. Since licensure is state-mandated, all Northwestern State University alternative certification programs lead to Louisiana licensure.

In addition to the MAT programs, Northwestern State University offers alternate certification in a practitioner format (Practitioner Teacher Program [PREP]). This on-campus, intensive summer program is available to candidates in a 1-year format. Candidates complete 9 total hours of graduate coursework in the summer and 6 hours of an internship and seminar in both the fall and spring semesters. A total of 21 graduate hours culminate in Louisiana licensure. Admission to PREP also requires full admission to both the Northwestern State University Graduate School and the College of Education and Human Development.

Although the MAT alternative certification programs have been available since 2006, enrollment has increased dramatically since the implementation of online coursework. Since fall 2007, enrollment has almost tripled (spring 2012 enrollment was 185 graduate students). Since the majority of the alternative certification programs are available online, Northwestern State University proudly boasts of completers in school districts from all parts of Louisiana. Principal feedback, anecdotal data from candidates and other school personnel and state-level value-added results illustrate that completers of Northwestern State University's alternative programs are successful in Louisiana classrooms.

Northwestern State University is a participant in the U.S. Department of Education TEACH grant program. This non-competitive grant allows candidates to receive a stipend to pursue teacher certification. In return, completers are required to teach for a minimum of 4 years within the first 8 years of completing the degree. This program is a significant help to students struggling for financial support. The requirements for receiving the grant are stringent (minimum 3.25 grade point average), but this incentive rewards hardworking students who need financial assistance to complete this graduate degree.

Clinical Component

Alternative certification candidates are required to participate in clinical field experiences within every course in the program. Since Northwestern State University's programs accommodate candidates who are either currently teaching or are outside the PK–12 school setting, clinical experiences are structured in ways to accommodate both groups of candidates. If currently employed as a teacher, MAT candidates must conduct a minimum of 25% of field experience hours outside their job assignment and in another school with significantly different demographics than their current placement. If not currently employed as a teacher, field experiences must come from a variety of sites with significantly different demographics. This program is practitioner-friendly, but field experiences must still reflect the unit's commitment to providing candidates opportunities to experience diverse learning environments. Each Louisiana teacher who will be observed by an MAT candidate must be recommended by the K–12 school building supervisor and approved by the Northwestern State University Office of Field Experience and Clinical Practice. Progress is monitored using PASS-PORT, a Web-based portfolio system. Principals recommend cooperating teachers for observations based on expertise, experience and ability to mentor. Course activities, including case studies and reflections, are used to link field experiences to the concepts within each course for maximum application. PASS-PORT allows the monitoring of candidates; if sufficient diversity is not seen in candidate submissions, modifications are made for subsequent field experiences within coursework. Another measure to ensure consistency and quality of field experiences in the MAT program is the inclusion of virtual field experiences with video and WebEx. Since the MAT coursework is offered online, Northwestern State University can post video clips, vignettes or classroom simulations to illustrate a particular concept or practice. These practices make learning more practical for the students and flexible to meet their immediate needs. In initial graduate MAT and all advanced programs, traditional comprehensive exams were replaced by portfolio oral defenses as an anchor assignment beginning in the fall of 2010. Initial graduate MAT and advanced teacher candidates critique and synthesize educational theory related to classroom practice based on their own applied research and field experiences. Presentations highlight the development and implementation of an action research project, program activities and reflection on personal professional growth. Requirements also include documentation aligning coursework, field experiences and teaching to appropriate professional content standards.

The internship begins only after the completion of all required coursework and the receipt of successful PRAXIS Principles of Learning and Teaching (PLT) scores. Candidates are responsible for securing employment at a Louisiana public school to begin the internship. To accommodate alternative certification candidates teaching in non-public schools, the College of Education and Human Development has adopted a set of guidelines that, if met, would allow a candidate to complete the internship requirement in the specified school.

The internship consists of two consecutive semesters. Candidates are assigned a university supervisor who has expertise in teaching and broad content knowledge. Orientation is provided for interns and their university supervisors each semester by the Office of Field Experience. The primary task of the university supervisor is to have regular, consistent contact with the intern to provide support, assess teaching ability and assist with acclimation into the classroom. At a minimum, the university supervisor makes four official visits to observe the intern teach each semester. It is expected that university supervisors will have much more extensive contact with the intern across the semester by phone, email and in-person meetings. This is over and above the support normally provided by the school district for a new teacher. In addition to supervision by the university supervisor and the orientation provided each semester of the internship course, requirements and materials are provided through an online platform and both the Office of Field Experience and Clinical Practice and the Office of Teacher Candidacy and Certification. Both offices are in regular contact with the interns. Graduates of Northwestern State University's alternative certification programs are successful in Louisiana classrooms.

Program Outcomes

From 2005 to 2008, program completers were as effective or more effective in four out of five subject areas (Noell, Burns, & Gansle, 2009). This means that their students' standardized test scores were equal to or better than the test scores of students taught by experienced teachers. This success continued in the following school year (2009–2010), with program completers being as effective as or more effective than experienced teachers in three of the five areas (Gansle, Noell, & Burns, 2010). The candidates were as effective as new teachers in the other areas. These data from the Value Added Teacher Preparation Program Assessment Model are required by the Louisiana Board of Regents and offer a quantitative benchmark regarding the effectiveness of the clinical experiences and the program as a whole. Candidates complete rigorous coursework and must show evidence of their ability to effectively teach children. (For more information on state requirements for teacher preparation value-added data, see the Louisiana Board of Regents website at http://regents.louisiana.gov/value-added-teacher-preparation-program-assessment-model/.) In addition, Northwestern State University received outstanding feedback from NCATE, with no areas of improvement.

Conclusion

The aforementioned five programs are examples of the diversity of nontraditional routes to certification. Alternative certification programs represent a myriad of innovative clinical practices, with program outcomes resulting in positive performance of graduates and high retention rates. Darling-Hammond (2000), in her report that examined the dilemma of teacher supply and demand for the National Commission on Teaching and America's Future, had two action steps for teacher preparation institutions: 1) the need for year-long internships and 2) the need for collaboration with local districts to support teacher internships, entry and induction. Each of the aforementioned programs addresses Darling-Hammond's (2000) action steps. Haberman (2010) believed that to transform teacher education, field and clinical experiences must require on-the-job mentoring and the use of effective teaching practices, which are demonstrated in the aforementioned programs. In addition, his call for accountability in teacher preparation programs is addressed in the outcomes of the aforementioned programs. There is more work to do, but the aforementioned programs exemplify an excellent starting point for taking the next steps. In terms of what those next steps should be, research is needed on the outcomes of teacher education programs and ways to examine the effects of preparation program practices on both short-term outcomes, such as achievement, and longer-term outcomes, such as high school completion rates, entry into post-secondary programs and completion of post-secondary programs. While describing clinical experiences is laudable, if those descriptions do not provide insight into best practices that will help students reach their desired outcomes, then perhaps our focus needs to shift. The aforementioned programs only touch upon those outcomes; a greater focus on outcomes is needed.

References

Clark, M. A., Chiang, H.S., Silva, T., McConnell, S., Sonnenfeld, K., Erbe, A., & Puma, M. (2013). *The effectiveness of secondary math teachers from Teach for America and the Teaching Fellows Programs* (NCEE 2013–4015). Washington, DC: National Center for Education Evaluation and Regional Assistance, Institute of Education Sciences, U.S. Department of Education.

Danielson, C. (2007). *Enhancing professional practice: A framework for teaching.* Alexandria, VA: Association for Supervision and Curriculum Development.

Darling-Hammond, L. (2000). *Solving the dilemmas of teacher supply, demand and quality.* New York: National Commission on Teaching and America's Future.

Darling-Hammond, L. (2006). *Powerful teacher education: Lessons from exemplary programs.* San Francisco, CA: Jossey-Bass.

FOCUS Transition to Teaching Program (2006–2012) & Georgia Teaching Force Program (2006–2012). Annual performance reports. Atlanta, GA: Georgia Professional Standards Commission.

FOCUS Transition to Teaching Program (2008, 2009) & Georgia Teaching Force Program (2010, 2011). Annual performance reports. Atlanta, GA: Georgia Professional Standards Commission.

Gansle, K., Noell, G., & Burns, J. (2010). Value added assessment of teacher preparation in Louisiana: 2005–2006 to 2008–2009 (sic) Overview of performance bands. Retrieved from http://regentsfiles.org/assets/docs/TeacherPreparation/200910ValueAddedAssessmentOverviewofPerformanceBandsFINAL82610.pdf

Georgia Professional Standards Commission (2007). Teacher new hire rates from non-traditional sources of supply. Atlanta, GA: Author.

Georgia Professional Standards Commission (2008). Georgia Assessment for the Certification of Educators (GACE). Atlanta, GA: Author.

Georgia Professional Standards Commission (2008, 2009, 2010, 2011). Teacher retention reports. Atlanta, GA: Author.

Georgia Professional Standards Commission (2010). Revised GaTAPP rule. Atlanta, GA: Author.

Georgia Professional Standards Commission (2012). GaTAPP guidelines. Atlanta, GA: Author.

Georgia Professional Standards Commission & Georgia Department of Education (2011). Georgia public school personnel report. Certified and classified personnel information report. Atlanta, GA: Author.

Georgia Teaching Force Program (2006–2012). Annual performance reports. Atlanta, GA: Author.

Gimbert, B., & Stevens, J. (March 2006). A study of a competency-driven alternative route to teacher certification in an urban hard to staff school system. Paper presented at the National Association for Alternative Certification Conference, Chicago, IL.

Guyton, E., Fox, M.C., & Sisk, K.A. (1991). Comparison of teaching attitudes, teacher efficacy, and teacher performance of first-year teachers prepared by alternative and traditional teacher education programs. *Action in Teacher Education, 13*(2), 1–9.

Haberman, M. (1994). Preparing teachers for real world urban schools. *The Educational Forum, 58,* 162–168.

Haberman, M. (1999). Increasing the number of high-quality African-American teachers in urban schools. *Journal of Instructional Psychology, 26,* 208–212.

Haberman, M. (2010). Proposal for making teacher education accountable. In V. Hill-Jackson & C.W. Lewis (Eds.), *Transforming teacher education: What went wrong with teacher training and how we can fix it* (pp. 121–152). Sterling, VA: Stylus Publishing.

Harvey, F., & Gimbert, B.G. (2007). Evaluation of nontraditionally and traditionally prepared teachers' pedagogical content knowledge and practice using performance-based evidence. *Journal of the National Association for Alternative Certification, 2*(1), 42–65.

Humphrey, D. C., Wechsler, M., & Hough, H.J. (2008). Characteristics of effective alternative teacher certification programs. *Teachers College Record, 110*(1).

Hunter, D. (July 2012). Education reforms: Discussing the value of alternative teacher certification programs. Education and the Workforce Committee, Washington, DC. Retrieved from edworkforce.house.gov/News/DocumentSingle.aspx?DocumentID=304099

Ingersoll, R.M., & Smith, T. (2003). The wrong solution to the teacher shortage. *Educational Leadership, 60*(8), 30–33.

Johnson, S.M., Kraft, M.A., & Papay, J.P. (2012). How context matters in high-need schools: The effects of teachers' working conditions on their professional satisfaction and their students' achievement. *Teachers College Record, 114*(10), 1–39.

Karge, B.D., Gleaser, B., Sylva, J., Levine, J., & Lyons, B. (2006). A critical reflection of the CSU Fullerton Alternative Certification Program. *National Association for Alternative Certification Online Journal, 1*(1), 23–35.

Karge, B.D., Lasky, B., McCabe, M., & Robb, S.M. (1995). University and district collaborative support for beginning special education intern teachers. *Teacher Education and Special Education, 18*(2), 103–114.

Lavadenz, M., & Hollins, E. (2015). Urban schools as settings for learning teaching. In E. Hollins (Ed.), *Rethinking field experiences in pre-service teacher preparation* (pp. 1–14). New York, NY: Routledge.

Marzano, R.J., Pickering, D., & Pollock, J.E. (2001). *Classroom instruction that works: Research-based strategies for increasing student achievement.* Alexandria, VA: Association for Supervision and Curriculum Development.

McTighe, J., & Wiggins, G.P. (2005). *Understanding by design.* Alexandria, VA: Association for Supervision and Curriculum Development.

National Council for Accreditation of Teacher Education (NCATE) (2010). *Transforming teacher education through clinical practice: A national strategy to prepare effective teachers.* Washington, DC: Author.

National Council for Accreditation of Teacher Education (NCATE) (2010–2012). Programs included in the NCATE review. Retrieved from http://www.ncate.org/BOE/ConductingtheVisit/ProgramsIncludedintheNCATEReview/tabid/86/Default.aspx

Noell, G., Burns, J., & Gansle, K. (2009). Value added assessment of teacher preparation in Louisiana: 2005–2006 to 2007–2008. Background and new results. Retrieved from http://www.laregentsarchive.com/Academic/TE/2009/2008-09VA%288.27.09%29.pdf

Paccione, A., McWhorter, B., & Richburg, B. (2000). Ten years on the fast track: Effective teacher preparation for nontraditional candidates. In D.J. McIntyre & D.M. Byrd (Eds.), *Research on effective models for teacher education: Teacher education yearbook VIII* (pp. 218–234). Thousand Oaks, CA: Corwin.

Peterson, K. (2012). *The complexity of teacher quality: A collaborative teacher preparation framework, digital images.* Governors State University.

Rasher, S., & Goold, R. (Spring 2011). *Governors State University Teacher Quality Partnership Grant #U405A10004: Partner residency school observations and interviews.* Wilmette, IL: OER Associates.

Rasher, S., & Goold, R. (February 2013). *Governors State University Teacher Quality Partnership Grant #U405A10004: Principal performance-based evaluation professional learning communities midyear evaluation.* Wilmette, IL: OER Associates.

Rosenberg, M.S., & Sindelar, P.T. (2005). The proliferation of alternative routes to certification in special education: A critical review of the literature. *Journal of Special Education, 39,* 117–127.

Sandlin, R.A., Young, B., & Karge, B.D. (1994). Regular and intern beginning teachers: Comparison of their development. In *The 1994 Yearbook of California Education Research* (pp. 157–168). San Francisco, CA: Caddo Gap Press.

Sears, S., Burstein, N., Ashton, T., & Murawski, W. (2009). Moving toward standards based alternative certification in special education. *Journal of the National Association for Alternative Certification, 4*(1), 54–72.

Shen, J. (1998). Alternative certification, minority teachers, and urban education. *Education and Urban Society, 31*(1), 30–41.

Stephens, C., Nweke, W., Afolabi, C., & Eads, J. (2006). The Georgia educator workforce 2006: Report of supply, demand, and utilization of teachers, administrative and student services personnel in Georgia public schools. Atlanta, GA: Georgia Professional Standards Commission.

Transition to Teaching Programs in Georgia (2006, 2009). Atlanta, GA: Georgia Professional Standards Commission.

Tyler, N.C., Yzquierdo, Z., Lopez-Reyna, N., & Flippin, S.S. (2004). Cultural and linguistic diversity and the special education workforce: A critical overview. *Journal of Special Education, 38,* 22–38.

University of West Georgia (2008). Evaluation report: Georgia teacher academy for preparation and pedagogy 2002–2008 (2010). Carrollton, GA: West Georgia Evaluation Center.

U.S. Department of Education (2011). Title 2 state reports. Retrieved from https://title2.ed.gov/Public/Home.aspx

U.S. Department of Education, Office of Postsecondary Education (2004). Meeting the highly qualified teachers challenge: The Secretary's third annual report on teacher quality. Washington, DC: Author.

Zeichner, K., & Conklin, H. (2005). Teacher education programs. In M. Cochran-Smith & K. Zeichner (Eds.), *Studying teacher education* (pp. 645–746). New York, NY: Routledge.

Zeichner, K.M., & Bier, M. (2015). Opportunities and pitfalls in the turn toward clinical experience in U.S. teacher education. In E. Hollins (Ed.), *Rethinking field experiences in pre-service teacher preparation* (pp. 20–46). New York, NY: Routledge.

Zeichner, K.M., & Schulte, A.K. (2001). What we know and don't know from peer-reviewed research about alternative teacher certification programs. *Journal of Teacher Education, 52,* 266–282.

PART II

Learning Teaching Situated in Context

> Teachers work on the problems involved in establishing and maintaining intellectual and social relationships with students and content by arranging the furniture and the schedule, planning lessons, working with students while students work independently or in small groups, instructing the whole class at once, linking lessons over time, covering the curriculum, motivating students to do what needs to be done to learn, assessing whether progress is being made, managing diversity of all sorts, and finally bringing the year to a close. Can these parts of teaching be learned in the abstract, as separate skills? Or does learning them depend on trying to do them with particular children in particular circumstances?
>
> (Lampert, 2010, p. 22)

The authors in this part of the book argue for situating learning teaching within the context of classrooms and communities for particular students. Central to this argument is the idea that context is essential for teaching and learning teaching—that learning teaching begins with understanding learners and the context in which they grow and develop. In this discussion, learning teaching refers to developing competence in applying teaching practices that facilitate students' academic, psychological and social development within the context of school and/or community. Learning teaching involves the translation and application of academic knowledge about learning, pedagogy and subject matter in ways that facilitate growth and development for a specific population of students learning in a particular context.

Situating learning teaching within the context of classrooms and communities serving particular students is grounded in a sociocultural perspective on learning and a social justice philosophical stance on envisioning the future. This perspective takes into consideration how students learn, how candidates learn teaching and the sociopolitical relationship among schools, communities and the larger society. This perspective takes into consideration the influence of candidates' early socialization on the ways in which they will appropriate knowledge in practice when facilitating learning for students from cultural and experiential backgrounds different from their own.

The tenets of the sociocultural perspective taken into consideration in the papers in this section are that: (a) learning and cognition are culturally mediated and supported through purposeful activity; (b) learning and the social context in which it occurs transform the person, resulting in a new identity; (c) learning is dependent on the productive use of cultural tools, artifacts, prior knowledge and experiences that are familiar to the learners and that form the basis for constructing new knowledge and understanding; and (d) understanding and expertise are developed through extended situated experience that is influenced by affordances, constraints, focus and guidance in a social context with others. The basic assumption is that these tenets of the sociocultural perspective apply to teaching and learning in different contexts and for different purposes, for learners at different levels in the process of knowledge construction, and for candidates learning teaching.

The premise that learning and cognition are culturally mediated and supported through purposeful activity is well documented in the research and scholarly literature on teaching diverse students. For example, Carol Lee (1995) reported on the use of a specific aspect of African American high school students' everyday language referred to as "signifying" to facilitate learning to interpret complex literary text. Moses, Kamii, Swap, and Howard (1989) combined students' everyday language and shared experience to facilitate learning basic concepts in algebra. Moll (1986) and McCarty (2002) demonstrated the importance of embedding learning experiences within the values and practices of students' home culture. Further, this research supports the premise that learning is dependent on the productive use of cultural tools, artifacts, prior knowledge and experiences that are familiar to learners and that form the basis for constructing new knowledge and understanding. These studies bring attention to particular aspects of students' background experiences that can be used to develop meaningful and productive learning experiences. However, more importantly, this research illuminates the need for teachers to be able to contextualize practice for particular students when developing skills and subject matter knowledge under specific conditions. This is consistent with Weiner's (2003) observation that "[successful] teachers display knowledge of students' lives outside of school to make connections, personal and intellectual, between school learning and lived-experiences" (p. 309). Learning to contextualize teaching practices in this way requires carefully guided experiences in classrooms with real students.

The premise that understanding and expertise are developed through extended situated experience that is influenced by affordances, constraints, focus and guidance in a social context with others is supported by research in urban schools and communities (Barton, 2003; Michie, 2009; Wilson, Corbett, & Williams, 2000). This research indicates that multiple factors within the social context for learning support the development of understanding and expertise. Moreover, other research on schooling for underserved students supports the premise that learning—and the social context within which it occurs—transforms the person and results in a new identity (Crosnoe, Johnson, & Elder, 2004; Nasir, Jones, & McLaughlin, 2011; Osterman, 2000; Packer & Goicocoechea, 2000). The findings from these research studies reveal the interconnectedness within the school context among student–teacher relationships and relationships among peers; feelings of belonging, acceptance and school connectedness; and student behaviors, personal and group identity, and learning outcomes. Other researchers identify the potentially negative impact on the academic, psychological and social development of students when there is a major disconnect between school practices and students' experiential backgrounds (Hemmings, 2003; Kennedy-Lewis, 2012; Nasir, et al. 2011; Noguera, 2003; Weiner, 2003).

The discussion so far has provided evidence for the usefulness of a sociocultural perspective in making sense of and facilitating the growth and development of traditionally underserved students. The evidence provided in this discussion indicates that learning for underserved students is best supported by meaningful and productive learning experiences directly linked to the learners' lives outside of school. Many teachers' cultural and experiential backgrounds differ from those of their students, and they may not live in the local community served by the school. Many teachers do not take the time to understand the students' experiential backgrounds, their everyday experiences and the community context in which students grow and develop. This difference in background experiences and lack of knowledge of the local community places many teachers at a disadvantage in making important connections between academic learning and students' lives outside of school and in supporting students' psychological and social development. This situation suggests the need for change in teaching practices and teacher preparation. The need for change is further supported by the low academic performance of urban and low-income students (National Center for Educational Statistics [NCES], 2013a) and in the reports of novice teachers that they feel underprepared for teaching in urban schools.

Historically, state and national accreditation standards for preservice teacher preparation programs have required that programs address diversity in the curriculum and experiences provided for candidates, and that candidates have experience with diverse populations in multiple aspects of the preparation program (National Council for the Accreditation of Teacher Education [NCATE], 2008). Evidence from the National Assessment of Educational Progress (NAEP) (NCES,

2013b) over several years indicates that the present level of preparation for teaching underserved students is inadequate. The tenets of the sociocultural perspective on which the chapters in this part of the book are based indicate that candidates need deep knowledge of the relationship between students' cultural and experiential backgrounds and meaningful and productive learning experiences. Further, the sociocultural perspective suggests that learning teaching in this way requires guided, focused and extended situated experience within the school and community context for particular students. The chapters in this part of the book provide examples of such contextualized experiences for learning teaching.

In the first chapter of Part II, the authors present examples of clearly focused and guided, subject-specific community-based *early field experiences* for candidates in a preservice teacher preparation program. These field experiences are consistent with the sociocultural perspective described earlier, where context is part of the text for learning teaching. The authors in this chapter employed a community-based experience as a natural setting for candidates to develop deep knowledge about learners and for learning how to interpret and translate this knowledge for facilitating learning. The candidates in secondary content area reading and English methods courses began the process of re-constructing the understanding of their own experiences as students, their understanding of teaching and learning and their understanding of the students with whom they interacted. The work of re-constructing knowledge within the context of students' daily lives would have been difficult to accomplish in a school or classroom context; however, this community-based field experience was an important part of making sense of the relationship among pedagogical practices, student attributes and learning outcomes.

In the second chapter in Part II, the author describes teaching as an *interpretive process*. This conceptualization of teaching forms the basis for clinical field experiences, employing the epistemic practices of focused inquiry, directed observation and peripheral participation. This interpretive process engages candidates in careful documentation of experiences and observations; dialogue among participants; and reflection on readings, dialogue and documentation. In this process, candidates learn the habits of interpretation, translation and application to practice the knowledge constructed during clinical field experiences. Ideally, the experiences the author describes are located in an urban community and in urban schools within this community. Candidates learn about schools as community agencies with a reciprocal impact on conditions in the community. Candidates learn to apply the interpretive process in teaching practice in clinical classrooms located within these urban schools. Clinical teachers work closely with teacher educators in developing the particular teaching practices highlighted in each of the eight rotations for candidates in the clinical classrooms. In this approach, learning teaching is a shared and reciprocal experience among teacher educators, clinical teachers and candidates.

In Chapter 7, the authors present a clinical classroom rotation approach used as a tool for facilitating the process of learning teaching consisting of three parts. The first part describes focused inquiry into the essential knowledge, skills and understandings of teaching practice as written into a pre-planned science lesson. The discourse concerning this lesson created a way for candidates to identify the implicit ideas, knowledge and skills of a practitioner, with the intention of facilitating an understanding of teaching as a complex practice. Second, directed observation guided candidates in collecting data from the enacted lesson, interpreting and translating the data to construct a deep understanding of teaching and learning in an urban classroom context. Here, candidates, practitioners and faculty engaged in a critical exploration of candidates' interpretations of real-time teaching. Practitioners and faculty then developed an understanding of what candidates understood in order to refine the learning experiences provided. Finally, candidates developed and enacted lessons based on the insight gained from the guided clinical experience. Through enactment of a lesson, candidates were able to refine their practice based on evidence of student learning and identify and address challenges that arose during enactment. In this way, clinical classroom rotations provided candidates opportunities to develop deep knowledge of the relationship among pedagogical practices, learner characteristics and responses, and learning outcomes.

The final chapter in Part II, Chapter 8, presents an ideological and theoretical conceptualization of a community-based schooling process for traditionally underserved urban students that locates the work of professional teaching within the ecosystem of a community collaborative supporting the growth and development of the whole child. In this conceptualization, in-service teachers are engaged in an "immersive" community experience where they develop deep knowledge of the everyday experiences of families and children and the opportunities and services available in the local community. Teachers engage with families, children and other community members to promote shared values such as civic responsibility, shared accountability and mutual respect. Teachers' knowledge of students and the community in which they grow and develop becomes the fabric for designing classroom learning experiences and developing a social context for supporting learning that builds upon and extends learning that occurs outside of school.

References

Barton, A. C. (2003). Kobe's story: Doing science as contested terrain. *Qualitative Studies in Education, 16*(4), 533–552.

Crosnoe, R., Johnson, M. K., & Elder, G. H., Jr. (2004). Intergenerational bonding in school: The behavioral and contextual correlates of student-teacher relationships. *Sociology of Education, 77*(1), 60–81.

Hemmings, A. (2003). Fighting for respect in urban high schools. *Teachers College Record, 105*(3), 416–437.

Kennedy-Lewis, B. L. (2012). What happens after students are expelled? Understanding teachers' practices in educating persistently disciplined students at one alternative middle school. *Teachers College Record, 114*(12), http://www.tcrecord.org ID Number 16723.

Lampert, M. (2010). Learning teaching in, from, and for practice: What do we mean? *Journal of Teacher Education, 61*(1–2), 21–34.

Lee, C. D. (1995). A culturally based cognitive apprenticeship: Teaching African American high school students skills in literary interpretation. *Reading Research Quarterly, 30*(4), 608–630.

McCarty, T. (2002). *A place to be Navajo: Rough Rock and the struggle for self-determination in indigenous schooling.* Mahwah, NJ: Lawrence Erlbaum.

Michie, G. (2009). *Holler if you hear me: The education of a teacher and his students.* New York, NY: Teachers College Press.

Moll, L. C. (1986). Writing as communication: Creating strategic learning environments for students. *Theory into Practice, 25*(2), 102–108.

Moses, R. P., Kamii, M., Swap, S. M., & Howard, J. (1989). The Algebra Project: Organizing in the spirit of Ella. *Harvard Educational Review, 59*(4), 423–443.

Nasir, N. S., Jones, A., & McLaughlin, M. (2011). School connectedness for students in low-income urban high schools. *Teachers College Record, 113*(8), 1755–1793.

National Center for Educational Statistics (NCES) (2013a). *The nation's report card: A first look: 2013 mathematics and reading* (NCES 2014-451). Washington, DC: Institute of Education Sciences, U.S. Department of Education.

National Center for Educational Statistics (NCES) (2013b). *Program for international student assessment.* Washington, DC: Institute of Education Sciences, U.S. Department of Education.

National Council for the Accreditation of Teacher Education (NCATE) (2008). *Professional standards for the accreditation of teacher preparation institutions.* Washington, DC: Author.

Noguera, P. A. (2003). Schools, prisons, and social implications of punishment: Rethinking disciplinary practices. *Theory into Practice, 42*(4), 341–350.

Osterman, K. F. (2000). Students' need for belonging in school community. *Review of Educational Research, 70*(3), 323–367.

Packer, M. J., & Goicocoechea, J. (2000). Sociocultural and constructivist theories of learning: Ontology, not just epistemology. *Educational Psychology, 35*(4), 227–241.

Weiner, L. (2003). Why is classroom management so vexing to urban teachers? *Theory into Practice, 42*(4), 305–312.

Wilson, B., Corbett, D., & Williams, B. (2000, October 30). A discussion on school reform—Case 1: All students learning at Granite Junior High. *Teachers College Record.* Retrieved October 28, 2008, from http://www.tcrecord.org/content.asp?contentid=10619

5

FOSTERING COMMUNITY-BASED FIELD EXPERIENCES IN TEACHER EDUCATION

Heidi L. Hallman and Terri L. Rodriguez

Introduction

This chapter describes the design and implementation of community-based field experiences that focus on disciplinary literacy learning and teaching for middle and secondary teacher candidates. Within the two programs described in this chapter, these experiences are framed as alternative placements where teacher candidates learn disciplinary literacy teaching outside of traditional content area classrooms. We refer to these experiences as *alternative* because we have noticed that beginning teachers' notions of community sites as non-school venues (i.e., not places where formal or academic learning usually occurs) influence their initial perceptions of the field assignment as removed from the "real work" of teaching (Hallman, 2012). However, like other teacher educators and researchers, we also notice how such experiences are invaluable and how they inform teacher candidates' learning in significant and distinct ways (Brayko, 2013).

Although the field experiences described in this chapter take place across the contexts of two different U.S. teacher preparation programs—one in the Midwest and the other in the mid-Atlantic region—we share a common goal of further examining their potential to contribute to teacher candidates' learning and to bolster evidence for the value of alternative community-based field placements within the traditional middle and secondary methods courses of university teacher preparation. As has been noted by others, teacher candidates who experience community-based field placements can be led to explore how school and community histories shape instructional practices and curricular goals and how families and schools interact within these contexts. However, it is important to note that both of the field experiences described in this chapter occurred during the professional stage of preparation. The majority of community-based field placements in teacher education programs are situated within or alongside foundations coursework (Brayko, 2013). This "historical divide" between methods and foundations coursework, as well as the separation between communities and universities, requires undoing if we are to re-imagine the preparation of teachers (Grossman, Hammerness, & McDonald, 2009).

Through this chapter, we propose that offering teacher candidates opportunities to experience community-based field assignments during a methods course—in contrast to traditional, classroom-based placements usually offered at this stage in their professional preparation—enables them to conceptualize their own learning and the learning of their students in new ways. We purposefully shift attention to learning and teaching literacy in the *disciplines*, or what is often narrowly framed within school contexts (especially in secondary schools) as the content areas of math, social studies, English and science (Shanahan & Shanahan, 2008). By considering expanded and more fluid conceptions of *content* and *literacy* while interacting with youth at community-based field sites, teacher candidates begin to more broadly conceptualize their own and youths' literate identities, knowledge and practices and regard them as pedagogical resources.

Conceptual Framework

Community-Based Field Experiences as Potential Sites of Learning

Early and diverse field experiences have been touted as one of the keys to successful teacher education programs (Darling-Hammond, 2006; Feiman-Nemser & Buchman, 1987; Sleeter, 2008; Zeichner, 2010). Such field experiences exist to promote teacher candidates' understanding and practice of culturally responsive pedagogy (Ladson-Billings, 2001) and bridge beginning teachers' reflection on the constructs of theory and practice present in the teaching act (Shulman, 2005). As field experiences in teacher education continue to be re-framed as important sites for teacher learning rather than merely spaces for candidates to "try out," demonstrate or apply things they have learned about (Zeichner, 1996), they move toward being conceptualized as productive sites for teacher learning. Cochran-Smith and Lytle's (2009) articulation that the site of one's teaching practice is a site for inquiry reiterates that field experiences are, indeed, critical sites for teacher learning.

The unique qualities of community-based settings as potential sites for teachers' learning (see Coffey, 2010), however, have been underexplored. Coffey (2010) suggests that community-based settings have the power to transform the ways that beginning teachers think about the effects of schooling in their students' lives and the extent to which social factors influence students' success in school. Community-based field sites, often contrasted with traditional "apprenticeship of observation" models of fieldwork (Lortie, 1975) within classrooms and schools, work toward the goals of broadening beginning teachers' conceptions of where student learning takes place and support the idea that teachers are not only part of a school but also part of a larger community. These goals are accomplished through the ways in which such experiences encourage "beginning teachers to contextualize students' lives as part of the fabric of the larger community" as they "emphasize that familiarity with students' communities is important to the work of teaching" (Hallman, 2012, p. 243).

In a previous paper, the first author of this chapter explores the "third space hybridity" of such spaces and their potential for contributing to teacher candidates' learning (Hallman, 2012). Drawing from Kirkland (2008), who calls for teachers to invite youths' lived literacies and everyday knowledge into teaching and learning spaces as "pedagogical third space" and conceptualizations of third space offered by Bhabha (1990) and Soja (1996) that transform an *either/or* viewpoint into a *both/and also* point of view, she rejects binaries such as school/community and practitioner/expert. Flessner (2008) discusses how such a transformation from an *either/or* viewpoint to a *both/and also* viewpoint can dissuade teacher candidates and teacher educators from recreating binary battlegrounds. Hallman (2012) points out that, like Kirkland (2008), Soja (2004) envisions the classroom as "an expanded world of learning and literacy practice" where "every space and place in the world becomes interpretable as a classroom" (p. xi). According to these authors, *third space* is already present rather than something that is (or can be) constructed. Thus, third space, as already present, "urges the possibility that teaching and learning are not confined to labels of in-school and out-of-school" (Hallman, 2012, p. 244). Consideration of this possibility suggests novel approaches to fostering community-based field experiences in teacher preparation.

Teacher Identity and Role

In addition to the opportunity that teacher candidates have to contemplate the roles of *teacher* and *learner*, we believe that an important affordance of community-based field experiences is the potential for candidates to begin to re-envision who they might become as a professional *self*. Alongside other scholars who study identity, particularly teacher identity (e.g., Alsup, 2006; Zembylas, 2008), both authors understand teachers and future teachers as produced as "particular types of professionals" (Zembylas, 2008, p. 124, italics in the original) who take up their teacher identity as a project of continuous "becoming" (Gomez, Black, & Allen, 2007) over time. Furthermore, teachers mediate their stories of *self* with the cultural and institutional expectations of what it means to be a teacher.

Oakes, Franke, Hunter Quartz, and Rogers (2006) assert that community-based field placements possess the potential for teachers to draw on local knowledge that extends outside the school. The notion of *expert* becomes not only a role for a teacher or teacher educator but rather a role that can be assumed by others in the community. As Portes and Smagorinsky (2010) remind us, the dominant model of classroom teaching into which teachers are socialized is one that adheres to a role of *teacher as authority*. Thonus (2001), similarly, reflects that the dominant model for socializing *tutors* (the label most often applied to teacher candidates in community-based field experiences) is one that differentiates tutor and teacher, with a tutor's role being distinct and different from a teacher's. Yet Thonus (2001) notes that this is, indeed, a tutoring mythology—a mythology that constrains the tutor's role, limiting it to "issues of personality and strategies of interpersonal interaction" (p. 61). Similarly, the role of *teacher as authority* bolsters a teaching mythology that constrains beginning teachers' views of an appropriate teacher's role (Hallman & Burdick, 2011). *Teacher as authority* remains a dominant force in beginning teachers' conceptualizations of themselves as future teachers. Through work in community-based settings, we question how teacher candidates might begin to challenge this model. In witnessing their understandings of the process of becoming teachers, we also consider the ways in which teacher candidates narrate their understandings of their growth as teachers.

Learning Teaching in Community-Based Spaces: Designing and Implementing the Experience

As noted, the field experiences we discuss take place at two different universities: Green State University (GSU) and Lafayette University (all names are pseudonyms). At GSU, teacher candidates in middle and secondary English/language arts enroll in a course called Teaching English in Middle/Secondary Schools during the semester prior to student teaching. At Lafayette, all middle and secondary teacher candidates take Content Area Reading prior to the content-specific methods course. The particular community-based experiences we explore in this chapter are integrated with these methods courses. This integrated approach of coursework and fieldwork allows for teacher candidates to understand that participation in a community-based setting is a viable way to learn about youths' literacy learning as a catalyst for instruction in literacy. Teacher candidates must translate their observations and perceptions about youths' literacy learning into instructional planning for one youth (in the community-based site) and then extend this into small group planning. The youth is studied as part of a small group, and this becomes a development process of learning about youths' literacies. Thus, the experience of learning teaching through participation in a community-based setting becomes a powerful learning experience for teacher candidates.

The process of learning teaching includes the development of deep observation and understanding, and a facet of this begins with teacher candidates' *peripheral participation* in a community-based site. The term *peripheral* is used not to limit the impact of candidates' roles in community-based settings but as a way to differentiate the role that they assume in such sites. Beginning teachers are not cast into the traditional role of *teacher* within these sites but rather use their more *peripheral* role to understand the assumed roles of *teacher* and *student* in more traditional classroom spaces. The *peripheral* role in the community-based site makes it possible for teacher candidates to recognize the assumed norms that are implied through the roles of *teacher* and *learner*, especially in content-specific courses.

The nature of teacher candidates' work in the community-based sites we explore is that of a sociologist. Traditionally, beginning teachers enter student teaching with few experiences in the field where they have observed, reflected and deliberated about possible decision making for students' learning; instead, they are launched through student teaching into an apprenticeship role, thereby often bypassing the critical work of observation and reflection. Shulman (2005) notes that teachers get a deep understanding of learning theory by observing students and then making decisions about teaching, using theory as an available tool to help them make sense of what is occurring. Teaching as interpretive practice (Hollins, 2011) asks teacher candidates to use data from their observations at field sites to construct plans for practice and reflect critically on how practices shape participation and identity.

Learning Teaching through Peripheral Participation

As discussed previously, a *peripheral* role in community-based field sites makes it possible for beginning teachers to recognize the assumed norms that are implied through the roles of *teacher* and *learner*. At GSU, beginning teachers' work at Family Partnership, a community organization that serves homeless families, was premised on the idea that teacher candidates' work with youth would expand beyond the traditional role of *teacher*. In this field experience, a cohort of teacher candidates worked with homeless youth through a partnership with the Family Partnership organization. Family Partnership, a national, nonprofit organization, was founded with the goal of helping low-income families achieve lasting independence. This model is oftentimes contrasted with a *shelter model* of assisting homeless individuals and families, as the program is founded on an integrated approach to addressing issues of homelessness. The organization works with a small group of families over the course of a period of 3 to 4 months with the intention of fostering families' independence. In the community of Cedar Creek, a mid-sized Midwest city, Family Partnership is one of several programs serving homeless individuals, and working with Family Partnership was purposeful, as the directors at Family Partnership had sought connections with GSU, intending to initiate an after-school initiative for the youth who were part of the Family Partnership program.

A cohort of 10 teacher candidates worked with students from Family Partnership throughout the course of one academic semester.[1] These beginning teachers completed at least 20 hours of tutoring/mentoring with young people, aged birth–17, at Family Partnership's after-school initiative for homeless youth. Over the course of the semester, the beginning teachers' work took place at Family Partnership's day center for homeless families. During the course of their work at Family Partnership, the beginning teachers were enrolled in the secondary English/language arts education program at GSU, and all were enrolled in an English education methods course and other education courses that comprised their teacher education program. Throughout the semester, these beginning teachers completed *anchor assignments*—assignments that connected the work they were doing in the field site to the teacher education program.

Participation with Family Partnership immediately asked beginning teachers to question what the role of *teacher* entailed. In fact, many times, taking the role of *peripheral* observer was unsatisfactory to beginning teachers, as they continuously questioned how the knowledge they were gaining directly translated into the act of teaching. For example, teacher candidate Bryce Adam wrote that sharing an experience drawing with 9-year-old Dominic helped Dominic "open up to him and create a more personal relationship." Yet despite having this success, Bryce wrote that there were difficult times working with children at Family Partnership. He wrote:

> The sheer resistance I got from a couple of the children reinforced my apprehensions about certain behaviors that aren't always the easiest to assuage and alleviate. Namely, it is the apathy and refusal to perform that shakes me . . . I will not make them fearful with empty discipline threats, so at least tutoring is less tense, in that regard, and allows for reciprocity.

At the end of the semester, Bryce noted that the experience at Family Partnership allowed him to witness a slow progression of students opening up to him, becoming engaged and then working with him. He noted that "as a teacher, it's the constant relationships with students" that is a key factor in the teaching act. Recognitions such as the ones made by Bryce were not uncommon for beginning teachers, as the assumed *traditional* role of teacher was concretized in their minds; at times, even the concept of building relationships with students did not coincide with the assumed role of *teacher*.

Like the English methods field experience at GSU, the urban community–based field experience at Lafayette University was similarly designed to promote teacher candidates' recognition of the assumed norms implied through the roles of *teacher* and *learner*, especially in relation to conceptions of content area teaching and literacy. Lafayette University is a private, religious, co-educational institution located in a large urban metropolis in the Rust Belt region of the United States. Given its demographic profile, which stands in stark contrast to that of the community in which it resides; the mission of the church/university as one oriented toward service and social responsibility; and the School of Education's commitment to preparing teacher candidates to enact culturally responsive and socially just peda-gogies, the second author of this chapter purposefully sought field sites that were located either within the same neighborhood as the university or whose demo-graphics closely aligned with those of the River District in which it resides. Two public libraries and one school where youth were already being provided with during- and after-school tutoring services were selected.

The field experience engaged 20 teacher candidates in facilitating digital book clubs (using e-reader technology) with volunteer youth during one semester. Since the teacher candidates in the course did not initially envision themselves as *reading teachers*, but rather assumed that their role was to teach *content knowledge*, the author asked them to first survey the youths' literacy interests and practices, select several pieces of young adult literature that reflected those interests and, finally, present these literature choices to youth who would then choose the text that they wanted to read together. Using young adult literature as a central cur-ricular resource, the author asked teacher candidates to make explicit connections between the texts, youths' discussions and lived experiences related to the text, and learning targets (content standards) within their respective disciplines.

Like the teacher candidates at GSU, these beginning teachers stressed that the relationships they were building with youth during the book club meetings were important for their learning. One teacher candidate who was facilitating a book club in the school library where he was also employed as a youth mentor said:

> They [the students] were excited to be there. They were. That might just be because they were trying to get out of [regular] class, but I had a relationship with the gentlemen that I worked with, and so they were more than eager to come down and read. I think the topic that we picked was one that was of interest to them. That was important to me, because if they don't want to be there, you're fighting an uphill battle. And one thing that I've learned over the years—you kind of have to pick your battles, and if you can make things easier on yourself you should by picking that book, encouraged read-ing, and our students read so little that that was an essential part of getting things on the right track from the beginning.

Another important goal of the course and field experience was to help teacher candidates explore conceptions of disciplinary literacies, both in their own under-standings of themselves as people who use literacy in particular ways for particular purposes (assemble their literacy "identity kits") (Gee, 2004) and as teachers of literacy. Through her experiences teaching this course, the second author often found that many secondary content area teachers view themselves as experts in a content area but not necessarily as literacy experts—they do not often envi-sion themselves as teachers of reading. In fact, many teacher candidates initially resist the notion that the course is required in their teacher education program.

Through the field experience, teacher candidates expressed changing understandings about the nature of content area literacy instruction and the possibilities it affords. Katie, a graduate student seeking initial certification to teach secondary science, had worked as a scientist in a lab for several years before making the decision to pursue a teaching degree. Through her experience with the book club, Katie's attention turned to the students and the choices they made in their reading as she questioned assumed norms about the role of *science teacher*. Katie said:

> I think the book club worked as a very interesting way to think about content area reading. Like, think about English class, that's where you do book clubs, or you do them at the library with a bunch of old ladies. You don't really think about doing it in a science classroom, a social studies classroom. And, I think opening that up as a possibility is a good idea.

In addition to re-conceptualizing the role of *teacher*, teacher candidates at Lafayette also re-envisioned their relationships with youth through the lens of *control* and teacher authority. Michael wrote in his field journal that the structure of the book club allowed students to "take control" in a way that would not have been possible in a classroom:

> This meeting was awesome. The students took complete control of the club and group discussion throughout the session. We thought that the students wouldn't have much to talk about because they had only read the first chapter, but we were fooled. These guys could talk for hours about the color of a character's jacket if we allowed them to.

In envisioning the space of the book club as student-led rather than teacher-directed, the teacher candidates recognized that students who are invested in selecting topics and texts, and who know that their opinions will be listened to and encouraged in debate, will want to continue the experience.

Learning Teaching through Structured Observational Fieldnotes and Interviews

One anchor assignment linked with peripheral observation was the writing of fieldnotes. Fieldnotes, for the beginning teachers working at Family Partnership, served as the link between describing what was happening, in a literal sense, and how these events connected to larger concepts about students' learning. In the Family Partnership experience, beginning teachers were asked to take fieldnotes after each session spent with youth at the day center. Then, bringing these fieldnotes to the methods class, discussion ensued with their peers about how to translate the meaning of such events into tangible action with the children at Family

Partnership. Through discussions with peers who were also working with youth at Family Partnership, beginning teachers began to experience how their perceptions of homeless youth affected their representations of these youth in their fieldnotes. The fieldnotes themselves became a text to question, and teacher candidates began to embrace the *peripheral* role of observer.

In the digital book clubs, teacher candidates also wrote detailed fieldnotes after each meeting. Through these guided observations, they began to see themselves as *learners* of youth and youth literacies as they made explicit connections to course readings and discussions. One way that teacher candidates expressed their learning was by demonstrating an awareness of assessment and how *learning about* who students are, what their interests are and what they know forms the basis for designing effective and relevant instruction. Michael, a beginning English teacher, wrote:

> From observing our students' discussion, we learned that they were enjoying the book so far. We also learned that they shared different views and opinions on the book's story and characters which allowed for great debate. When we asked students to support their claims from evidence from the book we were again surprised by what we learned. A few of our students were clearly advanced readers and had no issues supporting their rationales. Other students weren't so advanced.

Noting that he was "surprised" by what he learned (that some students were well able to support a claim, while others struggled with this), Michael continued his assessment of youths' reading skills by also attending to their fluency. He wrote:

> After a little encouragement, we had each student read for a little to gauge their reading skills and comprehension. Some students struggled tremendously and read very slowly. One student read so slow that he read each syllable of each word and had to follow his reading with his finger. Fortunately, our group was very respectful and no one made fun of each other. In fact, our advanced students helped our struggling students in time of need.

It is significant that not only did Michael learn important information about students' oral reading proficiencies but that he also learned that students are able to coach each other when provided with appropriate structures and supports to do so. Michael, like several other teacher candidates, was employed at the school in which this field placement was situated as a mentor teacher for African American youth. He was part of a cohort of young men who were hired by the district to work with small groups of sixth- to eighth-grade boys and concurrently earn their teacher certifications through the university. The second author often heard Michael and his colleagues talk about the difficulties of teaching within the contexts of this "troubled" urban school, where frequent administrative changes and a lack of resources often contributed to low student achievement. During digital book clubs, which were held in the library during the school day, Michael and his colleagues noted the contrasts between classrooms where students "made fun of each other constantly" and in the small group reading circle, where they often supported each other and were "respectful."

Like Michael, Dave, another beginning English teacher, was articulate about his role as a *learner* in the field site:

> I learn from observing. I learn from listening. If I have the opportunity, sure I can listen to the teacher all day, but as a student, would I really want to do that all the time? I don't really think that that's the way it would work, the best way that it would work. But, with the book clubs, you go in, and it's like a breath of fresh air because the kids would sit down, and they generally want to talk about the book with a little push, because right away they were a little, "Oh, you know, I don't know. What are we gonna read?" And they all want to read different things. That's understandable because how hard is it to get kids on the same level to do anything? But once we know—solidified the decision to read *Feed*—once we got it going, we read it—even as we started reading it, you could just tell that the kids were already making connections just 'cause of the questions that we prompted them. I just thought that was really cool.

In attending to students' choices about what they wanted to read and urging them to pose questions rather than following a traditional monologic discourse that is typical of most classroom talk, Dave noted how the session felt "like a breath of fresh air" and that he could see how having students "listen" to a teacher may not be the best way for many students to learn.

Learning Teaching through Guided Journaling

In the Family Partnership experience, beginning teachers were asked to move from writing fieldnotes to writing guided journal entries. Guided journaling was meant to incorporate both aspects of fieldnote writing and instructional planning, yet remain removed from designing concrete plans for deliberate action with students. Beginning teachers felt that guided journaling was an anchor assignment that asked them to move a step closer to *action* with working with students. Yet the guided journal entries were often where beginning teachers expressed their struggles. For example, beginning English teacher Aurora Brown struggled with what she viewed as occurring during the time designated for *tutoring* at Family Partnership. She wrote:

> Tonight at tutoring, I helped one of the students with her math homework and based on her worksheet, she was not struggling with the multiplication

tables. When we were working together, the student got very distracted by the other activities going on in the room. I think this was troublesome for her concentration because she felt like, "They aren't doing anything, why should I be productive?" I do not blame her for feeling like that and I wish the organization would set up a separate room for tutoring and education. As for now, the tutors work with students in the same space as they eat dinner, socialize, play games, etc. To most benefit the student's learning and success in school while in the program, I think the organization should focus more on these details and organize how they can best fit the needs of their students.

Aurora had many suggestions for Family Partnership and how the organization could change things in order to better benefit students. Though she was at the day center for only 2 hours each week, Aurora's journal entries consistently recommended such changes. Aurora began to shift her focus more toward herself and her role at Family Partnership mid-semester but continued to struggle with how to maintain a focus on self. Her questions concerning her identity as a tutor, mentor and teacher evolved over the course of the experience, and she wrote at the close of the semester:

> At the conclusion of my experience with Family Partnership, I have learned a lot about my beliefs as an individual, parent, and teacher. I also have a greater perspective on the reality of many families in the United States, specifically Cedar Creek. Although I do not regret working with the program at all, I do wish the organization would do internal interviews or 360-degree reviews in order to make Family Partnership more functional and useful for struggling parents and families. Overall, I had a good experience.

For Aurora, expectations and goal setting appeared to be a positive solution to what she perceived as the difficulties she experienced. Expectations, in her mind, would lead to better outcomes for all. Yet throughout Aurora's journal entries, there is rarely mention of the life circumstances of the children at Family Partnership. Because, as she says, "the tutors work with students in the same space as they eat dinner, socialize, play games, etc.," the experience lacked structure and the possibility of being "successful." To Aurora, the life circumstances of the children appeared to influence their learning in ways that could be identified and remedied.

Aurora's journal entries were met with questions from her peers. In the university-based methods class, several of Aurora's peers prompted her to re-think her characterizations of the circumstances of both the youth who were part of the Family Partnership organization and Family Partnership itself—a nonprofit organization working primarily with struggling families through the assistance of volunteers. Such discussions prompted Aurora to reconsider her initial perceptions of the program.

Like teacher candidates at GSU, those at Lafayette also used exploratory journal writing to reflect on their participation and perceptions of youth. As teacher candidates began to question and challenge their traditional role of *teacher as authority* and embrace a perspective that valued youths' knowledge and literacies, they also began to see how students themselves could "take control" of their learning and teach themselves and each other. Michael wrote:

> What was really cool was that—especially with the technology of the Kindle, which was what they had—they could pull up the vocabulary right there, and that allowed them—so, they were becoming better readers right on the spot. And, they were learning vocabulary there, and they were practicing reading.

This particular insight came about after the second author observed Michael asking an eighth-grade student to take out a piece of paper and pencil and write the words he did not know. He was to later look them up in the dictionary but continued reading at the moment. Michael later explained to Terri that this was the procedure he had observed in the classroom. The e-text they had selected was *Through My Eyes* by Tim Tebow (Tebow & Whitaker, 2011), and the youth's interest in reading was high. However, the author watched the student slowly struggle through each screen on the Kindle, frequently stopping to write on the paper next to him. This process was complicated because they were sitting in large easy chairs with narrow wooden side arms arranged in a circle for the book club discussion rather than at desks. When she showed Michael and the other students how to tap a word on the Kindle to see its definition, the student dropped his paper and pencil and immediately and intuitively began testing this feature of the digital text, effectively taking control of his own learning.

In addition to exploring changing perspectives about youth as learners, teacher candidates also wrote about their own changing beliefs about content area pedagogy. Katie, the prospective science teacher, wrote:

> I had never really done group discussion like that. Not where everybody has read the same thing. I mean, as sort of a teacher's assistant when I was in AmeriCorps, I did lead discussions like that, but I hadn't read the material really with the students, or it was just a poem. And, the experience of reading something longer like that, I think it made me think about, "Well, can I apply this to science? Could I read a journal article and then sit down with the students and talk about it?" And, I think it opened the door for bringing more controversial topics into the science classroom, because then there's not the discomfort with what a person believes. It opens it up to being able to be spoken about.

The book club in which Katie participated was facilitated by a local youth organization called the Gay, Lesbian, Straight Education Network (GLSEN). About half of the youth in this book club were openly gay, and the novel chosen for the book club featured a transgender protagonist negotiating his senior year of high school and coming out to his family, friends and the larger community. Katie articulated that the experience of discussing such issues with youth "opened the door" for her in terms of topics that she had previously thought might be taboo or forbidden for classroom discussion.

Learning Teaching through Informed Instructional Planning

Through discussions with peers who were also working with youth at Family Partnership, beginning teachers were able to collaborate with each other and design instructional plans for youth. These instructional plans were intended to be used with one child at Family Partnership with whom the beginning teacher had worked with consistently for a number of weeks. At the mid-point in the semester, beginning teachers had been able to assess many aspects of the literacy learning of the youth at Family Partnership; these included motivational and cognitive aspects. In the methods class, teacher candidates had studied the use of reading strategy work with youth, and often the instructional plans they created included concrete actions that would assist youth with learning literacy. Being passionate about designing reading and writing activities for youth at Family Partnership, beginning teachers were eager to incorporate the knowledge they had gained about both the lives and literacies of the students at Family Partnership into concrete instructional plans for students.

Creating instructional plans for the students at Family Partnership extended beyond the recommendation of learning activities for students. In fact, this anchor assignment fostered teacher candidates' realizations of how the community, the individual and learning are connected. Michele Christenot, a prospective English teacher, designed a series of comprehension activities that a student at Family Partnership could complete while reading the book *The Outsiders*. Connor, a sixth-grade student, was reading the book *The Outsiders* for his language arts class but was behind in his reading. Michele volunteered to work with Connor and design additional activities to assist him with reading the text. Her work with Connor was appreciated by both Connor and his parents but also had a great impact on Michele's perception of the connection between schools and families. Having lived in the community of Cedar Creek her entire life, Michele noted that she had always characterized the community of Cedar Creek as a comfortable and familiar place for herself. However, she began to see that the community had different meanings for the students she worked with at Family Partnership. In April, near the close of the semester, Michele noted that, through her participation in the Family Partnership field experience, she had learned that there was "little communication . . . between the schools and the Family Partnership organization itself." She said, "These kids received no counseling, little structure, and are often perceived as normal students in class." Michele's awareness of the issues of homelessness and the available resources led her to make the conjecture that it is, indeed, easy for some kids, such as the kids who are part of the Family Partnership program, to continue to "fall through the cracks." She related this especially to Connor, the student with whom she had worked the most while at Family Partnership.

When speaking with her peers in the methods class, Michele referred to her "breakthroughs" throughout the course of the semester. She claimed that, despite the chaos and frustration she experienced at times throughout the semester, "breakthroughs" were what propelled her to seek a commitment to the experience. Michele's ability to focus on "breakthroughs" confirmed her pursuit of a teaching career. She was able to observe the tangible difference she was making for the students she worked with, and this affirmed her work as both a tutor and a future teacher.

Katie, like Michele, experienced "breakthroughs" and articulated how leading a book club, from her perspective as a science teacher, helped her to acquire skills in reading pedagogy that had previously seemed outside her domain as a science teacher:

> I learned how to pitch a book. Because we all sat around and read the first chapter and then talked about what we liked about it, and I think that idea—I've never seen that done in the classroom. What if you could do that in a classroom? At the beginning of the school year even saying, "We're going to read 12 journal articles through the year. These are the possible subjects. Check off five of them and whichever one gets the most votes, we'll read." You don't think about that. And, I think that was something that the book club allowed me to think about, is that you don't have to be specific. You can cover things with the students having input.

In this "breakthrough," Katie's attention turned to the students and the choices they might make in their reading. For the first time, she considered their "input" as valuable in text selections for her course. Her experience also led her to become aware of how the structures of schooling, when uncritically accepted, hinder possibilities for learning.

Discussion

In the examples presented from both community-based experiences, teacher candidates began to recognize and question the way that structures in place interacted with the work they were able to undertake at the field site. For example, at GSU, teacher candidates questioned the organization of Family Partnership and what the organization "did" and "didn't do." At times, they blamed these structures for hindering their progress with students. In the case of Lafayette teacher candidates, they cited structures and others already in place (e.g., "old lady librarians") as hindering progress. As teacher educators, we recognized these comments as evidence of prospective teachers' continual focus on *self* and the agency they have with students. While we urged beginning teachers to consider nuancing their understanding of the ways structures, institutions and people interact with students, we recognized the value in identifying that such things have an impact on student learning.

Across both cases, we identified how anchor assignments that connected the work in the field sites to work in university-based methods classes urged prospective teachers to become more attentive to the relationship between teacher and students. Beginning teachers from Lafayette University recognized that the curriculum also played a part in this relationship, and negotiating how book choice within the digital book clubs fostered a different relationship between teacher and students became key in understanding what shifts in curricular choices impacted student engagement. One teacher candidate from GSU, Bryce Adam, recognized that "as a teacher, it's the constant relationships with students" that makes up the teaching act.

Implications

What Potential Do We See Community-Based Field Experiences Offering for Teacher Candidates' and Youths' Learning?

In both cases of alternative, community-based field experiences, teacher candidates were purposefully prompted to re-negotiate the relationship between *teacher* and *student* and contemplate what benefits such a re-negotiation might have to their future positions as classroom teachers. Such a contemplation is rarely undertaken early in beginning teachers' programs, as traditional field experiences provide a clear model for what constitutes the role of *teacher*. Despite this clear model, beginning teachers are often directed to assume this model rather than question it. Through critical questioning early in their teaching careers, beginning teachers are encouraged to be more cognizant of the roles and relationships involved in a teaching career.

Several students questioned their role as *tutor* at some point in both experiences. Some of their uneasiness stemmed from perceptions that they were en route to becoming a *teacher* and therefore were ready to shed the role of *tutor*.

This location of being a *not-yet* teacher placed them at an identity point difficult for them to define. Alsup (2006) writes about the creation of teachers' *borderland discourses*—discourses that challenge traditional teacher and student roles in the classroom. A community-based field experience encouraged the purposeful creation of such discourses as sites for contemplation of the role of teacher. In the case of teacher candidates at GSU, working with homeless youth urged them to question the dichotomy of tutor/teacher over the course of the semester, prompting them to arrive at some kind of resolution concerning the dissonances present in this dichotomy. Through focusing on the relationships they had with individual students—or "breakthroughs," as Michele called them—prospective teachers were able to witness the positive effects of their work with students. This affirmed their present and future work as teachers. Similarly, teacher candidates at Lafayette University turned their gazes toward students through the experience. As one beginning teacher said, "I learn from observing. I learn from listening. If I have the opportunity, sure I can listen to the teacher all day, but as a student, would I really want to do that all the time? I don't really think that that's the way it would work, the best way that it would work." Teacher candidates' understanding of the reciprocal relationship between teacher and students grew as a result of their questioning of how the roles of teacher and student interact with curriculum and pedagogy.

Teacher candidates' questioning of teacher–student roles to create a reciprocal relationship between the two resides at the heart of "third space" as conceptualized by Bhabha (1994). Bhabha's (1994) discussion of *hybridity* is critical to understanding the nature of third spaces and how this chapter operationalizes the idea of third space. Bhabha (1994) writes that hybridity points to "a difference 'within,' a subject that inhabits the rim of an 'in-between' reality. . . . [T]his borderline existence inhabits a stillness of time and a strangeness of framing that creates the discursive 'image' at the crossroads . . ." (p. 19). Hybrid understandings and moments, then, are created when binaries are challenged and new possibilities and spaces for meaning-making are created. The experiences that teacher candidates had in alternative, community-based field experiences are such hybrid spaces.

As teacher education programs continue to grapple with decisions about what field experiences matter for beginning teachers' growth, they must look beyond traditional school placements that offer a direct pathway to the role of teacher. Instead, embracing alternative, community-based sites for teacher learning can foster broader contemplation of students' learning and lives and can lead teachers early in their careers to view teaching as a process of inquiry rather than a pre-defined assemblage of techniques. Learning teaching, is, indeed, a process of inquiry. Viewing schooling as a complex arena where students' social, cultural and economic backgrounds interact begins with fostering such understandings with teacher candidates from the beginning of their teaching careers.

Glossary

Anchor assignments: Assignments that require teacher candidates to link learning teaching between the field site and the university-based teacher education class

Community-based field experiences: Field experiences in teacher education that take place in non-school venues (i.e., not places where formal or academic learning usually occurs). Community-based field experiences have the goal of prompting teacher candidates to explore how school and community histories shape instructional practices and curricular goals and how families and schools interact within these contexts

Peripheral participation in the field site: A short-term limited engagement in an experience that enables teacher candidates to gain an inside view of an approach or process used for a specific purpose in a particular setting or situation

Note

1 This initiative has been ongoing for six academic semesters. Each semester introduces a new group of prospective teachers into the Family Partnership program.

References

Alsup, J. (2006). *Teacher identity discourses: Negotiating personal and professional discourses.* Mahwah, NJ: Lawrence Erlbaum.

Bhabha, H. K. (1990). The third space. In J. Rutherford (Ed.), *Identity, community, culture, and difference* (pp. 207–221). London, United Kingdom: Lawrence and Wishart.

Bhabha, H. K. (1994). *The location of culture.* New York, NY: Routledge.

Brayko, K. (2013). Community-based placements as contexts for disciplinary learning: A study of literacy teacher education outside of school. *Journal of Teacher Education, 64*(1), 47–59.

Cochran-Smith, M., & Lytle, S. (2009). *Inquiry as stance: Practitioner research in the next generation.* New York, NY: Teachers College Press.

Coffey, H. (2010). "*They* taught *me*": The benefits of early community-based field experiences in teacher education. *Teaching and Teacher Education, 26,* 335–342.

Darling-Hammond, L. (2006). *Powerful teacher education.* San Francisco, CA: Jossey-Bass.

Feiman-Nemser, S., & Buchman, M. (1987). When is student teaching teacher education? *Teaching and Teacher Education, 3*(4), 255–273.

Flessner, R. (2008). *Living in multiple worlds: Utilizing third space theory to re-envision pedagogy in the field of teacher education.* Unpublished doctoral dissertation, University of Wisconsin-Madison.

Gee, J. P. (2004). *Situated language and learning: A critique of traditional schooling.* London, United Kingdom: Routledge.

Gomez, M. L., Black, R. W., & Allen, A. (2007). "Becoming" a teacher. *Teachers College Record, 109*(9), 2107–2135.

Grossman, P., Hammerness, K., & McDonald, M. (2009). Redefining teacher: Re-imagining teacher education. *Teachers and Teaching: Theory and Practice, 15*(2), 273–290.

Hallman, H. L. (2012). Community-based field experiences in teacher education: Possibilities for a pedagogical third space. *Teaching Education, 23*(3), 241–263.

Hallman, H. L., & Burdick, M. N. (2011). Service learning and the preparation of English teachers. *English Education, 43*(4), 341–368.

Hollins, E. (2011). Teacher preparation for quality teaching. *Journal of Teacher Education, 62*(4), 395–407.

Kirkland, D. (2008). "The rose that grew from concrete": Postmodern blackness and new English education. *English Journal, 97*(5), 69–75.

Ladson-Billings, G. (2001). *Crossing over to Canaan: The journey of new teachers in diverse class-rooms*. San Francisco, CA: Jossey-Bass.

Lortie, D. (1975). *Schoolteacher: A sociological study*. Chicago, IL: University of Chicago Press.

Oakes, J., Franke, M. L., Hunter Quartz, K., & Rogers, J. (2006). Research for high quality urban teaching: Defining it, developing it, assessing it. *Journal of Teacher Education, 53*(3), 228–235.

Portes, P., & Smagorinsky, P. (2010). Static structures, changing demographics: Educating teachers for shifting populations in stable schools. *English Education, 42*(3), 236–247.

Shanahan, T., & Shanahan, C. (2008). Teaching disciplinary literacy to adolescents: Rethinking content-area literacy. *Harvard Educational Review, 78*(1), 40–59.

Shulman, L. (2005). Pedagogies. *Liberal Education, 91*(2), 18–25.

Sleeter, C. (2008). Equity, democracy, and neoliberal assaults on teacher education. *Teaching and Teacher Education, 24*, 1947–1957.

Soja, E. (1996). *Thirdspace*. Malden, MA: Blackwell.

Soja, E. (2004). *Postmodern geographies: The reassertion of space in critical social theory* (2nd ed.). New York, NY: Verso.

Tebow, T., & Whitaker, N. (2011). *Through my eyes*. New York, NY: HarperCollins.

Thonus, T. (2001). Triangulation in the writing center: Tutor, tutee, and instructor's perception of the tutor's role. *Writing Center Journal, 22*(1), 59–82.

Zeichner, K. (1996). Designing education practicum experiences for prospective teachers. In K. Zeichner, S. Melnick, & M. L. Gomez (Eds.), *Currents of reform in preservice teacher education* (pp. 215–234). New York, NY: Teachers College Press.

Zeichner, K. (2010). Rethinking the connections between campus courses and field experiences in college- and university-based teacher education. *Journal of Teacher Education, 61*(1–2), 89–99.

Zembylas, M. (2008). Interrogating "teacher identity": Emotion, resistance, and self-formation. *Educational Theory, 58*(1), 107–127.

6

LEARNING TEACHING THROUGH CLINICAL ROTATIONS

Etta R. Hollins

A major challenge for classroom teachers and teacher educators is that of improving academic performance in the nation's public schools. This concern is related to the education of all students in the United States in comparison with peers internationally and comparisons among different subgroups within the United States. When compared internationally based on the 2009 Performance for International Student Assessment (PISA) administered to 15-year-olds in 65 countries and territories, the United States ranked 17th in reading, 34th in mathematics and 22nd in science (National Center for Education Statistics [NCES], 2012). Within the United States, students living in urban and rural areas, those from low-income families and those from certain ethnic minority groups have traditionally scored well below their white middle-class peers on standardized tests. Based on data from the National Assessment of Educational Progress compiled by the NCES (2012), the majority of students in the Trial Urban School Districts perform well below the national average.

Data from international comparisons indicate a need for improving teaching and learning for all students in the United States. NAEP data show that within the United States, there is a need to give particular attention to traditionally underserved students. Further, there is well-documented evidence of the unequal distribution of high-quality teaching and learning experiences. Public schools serving low-income and urban students are often underfunded, employ less qualified teachers and have significantly higher teacher turnover rates than public schools serving more affluent students (Zhou, 2003). Further, the influence of the quality of teaching on student learning outcomes is well supported in research showing that teaching has more influence on learning outcomes than social class status. This research shows further that it is difficult for elementary school students to recover from 2 consecutive years of low-quality teaching (Darling-Hammond, 2000). Further, evidence shows that in many low-performing elementary and secondary schools, there is at least one teacher who elicits excellent academic performance from students, and scattered across the United States are instances of high-performing schools serving a majority of low-income and ethnic minority students. The challenge for teacher educators is that of designing preservice teacher preparation programs that consistently prepare teachers who are capable of facilitating excellent academic performance for all students, including those from different cultural and experiential backgrounds.

Hollins (2011) presented a practice-based approach to teacher preparation for quality teaching in which teaching practice and teacher preparation employ an interpretive process. This approach was presented in two parts. The first part presented the knowledge, skills and habits of mind required for quality teaching. The second part presented a design for learning to teach emphasizing the epistemic practices of focused inquiry, directed observation and guided practice; an interpretive teaching process; and specific teacher preparation program qualities. Hollins (2011) states that:

> Practice-based teacher preparation. . . refers to the discursive processes, reasoning, and actions taken in interpreting and translating the experiences and responses of learners in authentic situations within and outside of classrooms as a way to construct understanding of the substantive relationship between learners, learning, pedagogy, and learning outcomes.
>
> (p. 403)

The following discussion presents an approach to practice-based preservice preparation that engages candidates in learning the interpretive practices of teaching through a series of clinical rotations.

Organizing Clinical Rotations for Learning Teaching

There are many different ways to think about and organize clinical rotations for learning teaching. In this discussion, a clinical rotation is one of several opportunities for candidates to make careful observations and to engage in peripheral participation or guided practice in the application of one or more key elements of teaching in a deliberately selected classroom context. Examples of key elements of teaching include planning instruction, enacting a learning segment, following specific procedures for particular approaches and facilitating learning in different organizational structures (individual, small group and whole class). Planning instruction can include the examination of a particular theoretical perspective on learning or a clear explanation of ways of conceptualizing the learning process. An important aspect of a clinical rotation is the attention given to developing deep knowledge and understanding of a particular element of teaching. This deep understanding provides the basis for flexibility and adaptability for different classroom contexts and different student learning needs. In the following discussion, clinical rotations will focus on (a) *teaching perspectives* and (b) *practices for facilitating student learning*. These clinical rotations are conducted in a clinical classroom specifically designated for this purpose.

The Clinical Classroom

This concept of a clinical classroom is based on the application of aspects of the clerkship employed in medical education. In medical education, the clerkship is a rotation through several different medical practices such as surgery or neurology over a specified number of weeks. During the clerkship, medical students observe specific procedures and have a limited involvement in the treatment of patients. In the clinical rotation for learning teaching practice, candidates conduct careful observations of specific pedagogical practices that are based on a particular theoretical perspective and engage in dialogue with the teacher as a way to develop deep understanding of the type of interpretive practice associated with teaching. Teaching does not presently have the level of codification and specificity of medicine; thus, clinical practice is adapted to the interpretive qualities of teaching. The intent is that candidates learn the ways of thinking associated with effective interpretive practice.

This sequence of rotations is intended to support candidates in constructing deep knowledge of teaching practice. In this first part of the discussion on learning teaching, the focus is on five frames of practice that constitute teaching perspectives: philosophical stance, theoretical perspective, curriculum content, epistemic practices and the teaching process. Each clinical rotation allows the candidate to focus on one particular frame of practice while gaining an awareness of the dynamic interaction among the different frames. Developing depth and breadth of understanding of productive professional practice requires knowledge construction within and across clinical rotations that is interrelated and cumulative. At the conclusion of each clinical rotation, candidates write a summary commentary synthesizing the knowledge constructed during that rotation, and as candidates progress through multiple rotations, these commentaries reflect the cumulative and progressive depth and complexity in their understanding of the interpretive practices of teaching.

Each clinical rotation for learning teaching employs the epistemic practices of focused inquiry, directed observation, peripheral participation and/or guided practice. Focused inquiry provides opportunities for candidates to develop the depth of knowledge necessary for understanding the learning experiences and tasks in the clinical rotation prior to participating. Focused inquiry includes reading the research and theory that supports the particular area of practice;

examining documented accounts and descriptions (videotape recordings, etc.); and interviewing practitioners and participants. During the directed observation, candidates attend to a teaching event, a learning segment or the social or physical context that is the focus of the clinical rotation. During directed observation, candidates make detailed documentation appropriate for the focus of the clinical rotation. Peripheral participation affords candidates opportunities for making sense of a teaching event, a learning segment or a social situation that illustrates the focus of the clinical rotation. This experience enables candidates to begin giving attention to how students interpret, translate and apply what they are learning or how students respond to the physical or social context in the classroom. Guided practice is a more involved enactment of a teaching segment or facilitation of a learning segment under the close supervision of an experienced teacher.

Teaching Perspectives and Frames of Practice

Teaching perspectives are made up of a particular ideology, personal perceptions, values, and moral and social commitments. Frames of practice are conceptual constructs through which teaching perspectives are translated into the everyday work of facilitating student learning. The frames of practice for teaching include the purpose of teaching (philosophical stance), the learning process (learning theory), the teaching process (planning and adapting instruction), epistemic practices (routines and procedures) and curriculum framing (representation and presentation). The quality of learning opportunities provided for students—and ultimately learning outcomes—are influenced by teaching perspectives. Improving learning outcomes for students in low-performing schools often requires changes in teaching perspectives in order to change teaching practices and the learning opportunities provided for students.

Rotation #1: Curriculum Framing

The purpose of this clinical rotation is to direct candidates' attention beyond subject matter knowledge to a deeper understanding of the structure of the discipline, perspectives represented in the curriculum and a purpose of learning that includes—but goes beyond—standards and specific objectives. The primary focus of this clinical rotation is the perspective or point of view represented in the curriculum, the purpose of studying the curriculum content and how the curriculum is organized for student learning.

During the *focused inquiry* part of this clinical rotation, the candidates examine (a) the structure of the discipline in which the curriculum content is located (the relationship among organizing ideas, concepts and principles); (b) how new knowledge is created and the rules for argumentation and critique in developing

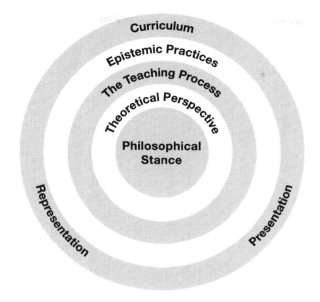

Candidates learn the professional practice of teaching through careful examination of curriculum representation and presentation, epistemic practices, the teaching process, theoretical perspectives on learning and the teacher's philosophical stance.

FIGURE 6.1 Learning teaching through clinical rotations

new knowledge; and (c) the relationship between the structure of the discipline and common core standards. These elements of the curriculum are examined and compared in relationship to different textbooks and supplemental material used in teaching the particular subject matter to students; to state content standards and curriculum frameworks; and to textbooks and materials used in university courses on methods of teaching the subject matter. Knowledge of the curriculum from these different sources provides a framework for making careful observations about how the curriculum is operationalized for students' learning.

During the *directed observation* phase of the clinical rotation, candidates attend to how the curriculum is operationalized for a particular group of students, including (a) the purpose of learning and the perspective represented; (b) how organizing ideas, concepts and principles are presented and how the interrelatedness is made explicit; (c) how curriculum content is linked to students' prior knowledge and everyday experiences; and (d) how students are supported in constructing knowledge of disciplinary discourse and practices that have application beyond the classroom. Further, candidates make observations about how learning segments fit into the structure of the discipline, how concepts are linked across learning segments and how learning experiences and tasks within and across learning segments are related to meeting the common core state standards.

During the *peripheral participation* phase of this clinical rotation, candidates work with a small group of students in carrying out part of a learning segment planned by the clinical teacher. The role and support candidates provide for students are predetermined by the clinical teacher. Candidates' roles could involve leading a discussion group, working with students to complete a particular task by providing appropriate support when needed or monitoring progress toward task completion. Candidates develop a narrative describing how the planned teaching segment addressed the points attended to during the directed observation.

While engaged in this clinical rotation attending to curriculum content, candidates are aware of other frames of practice, especially epistemic practices and the teaching process, but they are not engaged in a careful examination of these other frames. The clinical rotation that follows attends to epistemic practices.

Rotation #2: Epistemic Practices

The purpose of this clinical rotation is to develop an understanding of the importance of establishing a carefully designed and purposeful routine for teaching and learning that supports consistency and continuity across learning segments. The term *epistemic practice* refers to an easily identifiable and interrelated pattern of experiences comprising a teaching and learning routine, incorporating particular intellectual and academic practices, and developing particular habits of mind. Epistemic practices are not isolated activities or assignments. Examples of epistemic practices include literature circles; concept formation; the Four Blocks literacy model (guided reading, self-selected reading, writing and working with words); project-based learning; and disciplinary literacy. In this clinical rotation, attention to epistemic practices is linked to directed observation for item (d) in curriculum content—how students construct knowledge of disciplinary discourse and practices.

Disciplinary literacy is the epistemic practice used as an example in explaining this clinical rotation. In this context, disciplinary literacy refers to pedagogical practices that engage students in the discourse, documentation and notation; knowledge production, representation and application; and argumentation, critique and interpretation commonly practiced in the discipline as a way to construct deep knowledge of subject matter. In this example, students learn to use the tools of a particular discipline. For example, elementary school children can learn to use simple tools used by historians and other social scientists for inquiry, such as taking and collecting photographs, drawing maps and interviewing local residents. Using these tools can enable students to connect the study of a particular time period in state or national history with the local community to construct an original historical account based on the evidence collected. Children can raise questions about the language used in these accounts and how meaning might be inferred from such language usage as a way to challenge historical representation. Children can learn to critique these preliminary historical accounts by asking questions about what is known and what is unknown about the particular event or situation.

During focused inquiry, candidates review the scholarly literature on disciplinary literacy and the research on teaching the particular subject matter to students in different school contexts and from different cultural and experiential backgrounds. Candidates examine the relationship between research studies on disciplinary literacy and teaching students from different cultural and experiential backgrounds, including those from white middle-class backgrounds. Candidates interview the clinical teacher to determine his or her perspective on disciplinary literacy and for a clear explanation of its application in the clinical classroom, including procedures, routines and learning tasks. Candidates review data on students' academic performance in this particular discipline and identify patterns of strength and weakness in their learning. All of these data are combined with those previously collected in the community, school and classroom context to create a deeper and richer knowledge base for making interpretations and translations to practice in identifying learning tasks using a particular epistemic practice.

During directed observation, candidates give particular attention to the procedures, routines and learning tasks that make up the epistemic practice of disciplinary literacy. Candidates take note of how a learning segment is introduced, supported and concluded and the relationship of experiences across several learning segments. Candidates make careful documentation of particular teaching events that include giving directions, explanations for learning tasks, examples and models, learning materials, assignments and dialogue with the whole class and small groups of students. Candidates carefully describe the patterns of teaching events and learning tasks that provide evidence of the implementation of the particular epistemic practice.

In this clinical rotation, the clinical teacher identifies appropriate ways for candidates to engage in peripheral participation when learning the epistemic teaching practice. This participation might include working with individuals or small groups of students, reviewing and responding to products from students' learning tasks, assembling materials for specific learning tasks or developing examples and models used in a learning experience or a learning task. Candidates may be involved in planning a learning segment using the particular epistemic practice. Peripheral participation is expected to provide candidates opportunities to gain experiential knowledge of the particular epistemic practice.

Rotation #3: The Teaching Process

The third clinical rotation in this sequence is focused on the teaching process. The purpose of this rotation is to make the anatomy of pedagogical practice visible to candidates. The teaching process consists of a sequence of interrelated actions that include planning a learning segment, enacting the plan, observing and interpreting students' responses to the learning segment, translating information from observations on students' responses into pedagogical practice, planning a new learning segment that incorporates the new information about students' responses and enacting the new segment. The teaching process represents a holistic view of teaching that was not attended to in the clinical rotation on epistemic practice but was present.

Focused inquiry in this clinical rotation has two parts that are directly related to planning a learning segment: the curriculum and epistemic practices. Candidates inquire about (a) how the curriculum in the learning segment is represented; (b) how organizing ideas, concepts and principles are represented and presented and how interrelatedness is made explicit within the learning segment; (c) how curriculum content is linked to students' prior knowledge and everyday experiences; and (d) how the representation of curriculum content supports students in constructing knowledge of disciplinary discourse and practices during the learning segment. Regarding epistemic practices, candidates inquire about the routines and procedures of teaching practice and student learning and the habits of mind that are expected to result.

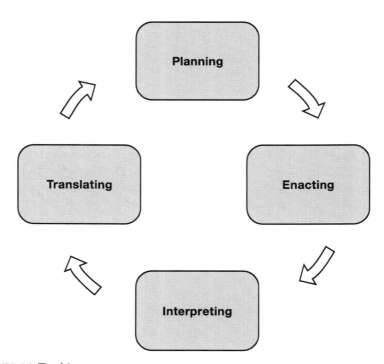

FIGURE 6.2 Teaching process

The directed observation in this third clinical rotation is much more complex than the first two because it integrates knowledge from all three. This directed observation is focused on understanding how the curriculum and epistemic practices are integrated into the teaching process to facilitate learning and how pedagogical practices are adjusted on the basis of learners' responses in order to optimize learning. Specific learning segments are carefully examined to determine how curriculum content is made meaningful for learners; how organizing ideas, concepts and principles are made accessible to a diverse group of learners; and how learners construct deep knowledge of disciplinary discourse and practices. Candidates examine the interrelatedness of the routines and procedures in the epistemic practice employed and the teaching process where adjustments are made on the basis of students' responses in order to optimize learning.

Peripheral participation in this third rotation consists of planning the next learning segment after observing a sequence of several segments. The plan for this learning segment takes into consideration all that has been observed in the previous learning segments about the curriculum, epistemic practices, the teaching process and students' responses to several previous learning segments. The candidate's plan for the particular learning segment is discussed in two parts: First, the candidate's observations about students' responses are discussed in comparison with the observations made by the clinical teacher. Second, the candidate's plan for a learning segment is discussed in comparison with that developed by the clinical teacher. These comparisons are expected to increase the candidate's awareness of strengths and weaknesses in his or her ability to observe, interpret and translate observations of teaching practice and students' responses to learning experiences into pedagogical decisions about subsequent learning experiences provided for students. Planning and analyzing a learning segment allows the candidate to demonstrate progress in constructing a deep understanding of teaching practice.

Rotation #4: Theoretical Perspectives on Learning

The fourth rotation in this sequence is focused on a theoretical perspective on learning. The purpose of this rotation is to help candidates think deeply about their understanding of the learning process; to enable candidates to infer the theoretical perspective on learning that is operationalized in a teaching event or a learning segment; and to apply a theoretical perspective when planning learning segments, interpreting students' responses to a learning experience and making adjustments in teaching practice in order to optimize learning.

In this clinical rotation, a theoretical perspective explains the learning process and serves as a guide for planning, evaluating and adjusting learning experiences. For example, the sociocultural perspective explains the learning process as cognitive and social engagement that employs historical, cultural and experiential knowledge as a basis for assimilating, accommodating or constructing new understanding or new knowledge in a context of joint productive activity with others. Based on this perspective, learning takes place in a cultural and social context, is mediated by language and other cultural symbols and tools and is linked to a historical setting. Learning is participatory, interactive and distributed among participants in a particular context or community. Knowledge is co-constructed with others and is internalized, appropriated and transformed. Identifying and employing a theoretical perspective on learning provides candidates with opportunities for developing a broader framework for understanding teaching practice through focused inquiry, directed observation and peripheral participation.

During the focused inquiry part of the clinical rotation on theoretical perspectives, candidates carefully examine the scholarly literature for definitions, basic tenets, concepts, principles and researched examples applying the particular perspective that will be observed in the clinical classroom. Candidates engage in dialogue with the clinical teacher focused on (a) how he or she thinks about and uses the theoretical perspective in planning and making adjustments in learning segments; (b) examples applying the theoretical perspective in everyday classroom practices; and (c) particular aspects of the theoretical perspective that can be observed in the classroom.

In this clinical rotation, directed observation in the clinical classroom engages candidates in documenting the application of the theoretical perspective in the way the curriculum is represented and presented, the epistemic practices that provide the procedures and routines for teaching and learning, and the teaching process that is the cycle of pedagogical analyses and actions that constitute enactment of teaching events and learning segments. This is a meticulous process that engages candidates in examining teaching practice through a particular lens that reveals the extent of continuity and/or discontinuity across different elements of teaching practice. In some instances, candidates may be able to observe and document how factors involved in continuity and/or discontinuity across different elements of teaching practice influence the quality of student learning and learning outcomes.

In the peripheral participation aspect of this clinical rotation, candidates observe three to five connected learning segments enacted by the clinical teacher, which may include those learning segments from the directed observation. Afterward, candidates are to plan the next learning segment in the sequence by integrating knowledge from this clinical rotation on theoretical perspectives and that from all previous clinical rotations. The planned learning segment includes a narrative that explains how continuity in the application of the theoretical perspective has been maintained across other frames of teaching practice in the way the curriculum is represented and presented, the epistemic practices that provide the procedures and routines for teaching and learning, and the teaching process that is the cycle of pedagogical analyses and actions that constitute enactment of teaching events and learning segments. The planned learning segment and the narrative are to be shared among team members and with the clinical teacher for the purpose of careful analysis and feedback. Candidates learn the strengths and weaknesses in their ability to apply a theoretical perspective across frames of practice and how this contributes to continuity and/or discontinuity in their teaching.

Rotation #5: Philosophical Stance

The fifth rotation in this sequence is focused on philosophical stance, which refers to the vision and purpose of school learning in relationship to the benefits for students, and individuals and groups in the larger society. The purpose of this clinical rotation is to increase candidates' awareness of the power of their own personal philosophy, ideology, perspectives and values in influencing what and how students learn in the classroom, the learning opportunities provided for students and determining who has access to what knowledge and who does not. At the core of a philosophical stance are moral judgments and moral commitments. The vision and purpose of school learning include what and how students will learn; how academic knowledge and skill are appropriated and used in everyday life; and how students' academic competence, personal values and identity, and career goals and aspirations are influenced. A teacher's philosophical stance is related to the value of knowledge and what knowledge is of value; personal, social and political values and perspectives; and perspectives on power relationships in the society. The philosophical stance combines or integrates social commitment, personal ideology and reasons for joining the profession with knowledge of teaching practice. The philosophical stance is the overarching framework for teaching practice.

Candidates begin the focused inquiry for this rotation by writing an introspective narrative addressing the following questions: (a) In your opinion, what is the most important aspect of school learning? Explain why this aspect of school learning has such high value; (b) How are students expected to use the knowledge and skills from school learning in their everyday lives now and in the future? and (c) What is the best approach to determining who should have access to the highest-quality public education? The candidates ask the clinical teacher to address the same three questions. Candidates engage in dialogue on their responses to the questions among peers and with the clinical teacher. This discussion will reveal different perspectives and ideologies among group members. Candidates discuss the benefits and risks of the different perspectives.

The second part of the focused inquiry is to examine at least two perspectives on teacher ideology from the scholarly literature (e.g., Abbate-Vaughn, 2004; Moje, 2007). Abbate-Vaughn (2004) provides examples of the application of a philosophical stance or ideology. Moje (2007) differentiates between socially just pedagogy and pedagogy for social justice, each of which is a philosophical stance. Moje (2007) raises an important question for candidates to consider: "Further, what would it look like to fuse the moral and intellectual to produce a subject-matter instruction that is not only socially just but also produces social justice?" (p. 1). Understanding the fusion of moral perspectives and commitments with the intellectual in teaching practice is at the heart of the work in this clinical rotation. After reading the selected articles from the literature, the cohort and the clinical teacher return to the discussion on philosophical stance. The first part of this discussion addresses a comparison between each candidate's philosophical stance and the examples provided by Abbate-Vaughn (2004). In this discussion, candidates compare, contrast and make suggestions for changes in their philosophical stances. The second part of the discussion is focused on Moje's (2007) point about the fusion of the moral and the intellectual in teaching practice. Candidates discuss how this fusion happens in situations involving each participant's philosophical stance. In these discussions, candidates construct the background knowledge for examining their own philosophical stance and for making observations about a philosophical stance implemented by the clinical teacher.

The clinical observation in this rotation is very complex because it simultaneously considers the four other frames—the curriculum, epistemic practices, the teaching process and the theoretical perspective. Candidates have had opportunities to make observations of each frame of practice separately. This has encouraged deep understanding of each frame. In directed observation for this clinical rotation, candidates examine the influence of philosophical stance on each frame in an effort to understand the power and influence of this last frame. In relationship to the curriculum, candidates make observations about the knowledge that has the greatest value, how students are expected to use this knowledge in the present and the future, and the quality of knowledge to which students have access and why. Regarding epistemic practices, candidates make observations about the behaviors, academic competencies and habits of mind that are encouraged and supported. Candidates examine the planning and enactment of a learning segment and the interpretation and translation of students' responses during the learning segment to identify the relationship of adjustments in instruction to the knowledge valued and the behaviors and competencies encouraged.

The theoretical perspective on learning guides the representation and presentation of the curriculum, the selection of epistemic practices and the teaching process. The application of the theoretical perspective is influenced by the teacher's philosophical stance. Candidates examine the application of the theoretical perspective to determine the influence of the philosophical stance. After completing observations and documentation, candidates develop a written report and discuss their findings with the clinical teacher to determine consistency and inconsistency in perceptions.

Peripheral participation in this clinical rotation engages candidates in planning a learning segment that builds upon and extends the sequence being enacted by the clinical teacher but that presents a different philosophical stance than that documented in the practices of the clinical teacher. The candidate may choose from among those stances described in the literature from the focused inquiry experience or from another source. The narrative that accompanies the learning segment uses the philosophical stance to explain (a) the most important aspect of school learning and why this aspect of school learning has such high value; (b) how students are expected to use the knowledge and skills from the learning segment in their everyday lives now and in the future; and (c) the best approach to determining who should have access to the highest-quality public education. The discussion of the candidates' planned learning segments is focused on the significance of the teacher's philosophical stance on what students learn, the learning experiences and tasks provided and the sense students make of what has been learned.

Facilitating Student Learning

This clinical rotation sequence is intended to support candidates in constructing deep knowledge for facilitating student learning. This clinical rotation sequence addresses the *context* and *conditions* for student learning. The *context* for student learning includes the social arrangements for learning, such as the individual, small groups and the whole class; students' cultural and experiential backgrounds; and the social dynamic among students and between the teacher and students. The *conditions* for learning include the learning goals; what the learner knows in relationship to the learning goals and how the learner makes sense of what he or she knows; what learners need to know to achieve the learning goals; and what experiences and/or learning tasks will be the most meaningful to the learner. These aspects of teaching and learning are equally important and need a similar structure in a clinical rotation to support deep understanding.

Rotation #6: Working with Individual Students (Differentiated Instruction)

The purpose of this clinical rotation is to deepen candidates' understanding of the interrelatedness of the context for learning, the conditions for learning, developing meaningful and productive learning experiences and tasks and accomplishing learning goals. This clinical rotation is focused on facilitating learning for students with learning challenges. These challenges can originate from a variety of sources, including cumulative learning deficits based on misconceptions, gaps in academic knowledge and skills or cognitive processing issues of various types. The source of the learning challenge may not have been formally determined, but the challenge is evident in records of the students' academic performance and in work samples.

During focused inquiry in this clinical rotation, each candidate selects one student with learning challenges and develops a student profile. The student profile is based on an interview with the student, records of past academic performance and

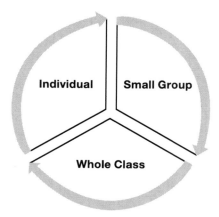

FIGURE 6.3 Interrelated participation structures for learning

recent student work samples. The interview with the student is focused on pertinent background experiences within and outside school, learning preferences, personal interests, special talents and skills and the student's perception of the challenges in schoolwork. Candidates examine records of the student's prior performance to identify beginning points of a downward slope as indicators of gaps in knowledge and skills that impact present learning. Recent samples of the student's work are examined to determine specifically related misconceptions, gaps in knowledge and skills and incomplete knowledge of concepts in the present learning segment. Each candidate develops a written profile of the target student.

During directed observation, the candidate shadows the student for whom the profile was developed. The purpose of the shadowing is to better understand the impact of misconceptions and gaps in knowledge and skills and to become familiar with the student's thought processes related to the present learning task or experiences. Shadowing allows the candidate to make observations about the student's use of prior knowledge, learning preferences, personal interests, special talents and skills and approaches to challenges in schoolwork. The results of these observations enable the candidate to develop a learning trajectory for the target student based on the goals for the learning segment, knowledge gaps and misconceptions, learning experiences and tasks to address the learning gaps and misconceptions, and learning experiences and tasks for constructing new knowledge and understanding.

In the first part of peripheral participation in this clinical rotation, the candidate develops and enacts two sequential learning segments for the target student based on the findings from the focused inquiry and directed observation. Knowledge of the target student's learning trajectory will be interpreted and translated into plans for learning using a theoretical perspective from Clinical Rotation

#4, knowledge about curriculum representation and presentation from Clinical Rotation #1 and epistemic practices from Clinical Rotation #2. This translation process is expected to result in meaningful and productive learning experiences and tasks for the target student. However, this proposition will be tested through engagement in the teaching process from Clinical Rotation #3—planning and enacting a learning segment, interpreting and translating the target student's responses to learning experiences and tasks and making adjustments to optimize learning.

The second part of peripheral participation involves an analysis and evaluation of the learning segment based on the concept of a philosophical stance from Clinical Rotation #5. The first part of this evaluation is a determination of the extent to which the target student accomplished the learning goals. The second part of the evaluation is a determination of the extent to which the target student can apply the new knowledge as anticipated in an academic setting and in everyday life.

Rotation #7: Working with Small Groups of Students

The purpose of this clinical rotation is to continue to deepen the candidates' understanding of the interrelatedness of the *context* for learning, the *conditions* for learning, developing meaningful and productive learning experiences and tasks and accomplishing learning goals. This particular clinical rotation introduces a more complex social dynamic in teaching and learning than was present when working with an individual student.

An important aspect of focused inquiry in this rotation is research on the significance of the social dynamic among students in the classroom. Candidates are encouraged to examine the research on the impact of peer relationships and relationships between students and teachers on students' academic performance (Hemmings, 2003; Farmer et al., 2010). Candidates inquire into the rationale or theory used to create the small group, including the anticipated interaction among different student attributes, and the expected contribution of each student to the learning experience or task based on particular attributes. In this clinical rotation, focused inquiry requires the candidate to collect the same information on each member of the small group as was collected on the individual student in Clinical Rotation #6. Additionally, the candidate inquires into the relationship among members of the group, each group member's perceived status in the class and within the small group and each member's relationship with the clinical teacher. This information will be collected during individual interviews. Candidates examine the curriculum content, learning experiences and learning tasks in relationship to what is known about learners in the small group. The purpose is to determine how the content is framed, and learning tasks are designed to incorporate the learners' prior knowledge, experiences, interests and learning preferences.

During directed observation, candidates focus on how the dynamic interaction of differences in experiences, perceptions and preferences among individual members of the small group mediate the negotiation of learning experiences and tasks, and the role each group member assumes. Candidates observe the extent to which learning experiences and tasks enable learners to accomplish the expected learning outcomes and identify adjustments that might optimize learning. Further, candidates observe and make inferences about the extent to which the clinical teacher's theoretical perspective on learning is evident in learning experiences and tasks within the small group setting and how the teacher's philosophical stance has been internalized and actualized in the mediated negotiation among small group members.

Peripheral participation involves candidates in facilitating learning in a small group. The actual role of facilitation is determined by the clinical teacher and is appropriate for supporting student engagement in the learning experience or task and the students' social and emotional development. This role should span several learning segments. While facilitating student learning in the small group, the candidate gives careful attention to the social dynamic among group members, the extent to which each student participates and benefits from the experience or task, and those aspects of individual student profiles that influence the student's own learning and that of others.

Rotation #8: Working with the Whole Class

The purpose of this clinical rotation is to continue to deepen the candidates' understanding of the interrelatedness of the *context* for learning, the *conditions* for learning, developing meaningful and productive learning experiences and tasks and accomplishing learning goals. This particular clinical rotation introduces a more complex social dynamic in teaching and learning than was present when working with an individual student or a small group.

An important aspect of focused inquiry in this rotation is research on the significance of the social dynamic among students in the classroom. Candidates are encouraged to examine the research on peer relationships and relationships between students and teachers, organizing and managing learning in the classroom and students' learning outcomes (Hemmings, 2003; Farmer et al., 2010). During focused inquiry, candidates discuss with the clinical teacher the power and social relationships among students, how these relationships are managed, how students' emotional and social development is facilitated and how social and power relationships influence the planning of learning experiences and tasks. Candidates inquire into how different parts of learning experiences and tasks fit together across learning segments to support student learning and how learning experiences and tasks are connected to students' prior knowledge, experiences, interests and learning preferences.

Directed observation in this clinical rotation is more complex than that in the focus on the individual student or the small group. This observation combines attention to individuals within and across small groups with the whole-class dynamic and the impact of individuals on the whole class as influenced by teacher-orchestrated social arrangements. Candidates observe the behavior of individual students in different social situations and the impact of these different social situations on individuals and small groups and patterns in learning and responding across the whole class.

Peripheral participation in this clinical rotation involves candidates in planning and enacting one learning segment for a whole class. This learning segment should fit the sequence planned by the clinical teacher. The learning segment should be consistent with the curriculum content, epistemic practice, theoretical perspective and philosophical stance operating in the classroom. This learning segment may include individual, small-group and whole-class learning experiences and tasks as appropriate for accomplishing the expected learning outcomes.

Summary

The discussion in this chapter presented an approach to learning teaching through clinical rotations employing a practice-based perspective positioned within an understanding of teaching as an interpretive process. Learning teaching engages candidates in this interpretive process through application of the epistemic practices of focused inquiry, directed observation and guided practice. The clinical rotations occur in clinical classrooms located in public schools that are specifically designated for this purpose. The clinical rotations are organized into two parts: (a) teaching perspectives and frames of practice and (b) facilitating student learning.

Teaching perspectives are embedded within frames of practice that inform approaches to facilitating student learning. Teaching perspectives comprise a particular ideology, personal perceptions, values, and moral and social commitments. The frames of practice are the conceptual constructs through which teaching perspectives are translated into the everyday work of facilitating student growth and development. These frames of practice include the philosophical stance, theoretical perspective, teaching process, epistemic practices and curriculum framing.

The process for facilitating student learning is accomplished with the support of an appropriate context and conditions. The context for facilitating student learning includes social arrangements, such as individuals, small groups, and the whole class; students' cultural and experiential backgrounds; and the social dynamic among students and between the teacher and students. The conditions for learning include the learning goals; what the learner knows in relationship to the learning goals and how the learner makes sense of what he or she knows; what learners need to know to achieve the learning goals; and what experiences and/or tasks will be the most meaningful for the learner.

Conclusion

The discussion in this chapter presented a clearly delineated interpretive process embedded in clinical experiences for learning teaching that are developmentally sequenced. Concepts are interconnected, knowledge is cumulative and learning is mutual and reciprocal among candidates and mentors. In this process, candidates learn teaching, and mentors gain deeper understanding of their own practice. This approach enables teacher educators to contribute to improving the quality of teaching and learning in P–12 schools while preparing the next generation of classroom teachers.

Further, this systematic approach to clinical experiences for learning teaching provides an exemplar that can be used in designing entire preservice teacher preparation programs. Foundations courses can be linked to clinical experiences by supporting candidates in constructing related knowledge of the historical, sociological and theoretical context for schooling in the local community and the larger society. The pedagogical approaches presented in methods courses can go beyond propositional and procedural knowledge to include conditional knowledge linked to clinical experiences for learning teaching in classrooms. The epistemic practices of focused inquiry, directed observation and guided practice or peripheral participation can be applied in courses and experiences across the program.

References

Abbate-Vaughn, J. (2004). The things they carry: Ideology in an urban teacher professional community. *Urban Review, 36*(4), 227–249.

Darling-Hammond, L. (2000). Teacher quality and student achievement: A review of state policy evidence. *Education Policy Analysis Archives, 8*(1). Retrieved from epaa.asu.edu

Farmer, T.W., Petrin, R.A., Robertson, D.L., Fraser, M.W., Hall, C.M., Day, S.H., & Dadisman, K. (2010). Peer relationships of bullies, bully-victims, and victims: The two social worlds of bullying in second-grade classrooms. *The Elementary School Journal, 110*(3), 364–392.

Hemmings, A. (2003). Fighting for respect in urban high schools. *Teachers College Record, 105*(3), 416–437.

Hollins, E.R. (2011). Teacher preparation for quality teaching. *Journal of Teacher Education, 62*(4), 395–407.

Moje, E.B. (2007). Developing socially just subject-matter instruction: A review of the literature on disciplinary literacy. *Review of Research in Education, 31*(1), 1–44.

National Center for Education Statistics (NCES) (2012). *The nation's report card: Trends in academic progress 2011.* Washington, DC: Institute of Education Sciences, U.S. Department of Education.

Zhou, M. (2003). Urban education: Challenges in educating culturally diverse children. *Teachers College Record, 105*(2), 208–225.

7

A CLINICAL CLASSROOM PROCESS

Antoinette S. Linton and Richard K. Gordon

Introduction

Many urban students will come from a variety of cultural backgrounds, speaking an array of different languages (August & Haketa, 1997). By the year 2030, 40% of all public school students in the United States will come from diverse cultural and linguistic backgrounds (Thomas & Collier, 2001). Teacher preparation programs are charged with the responsibility of preparing candidates with the knowledge and skills to facilitate the desired learning outcomes for urban students. Better teacher preparation translates into better teaching and improved learning outcomes for urban students.

Teacher education programs have attempted to create well-planned learning experiences for learning how to teach. For example, Wilson and Anson (2006) wrote about the use of microteaching as a way to contextualize the complexities of teaching and learning for candidates. The researchers described a 7-week process in which pairs of candidates teach simplified 30-minute lessons with small groups of students (6–8) from the local school. Candidates teach and then reflect on the learning outcomes of the students. This particular experience fostered a professional understanding of the complexities of teaching and learning for preservice candidates. However, the research report did not address the effects on student academic performance. Hollins (2011b) described how an epistemic practice focused candidates' inquiries about learning and teaching and facilitated the development of effective teaching practices that positively affected urban student academic performance.

In this study, a faculty member at a local southern California university and a practitioner at a local urban secondary school explored an embedded signature assessment called a clinical classroom rotation that promotes intentionally linking teaching practice to expected student learning outcomes by using focused inquiry, directed observation and guided practice (Hollins, 2011b) when learning how to teach. The clinical classroom rotation has three parts: *focused inquiry* about a particular skill or body of knowledge; *directed observation* of a predetermined conceptualization of teaching practice planned and enacted within a clinical classroom by a practitioner; and the guided enactment by the candidate within the field experience classroom. The practitioner is defined as a trustworthy content expert whose intentionality and integrity of practice consistently facilitate the desired learning outcomes for urban students. The practitioner and the university faculty determined the focus of and collaboratively planned the clinical classroom rotation. Candidates were expected to interpret and translate the observational data gathered from the directed observation of the practitioner into knowledge, skills and understanding for the urban classroom during an embedded signature assessment.

The first part of the clinical rotation centers on *focused inquiry*. *Focused inquiry* is an investigation into particular phenomena that influence the processes and conditions for learning within and outside classrooms (Hollins, 2011b). For the clinical classroom rotation, the focus was on how teaching practice and curriculum enactment, grounded in a theoretical perspective, provided students access to ensure strong academic performance. Candidates were given a lesson plan, materials and rubrics to examine and discuss with the practitioner prior to enactment. Candidates were given opportunities to ask questions about the materials and to begin constructing an understanding of the relationship among learner characteristics, pedagogical practices and the intended learning outcomes of the lesson (Hollins, 2011b).

During *focused inquiry*, the candidates, the practitioner and the university faculty constructed a directed observation form. Directed observation was the primary tool used to focus candidate attention on the curricular materials, the pedagogical choices of the practitioner and the responses of the students. Candidates wrote their observations, questions and anecdotal evidence gathered from the observation on the form. Observational data were then interpreted and translated by the candidates with guided assistance from the practitioner and the university faculty.

The second part of the rotation consisted of candidates conducting a directed classroom observation where they witnessed the learning process, took note of the patterns of instruction and began to make sense of how these patterns influence learning opportunities for urban students (Hollins, 2011b). Candidates actively interpreted the particular aspect of teaching and learning enacted and afterward were given opportunities to ask questions and receive one-on-one time with the practitioner to gain insight into the in-the-moment pedagogical decisions made during the lesson.

The final part of the clinical rotation took place in the mentor teacher's classroom during field experience. Here, guided by the mentor teacher, faculty and practitioner, candidates incorporated ideas concerning practice translated from *directed observation* into a lesson and then taught. Candidates were encouraged to define their practice based on evidence of student learning and identify challenges that arose during enactment. These challenges were then brought back to the university, where the candidates and the university professor identified approaches for meeting the challenges. In this way, clinical classroom rotations provide candidates opportunities to develop a more sophisticated understanding of how to utilize different social, theoretical and philosophical perspectives to facilitate urban student learning (Hollins, 2011a).

The purpose of this embedded signature assessment approach was to explore the use of the clinical classroom rotation process as a mechanism for developing teaching practice that has a positive impact on urban science student academic performance. Through the clinical classroom rotation, teacher educators develop an awareness of candidates' strengths and weaknesses concerning the knowledge, skills and understandings needed to teach in urban settings, while candidates simultaneously develop an awareness of the complexities associated with facilitating meaningful and productive learning experiences for urban students.

The embedded signature assessment served two purposes: (1) it was a learning experience for candidates and (2) it was a way for faculty to assess candidates' progress in learning to teach urban students and to assess the effectiveness of program practices. Two focus questions guided the exploration: (1) What information can be gathered about candidate knowledge and skills from the focused inquiry and directed observation of the clinical classroom rotation? and (2) How are responses elicited from the candidates during *focused inquiry* and *directed observation* used to construct learning experiences that enable candidates to effectively teach urban students? Our ultimate goal in this work was to use the answers to these questions to help improve clinical classroom experiences for candidates.

Conceptual Framework for the Clinical Rotation

Preservice teacher candidate learning is socially and culturally constructed and needs to be understood within a particular experiential and cultural context (Cochran-Smith, 2000). Understanding and facilitating this process of candidate learning requires the use of a construct or tool for organizing and interpreting observations and explaining and predicting reactions and outcomes (Hollins, 2011a). The challenge in this clinical rotation was in the design of mediated action and tools that could focus candidate dialogue and experiences and then reshape existing knowledge, beliefs and practices related to teaching and learning (Johnson & Golombek, 2003; Hollins, 2011a). Fernandez and Chokshi (2002) present a carefully guided experience that mediates the social and cognitive outcomes of teachers when they participate in a lesson study.

Fernandez and Chokshi (2002) point out that lesson study is a tool for evaluating the effectiveness of a particular learning event while actively participating in the collaborative process of lesson planning, teaching–observing and reflective debriefing. When the planning portion of a lesson study is combined with Hollins' (2011b) *focused inquiry* into a lesson plan, it provides an opportunity to make candidates' implicit ideas about teaching and learning explicit. During *focused inquiry*, the group was expected to develop suitable criteria for recognizing whether or not the learning episode provided evidence of effective teaching for urban students, as measured by students' academic performance (Windschitl, 2002).

Second, careful observation of the lesson was a data-gathering opportunity that helped answer focus questions concerning the lesson (Fernandez & Chokshi, 2002). Fernandez and Chokshi's (2002) careful observation was expanded to include Hollins' (2011b) *directed observation*. *Directed observation* was particularly important because it provided a way for candidates to examine and record patterns of actions made by the practitioner and the responses elicited by the students.

Finally, feedback sessions immediately after *directed observation* offered the group opportunities to ask the practitioner about the pedagogical decisions that were made in the moment that characterized the lesson from start to finish (Fernandez & Chokshi, 2002) and to engage in critical exploration of the meanings behind both the questions and answers (Ladson-Billings, 1996). The goal of these Q&A sessions was to provide candidates insight into the different social, theoretical and philosophical perspectives (Hollins, 2011a) that are used to understand one's own teaching practice, perceptions and values (Ladson-Billings, 1996). This supports candidates developing the insight, habits of mind and norms for engaging in meaningful professional discourse (Hollins, 2011a).

Inquiry into Practice

Division K of the American Educational Research Association (AERA) and the National Council for Accreditation of Teacher Education have challenged a selected group of university researchers from teacher education programs, the National Education Association, the Association of Teacher Educators and practitioners to develop a better way of preparing teachers in urban schools, especially high-poverty urban schools. This collaborative group of researchers and stakeholders was encouraged to interpret practices in medical education to improve the process of clinical practice for urban teacher residency (UTR) programs. It was reasoned that medical practices were useful in underscoring the importance of establishing clear routines and procedures in residency programs to consistently apply learning theories in practice and provide a process for cognitive and intellectual growth for teaching practice (Hollins, 2011a). We present this approach as a way to integrate practices found in medical education into teacher education through the use of this clinical classroom rotation, with the intention of introducing a process of developing teaching practice that facilitates meaningful and productive learning experiences for urban students.

Our inquiry focused on the clinical classroom rotation whereby 19 math and science candidates enrolled in an UTR program and participated in a lesson study that was grounded in socioculturalism and facilitated with structured dialogue. All UTR candidates were enrolled in a curriculum theories course and were actively teaching at least twice a week in a mentor teacher's classroom.

The observation and debriefing took place in a biology classroom located within an urban high school in southern California. The ethnic composition of the school was 55% African American and 45% Latino. The practitioner was an African American woman identified as highly qualified and credentialed to teach biology in the state of California with 12 years of teaching experience.

The clinical classroom rotation as an embedded signature assessment allowed for a close examination of individual candidate experiences pertaining to learning how to teach. By interpreting a practitioner's in-the-moment pedagogy, candidates were encouraged to attend to specific aspects of the lesson using knowledge learned in coursework and then translating this to future practice in fieldwork. Candidates' interpretations were collected and organized using the *directed observation* form, which made analysis of candidates' ability to attend to and interpret practitioner in-the-moment pedagogy possible. The candidates and practitioner also debriefed after the enactment of the lesson to ask clarifying questions and go deeper into the practitioner's thinking.

To assess candidates' ability to attend to and interpret the teaching process, we utilized knowledge regarding learning theory, facilitating student learning, epistemic practice, curriculum and teacher processes. Our aim was to observe patterns in the elicited responses from candidates concerning theories of learning, facilitating student learning, epistemic practice, curriculum and teaching processes. Using NVivo qualitative software, responses to these prompts were coded into groups of skills described and cross-referenced with the type of knowledge reported to support the description (Tables 7.1 and 7.2).

The initial round of coding included categorizing the responses reported on the *directed observation* forms. Each category was examined for a second time, looking for specific evidence of candidates' description of the practitioner's focus on the *nature of science* approach to the curriculum, where the scope and sequence of the learning experiences are based on web-like biological themes that include big ideas such as patterns, systems, processes and relationships grounded in a constructivist perspective of learning. Subcategories or subcodes were based on descriptions of the skills in the literature and initial coding of the

TABLE 7.1 Categories of Skills Described by Candidates

Skills	Indicators
Knowledge of a Theoretical Perspective	• Practitioner decision making • Constructivist perspective of learning • Discourse strategies of students and practitioner in a science classroom
Knowledge of Facilitating Student Learning	• Teacher–student and student–student interactions
Knowledge of Curriculum Content	• *Nature of science* stance of curriculum
Recognition of Teaching as an Epistemic Practice	• Practitioner decision making • Alignment of planning with enactment
Recognition of Teaching Processes	• Knowledge of content-specific pedagogy • Use of routines • Use of rubrics

TABLE 7.2 Categories of Knowledge Applied by Candidates

Knowledge	Indicators
Proficient Knowledge for the Observation	• Inquiry as opportunity for students to pose questions, collect and work with their own data, design investigations and make claims with instruction • Constructivist theory of learning is enacted when students develop their own ideas, rules and strategies for solving problems and can articulate this to each other and to the teacher • Teacher provides evidence of adjusting the instruction in response to student ideas and reasoning • Sound subject matter knowledge, concepts are integrated, language of the discipline is used • Activities are appropriate for level of students' growth and development
Developing Knowledge	• Inquiry strategies are primarily opportunities to collect data through observation or experimentation and are teacher-centered • Constructivist theory of learning implemented when students help each other and can articulate the learning objective • Science has some empirical and tentative aspects and includes specific ideas • Candidates view science as a process only—not as a way of knowing

responses in this inquiry. Descriptions of the subcategories for each component of skills were as follows:

- The skills needed to sustain a positive learning environment include the ways in which a practitioner alters pedagogy to help students construct deeper understanding of principles, concepts and ideas (Hollins, 2011b). The skills also include how the teacher interacts with students and critiques the interactions according to knowledge of child growth and development (Hollins, 2011b).
- Practitioners enact their theoretical perspective of learning and their philosophical stance on the curriculum (Hollins, 2011b). For this inquiry, the practitioner's theoretical perspective on learning was constructivist, and the philosophical stance on the curriculum was a nature of science perspective.
- The practitioner has the ability to utilize frameworks and a developed epistemic practice to facilitate students' developing and evaluating knowledge and provide social processes and context for communicating knowledge (Hollins, 2011b).

The responses were transcribed and mapped, marking places where candidates made their thinking about knowledge and skills explicit. The first step in analyzing the data was to fracture or chunk the material (Ward & McCotter, 2004). Second, the use of generative questions allowed for a more detailed analysis of the data. Third, data were then subcoded for details that addressed the characteristics of teacher knowledge and skills. Finally, conceptual density was achieved when we continued to use the generative questions to guide the data analysis until the matrix provided good descriptions of all the chunks and was consistent with the guiding frames that were identified for the types of categories.

Findings from Inquiry

Knowledge of a Theoretical Perspective

Constructivist Learning Theory

Constructivist learning theory explains learning as a cultural product and knowledge as shaped by micro- and macrocultural influences that evolve through increasing participation within different cognitive and social contexts (Windschitl, 2002). The purpose of this category in the embedded signature assessment was to observe whether or not candidates could infer the theoretical perspective on learning that was operationalized during the teaching events (see Chapter 6). Responses in this category were analyzed for descriptions of how students made decisions about engaging in scientific inquiry into the surface area–to–volume ratio. Three overall responses were identified in the observations: (1) candidates' ability to identify students posing questions, hypothesizing and analyzing data as evidence of the learning theory that was operationalized; (2) candidates' ability to describe the inquiry process connected to student decision making as developing knowledge of learning theory; and (3) candidates' inability to connect biology students' elicited responses and actions with the learning theory that was operationalized. One candidate reported that the practitioner made sure that instruction elicited students' use of "meaningful language based social interactions to help with cognition." The candidate supported this observation with more evidence, stating that "the practitioner made use of students' prior experiences and knowledge."

The remaining candidates had difficulty recognizing constructivist learning theory. The reports from the observation forms indicated that 12 candidates attended to student completion of the fill-in-the-blank portions of the lesson, making measurements and calculations and handling the laboratory materials. Five candidates reported that students collected data to support or reject hypotheses and answer questions based on data collected and that students worked in groups to "help each other." These candidates also reported that the classroom routines were enacted to increase students' levels of responsibility.

Discourse Strategies

The focus on discourse strategies as a measure of learning theory is rooted in Vygotsky's concept of the "zone of proximal development"—the notion that developing mental functions must be fostered and assessed through collaborative activities in which learners participate in problem-solving tasks and the use of discourse as a cultural tool (Windschitl, 2002). From this premise, the lesson was planned to demonstrate how the practitioner creates activities for students that are approximations of science practice that lead to certain types of discourse. To be categorized as proficient, candidates were expected to attend to and make note of the questions asked by the practitioner and other indicators that students had been taught explicitly how to work together and engage in discourse during the lesson. Students demonstrated this by clarifying instructions for fellow students and by explaining student roles and procedures during the laboratory activity.

From the recorded responses, it was determined that four candidates attended to student-to-student discourse used to clarify procedures. Two candidates attended to the warm-up question and the use of visual aids to facilitate student participation. One teacher mentioned that students were asked to describe the relationship between hypotonic solutions, hypertonic solutions and osmosis. Altogether, eight candidates described some aspect of student discourse and the strategies used to facilitate the use of academic language. Although all candidates received university instruction concerning the importance of learning environments that facilitate discourse, candidates were unable to consistently attend to the evidence of this skill during the *directed observation*.

Knowledge Facilitating Student Learning

Teacher–Student and Student–Student Interactions

The purpose of this category was to determine the depth of the candidates' understanding of the interrelatedness of the context for learning, the conditions for learning and how both students and the practitioner participate in the learning experience to make meaning and to accomplish the learning goals (see Chapter 6). To determine whether candidates' responses in this category could be described as proficient, responses were analyzed for the candidates' ability to recognize how students were grouped to facilitate discussion and noted how both teachers and students used socially and culturally influenced questions, analogies and examples to make meaning of the learning episode.

Candidates were able to describe two forms of teacher–student interactions and provided one general description of student–student interaction. Candidates interpreted teacher–student interactions as (1) behavior-oriented and (2) interactions that facilitated student responses. Three out of 19 candidates described teacher–student interactions as "disciplinarian," "enforcing the rules" and "enforcing the rules set." These candidates were described as having a developing knowledge of teacher–student interactions.

Four out of 19 candidates attended to specific student–student interactions. One candidate noted that students aided each other as the practitioner walked around the room checking for answers to the warm-up question; however, student-attempted use of academic language, the ability to clarify directions and the analogies and examples used by students were not described. There were no records of the questions that students or the practitioner asked, analogies, elaborations or examples used that helped both the practitioner and the student make sense of the learning situation.

Knowledge of Curriculum Content

Nature of Science Perspective of Curriculum

The purpose of this category was to determine if candidates could recognize how the curricular perspective was enacted in the science classroom. The nature of science perspective takes the stance that science is an integrated field of knowledge with connections and themes that might be hierarchical or web-like and includes big ideas such as patterns, systems, processes or relationships (Schneider & Plasman, 2011). In this view, teachers are representative of canonical science and, as such, are disciplinary practitioners who process intellectual skills and dispositions for students (Windschitl, 2002). Thus, teachers engage students in scientific discourse, plan and enact learning experiences that are relevant to the discipline and use tools commonly available to practitioners in the field.

Tools include academic language, science equipment and scientific text. It was expected that candidates would demonstrate an understanding of the purpose of the curriculum as the facilitation of students' understanding of biology from the nature of science perspective. Candidates were to recognize how students used the formal laboratory rubric and concept maps as tools for understanding science as a process.

All candidates reported that the activity observed was a completion of laboratory procedures. For some candidates, the purpose of the laboratory activity was to follow the procedures for collecting data to support or reject a hypothesis. One candidate described the activity as the "filling out of the laboratory sheet where students could use the formulas to determine certain data." Another candidate stated that students were using the blocks (cell process) to measure and make connections to justify former hypotheses/findings about cells and surface area. These responses were categorized as "developing." Overall, no proficient indicators about the understanding of the purpose and construction of the curriculum were reported.

Recognition of Teaching as an Epistemic Practice

Practitioner Decision Making

The purpose of this category was to observe whether or not candidates could identify the interrelated patterns of experiences comprising the practitioner's teaching and learning routine from the lesson plan reviewed during *focused inquiry*. Candidates were offered a clear explanation of the plan, including procedures, classroom routines and learning tasks.

To determine whether candidate responses were proficient, responses were analyzed for descriptions of the practitioner's reasoning to enact the lesson. Proficient candidates were to identify factors within the learning episode that allow biology students to engage in scientific inquiry. In addition, candidates were to observe which classroom routines and rituals were put in place for the learning episode. Three overall responses were identified for this section: (1) the enactment of the lesson resulted in candidates not identifying specific aspects of the lesson that facilitated inquiry; (2) candidates reported the purpose of the activity as a way to develop general skills for students; and (3) candidates reported hands-on activities, group work and the use of academic vocabulary as indicators of practitioner decision making. Only one teacher described evidence that the lesson was grounded in social constructivist learning theory and that the purpose of the lesson was met because "students expressed their prior knowledge and previous learning experiences." However, the candidate did not provide evidence that this approach was to facilitate student engagement in scientific inquiry.

Teaching Processes

Knowledge of Content-Specific Pedagogy

The purpose of this category was to observe whether or not candidates could recognize the components of practitioner pedagogical practice. During the *direct observation*, candidates were to observe the enactment of the lesson and how pedagogical practices were adjusted to clarify organizing ideas, concepts and principles (see Chapter 6). During the lesson, the practitioner employed strategies for facilitating student construction of research questions and hypotheses and collecting and organizing data. Students were provided multiple representations of cellular surface area–to–volume ratio as represented by diagrams, charts, blocks and verbal explanations. To address any challenges that may have occurred during the lesson, students were encouraged to strategically use these representations and make note of their own decision making while using strategies. To determine whether candidate responses were proficient, responses were analyzed for descriptions of student usage of concept maps, academic vocabulary, use of the wooden blocks as representations of cells and student discourse.

Candidates were able to recognize strategies used to facilitate student learning but did not recognize how these strategies were used to facilitate student decision making and mastery of the scientific process. Thirteen out of 19 candidates reported teacher use of one or more of the learning strategies. Lacking were descriptions of students' use of the tools to formulate questions, hypothesize, experiment and engage in argumentation as the process of scientific inquiry (Duschl, 2008). Even though candidates were given the planning documents that explained the strategies used during enactment, candidates did not report a connection between the facilitative strategies (i.e., concept maps) and the overall concepts of constructing scientific knowledge about cellular dynamics by the students.

Use of Rubrics to Facilitate Student Learning

To be determined as proficient in this category, candidates were to attend to and record the use of rubrics by students to engage in the inquiry process with little assistance from the practitioner. From the recorded responses on the directed observation forms, it was determined that candidates were not able to attend to the use of rubrics as a way to mediate student inquiry skills. During the lesson, candidates were to observe students collecting and analyzing data with the understanding that the earlier steps in the experimentation process had taken place. Candidates' directed observation forms did not provide evidence that this knowledge was considered. For example, one candidate stated that the practitioner processed ideas and thinking skills for students for the gradual release of responsibility during the lesson. A response was categorized as developing due to the attendance to students' independence during the laboratory activity; however, there was no mention of the inquiry process as represented by the rubric. Another candidate reported a "pre-lab" activity but gave no evidence that this was part of an ongoing inquiry skill development facilitated by the formal laboratory rubric.

Use of Routines

To be considered proficient within this category, candidates' responses were to include the enactment, observation and interpretation aspects of teaching practice that could be observed during instruction (Hollins, 2011b). During the enactment phase, biology students were to come in, complete their warm-up and discuss their hypotheses based on activities completed prior to the lesson. Second, biology students engaged in an experimentation routine that included measuring blocks (simulated cells of different sizes), calculated the surface area–to–volume ratios and gathered data to support or reject their hypotheses to expand their knowledge of cell structure, function and dynamics in the solution. During this time, candidates were to note how the practitioner used the experimentation routine as a formative assessment technique to collect data on student skills and understanding of the topic. Finally, candidates were to notice how the learning activity was ended and how students were given an opportunity to reflect on their learning.

Candidates were able to recognize the use of the warm-up to facilitate student engagement within the science process. Eight out of 19 candidates attended to the teaching process—specifically the classroom procedures and routines enacted. Of the eight, two candidates stated that the teaching process was used to "enforce the rules." One candidate described a portion of the enacting process as an "implementation ritual" and noticed that the ritual was used to familiarize students with release questions for the state assessment.

Discussion

We used Hollins' (2011b) description of knowledge, skills and habits of mind required for quality teaching and Schneider and Plasman's (2011) review of science teachers' pedagogical content knowledge development to analyze candidates' interpretive abilities concerning knowledge of teaching and learning. For example, although candidates at the time of the clinical classroom rotation had participated in coursework concerning learning theory, teaching processes and curriculum and were in field placements, the only clearly developed knowledge category was knowledge of curricular content, in which all 19 candidates could be classified as developing. Table 7.3 displays candidates' responses demonstrating areas of proficiency, development and pre-developing; the majority of the skills and knowledge for interpretative practice lie within the pre-developing stage and are in serious need of academic attention.

TABLE 7.3 Candidates' Responses within Teacher Knowledge Categories

Knowledge Category		*Number of Candidates Who Responded*		
		Proficient	*Developing*	*Pre-developing*
Knowledge of a Theoretical Perspective	Enactment of learning theory	1	2	16
	Discourse strategies		8	11
Knowledge of Facilitating Student Learning	Teacher–student interactions		3	16
	Student–student interactions		4	15
Knowledge of Curricular Content	Nature of science		19	
Teaching as an Epistemic Practice	Practitioner decision making	1	6	12
Teaching Processes	Knowledge of content-specific Pedagogy	3	13	6
	Use of routines		8	11
	Use of rubrics to facilitate learning	3	7	12
	Inquiry strategies		5	11

Using Focused Inquiry and Directed Observation

The enactment of *focused inquiry* and *directed observation* in a clinical classroom allowed access to the type of knowledge and understanding candidates used to interpret a learning episode. During the observation, candidates reported pre-developing and developing knowledge of the skills needed to facilitate urban student academic performance. Analysis of candidates' responses revealed that knowledge of *teaching processes* and *curricular content* was most developed for the group. Other categories of knowledge are in need of intensive re-planning and re-teaching within the preservice program.

Using *focused inquiry* and *directed observation* as epistemic practices for learning how to teach allowed teacher educators to observe patterns in the responses of the candidates and make meaning of the responses elicited. *Focused inquiry* allowed the practitioner to provide an in-depth look at the social, theoretical and philosophical perspectives that inform teaching practice. Taking a sociocultural perspective, learning what a practitioner is thinking and why they are thinking in a particular way became a resource for continued candidate development (Gallucci, DeVoogt Van Lare, Yoon, & Boatright, 2010). The learning process was reciprocal because the practitioner interpreted the questions and ideas from the group of candidates, and this became the data the practitioner used to interpret and translate candidate learning from planned learning experiences, including the clinical classroom rotation, the university coursework and the candidates' fieldwork experience.

Directed observation gave practitioners and university faculty a glimpse of how candidates' interpretive practice was developing. Candidates' responses about learning theory, facilitating student learning, curriculum, epistemic practices and teaching processes were made explicit. By engaging in conversations with candidates during the debriefing and analyzing their written responses, practitioners and university faculty constructed understandings about (1) targeted learning episodes based on relevant data and (2) immediate refinement or creation of learning materials needed to further candidate learning. After analyzing candidate responses, we found that one candidate attended to three components of the knowledge required for quality teaching at the proficient level when compared to other candidates. This realization laid the groundwork to address the knowledge for quality teaching that candidates were learning in university coursework.

Proficient Knowledge of One Teacher Candidate

The candidates' responses elicited from *directed observation* revealed only one candidate with proficient knowledge. This analysis raises questions regarding the conditions that are necessary to adequately learn teaching. The results suggest that candidate learning overall is in need of remediation. Candidate learning can be mediated through the use of teaching and cultural tools that are shared across a preservice program. At the time of this inquiry, the clinical classroom and the university coursework were interconnected for just 2 weeks. It is suggested that coherency, continuity and consistent learning opportunities across all three areas are needed to sustain effective learning opportunities for candidates.

Turning to the conceptual implications of this assessment, we draw attention to the coherency, consistency and continuity for learning how to teach.

Conclusion

Our work presents evidence that enacting *focused inquiry* and *directed observation* provides a clearer understanding of what candidates know and understand about teaching practice and what they still must learn. With this information, learning experiences constructed by universities and public schools can extend candidate knowledge of teaching and learning and address the misunderstandings and pre-developing knowledge in more strategic ways. By using the clinical classroom rotation as an embedded assessment, university faculty and practitioners can gather information about a number of key components of teaching practice that candidates understand. Further research is needed on the effectiveness of the scope and sequence of the preservice education program curriculum in addressing the learning needs of candidates as determined by responses elicited during the embedded signature assessment.

Our results have a number of implications for UTR programs regarding facilitating learning to teach in urban schools. First, our findings indicate that when planning a clinical rotation, practitioners and university faculty should consider focusing on one or two aspects of teaching practice to help candidates improve their skills when attending to, interpreting and translating practitioner teaching practice. Specifically, aspects of teaching practice attended to during the clinical classroom rotation could be linked to the coursework curriculum of the UTR program. Second, by using Hollins' (2011a) epistemic practice for teaching and learning, university faculty can interpret and translate candidate responses and re-plan and re-enact aspects of the curriculum that address the challenges that candidates are experiencing. In this way, we can develop a deeper understanding about what aspects of preservice education make a greater impact on candidates learning how to teach.

In conclusion, the proposed clinical classroom rotation process as an embedded signature assessment is based on research and theory in teacher education and research concerning the enactment of lesson study in K–12 schools. The result is a proposal for a process that features *focused inquiry* around a key component of teaching practice; *direct observation* of a practitioner in a clinical classroom; and guided practice for the planning, enactment, observation, interpretation and translation of a lesson by university faculty, practitioners and mentor teachers. These practices are thought to mirror those that candidates are expected to apply in K–12 schools.

References

August D. & Hakuta, K. (1997). *Improving schooling for language-minority children: A research agenda.* Washington, DC: National Academy Press.

Cochran-Smith, M. (2000). The future of teacher education: framing the questions that matter. *Teaching Education, 11*(1) 13–34.

Duschl, R. (2008). Science education in three-part harmony: Balancing conceptual, epistemic, and social learning goals. *Review of Research in Education, 32*(1), 268–291.

Fernandez, C., & Chokshi, S. (2002). A practical guide to translating lesson study for a U.S. setting. *Phi Delta Kappan, 84*(2), 128–134.

Gallucci, C., DeVoogt Van Lare, M., Yoon, I., & Boatright, B. (2010). Instructional coaching: Building theory about the role and organizational support for professional learning. *American Educational Research Journal, 47*(4), 919–963.

Hollins, E. R. (2011a). The centrality of a theoretical perspective on learning to teach. In I. M. Saleh & M. S. Khine (Eds.), *Teaching teachers: Approaches in improving quality of education* (pp. 323–341). New York, NY: Nova Science Publishers, Inc.

Hollins, E. R. (2011b). Teacher preparation for quality teaching. *Journal of Teacher Education, 62*(4), 395–407.

Hollins, E. R., & Torres Guzman, M. (2005). Research on preparing teachers for diverse populations. In M. Cochran-Smith & K. M. Zeichner (Eds.), *Studying teacher education: The report of the AERA panel on research and teacher education* (pp. 477–548). Mahwah, NJ: Lawrence Erlbaum.

Johnson, K. E., & Golombek, P. R. (2003). "Seeing" teacher learning. *TESOL Quarterly, 37*(4), 729–737.

Ladson-Billings, G. (1996). Silences as weapons: Challenges of a black professor teaching white students. *Theory into Practice, 35*(2), 79–85.

Schneider, R., & Plasman, K. (2011). Science teacher learning progressions: A review of science teachers' pedagogical content knowledge development. *Review of Educational Research, 81*(4), 530–565.

Thomas, W. P. and Collier, V. P. (2001). *A National study of school effectiveness for language minority students' long-term academic achievement* (CREDE Report). Retrieved from the University of Southern California, Department of Education website: http://www.usc.edu/dept/education/CMMR/CollierThomasComplete.pdf.

Ward, J. R., & McCotter, S. S. (2004). Reflection as a visible outcome for preservice teachers. *Teaching and Teacher Education, 20*(3), 243–257.

Wilson, G. and Anson, J. (2006). Reframing the practicum: constructing performative space in initial teacher education. *Teaching and Teacher Education, 22*(3), 353–361.

Windschitl, M. (2002). Framing constructivism in practice as the negotiation of dilemmas: An analysis of the conceptual, pedagogical, cultural, and political challenges facing teachers. *Review of Educational Research, 72*(2), 131–175.

8

COMMUNITY IMMERSION TEACHER DEVELOPMENT

Pragmatic Knowledge of Family and Community in Professional Field-Based Practice

Peter C. Murrell, Jr., Jessica Strauss, Rachel Carlson and Maritza Alcoreza Dominguez

Introduction

After decades of research and debate on how to prepare teachers for the demands and challenges of teaching in under-resourced urban communities, very little headway has been made in generating a comprehensive approach for doing so (Darling-Hammond, 2010; Noguera, 2003). One reason for this is that teacher preparation curricula, by and large, fails to conceptualize school success and child development in terms that draw on what Luis Moll has called *funds of knowledge*. The challenge to the practical and professional knowledge of teachers is to understand just how social, cultural and experiential factors *outside of school* support or impede individuals *in* school. This proposed research seeks to do that through action and engagement with the actual distressed neighborhoods and schools and clinical experience that frames school success in terms that include the substantial impact of conditions outside the school walls. In the last decade, there has been increasing interest among teacher educators in community-immersive field experiences in which candidates develop community-based practical teacher knowledge by personally engaging school communities and families (Boyle-Baise & McIntyre, 2008; Cooper, 2007; Marks, Louis, & Printy, 2000; McLaughlin & Talbert, 2001, 2006, 2007; Shaakir-Ansari & Williams, 2009). Virtually every school reform model includes a component that focuses on building collaborative leadership within school communities (Henderson et al., 2007;

McLaughlin & Talbert, 2007; Shaakir-Ansari & Williams, 2009; Warren & Mapp, 2011; Zygmunt-Filwalk et al., 2010). Similarly, there has been a mounting interest in conceptualizing the professional activity that takes place in a *community school*; this comprehensive framework would allow practitioners to account for how a multiplicity of factors combine and interact as determinants of a child's well-being and academic success (Santiago, Ferrara, & Quinn, 2012). To formally define this concept:

> A community school is a network of prevention and intervention services and programs that promote student achievement and family well-being by breaking down barriers and removing obstacles to success. A community school enhances the school experience by establishing and maintaining public and private partnerships with the school. Its integrated focus on academics, health, and social services, youth and community development and community engagement leads to improved student learning, stronger families, and healthier communities. Schools become the centers of community and are open to everyone.
>
> (Park Heights Renaissance Corporation Five-Year Strategic Plan, 2006, p. 11)

Our comprehensive framework, depicted in Figure 8.1, seeks to: (1) make relevant research and theory intelligible and usable by ordinary people and (2) provide a theory of action—a means by which experts and ordinary people can collaborate on equal terms to map the problems and the resolutions of dilemmas. This comprehensive framework will allow practitioners to account for how a multiplicity of factors—*conditions* and *contexts*—combine and interact as determinants of a child's well-being and academic success. Without a comprehensive framework, the experiences of students may not be accurately interpreted. What might be missing is how specific environmental inputs (e.g., upcoming high-stakes assessments) constitute adverse experiences for some students but not for others. On this account, test anxiety and troubling classroom behavior exhibited by individuals may be symptoms of much larger issues of emotional disease in the school, stemming from conditions and contexts related to in-school and out-of-school experiences. We may also be missing the inputs that promote optimal development.

This comprehensive framework is an extension of several key grounded theoretical frameworks—including ecological systems theory (Bronfenbrenner, 1979)—with a focus on the *contexts* and the *conditions* that children and youth navigate combined with the new turn in human development with a focus on situated identity theory (Murrell, 2007). It is focused on improving the often complex methodology of studying resilience and resiliency among urban youth, specifically with attention paid to social and cultural contexts and individual *conditions* (e.g., prior experiences inside and outside the classroom, personal strengths,

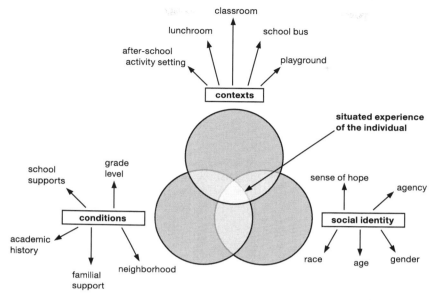

FIGURE 8.1 Comprehensive conceptual framework for educational resilience and resiliency

personal histories of trauma and stress, etc.) that concurrently define social identities and identities of achievement.

This chapter describes an initiative for providing immersive field experiences to urban educators drawing on this comprehensive framework and predicated on the most pressing and strident issues, dilemmas and challenges in urban settings. We describe an *immersion model* that builds upon what we know about building a new professional learning community that has as its foundation the following:

1. The situating of learning practice *for* urban schools *in* urban schools by creating new structured knowledge development in professional learning communities that include teachers, family members and community partners.
2. The focus on the development of teachers through a consistent and systematic *appraisal of practice* in the new professional learning community informed by rich and deep community and family engagement.
3. The focus on the development of practice through an evidence-based *systematic appraisal of the benefits to children in the school* served.
4. The focus on developing the *human systems and social practices* that make the professional learning community work.

One project is termed the Learning in Neighborhood Context (LINC) Project and centers the development of teachers on the concerted cultivation and development of urban children and youth. The companion project within which the practical wisdom from clinical experience is generated is called Learning Ignited by Families and Teachers Together (LIFTT). These projects will be discussed later in the chapter.

Rationale

Children growing up in 21st-century America must learn to navigate an unprecedented multiplicity of social, political, economic and personal challenges. In recent years, we have seen a doubling in instances of obesity, asthma and diabetes in children. We have also seen a dwindling of access to safe and effective schools and an increase in the number of children in poverty. These challenges are particularly daunting for youth of color in city schools and neighborhoods. For many of these children, our society is curtailing opportunity and resources and narrowing expectations for school attainment and academic success, while at the same time instituting policies that result in increased school failure, incarceration and despair. Forces of poverty and racism—if not engaged, explored, comprehended and confronted—could further affect their futures.

We argue that this imperative should be the critical core of teacher development and preparation. More than ever, young people need to be supported and anchored as they navigate a world filled with powerful influences. Youth living in low-income, urban areas often lack both the *navigation* and *negotiation* skills necessary to *build resiliency* in the face of the often chronic exposure to stress and the adverse nature of many of their life experiences. The environments these children were born into often harbor an overwhelming number of emotionally and physically distressing situations. We are not preparing nearly enough educators with the practical wisdom required to promote academic success and optimal growth experiences for this population. The communities within which these children are growing up are not, however, only sources of stress and oppression on which we often focus. They are also the sources of wisdom, effective struggle, resilience and historical overcoming upon which children and the adults who support their development can draw in the cultivation of successful personal and academic identity. Thus, professional knowledge, experience and wisdom of practice have to be based upon a situated understanding of community contexts in terms of both advantages and adversities.

Academic identity "is a form of social identity through which the learner projects, maintains and improvises an image of self as a learner—particularly as an academically able individual" (Murrell, 2009). This is also fundamentally important to student achievement. A student's academic identity affects his or her confidence, motivation and resiliency as a learner. It includes a dimension of *transpersonal* identity in which students gain the agency to shape their identity in dynamic interaction with others. For African American and Latino learners in particular, this transpersonal dimension is closely interwoven with deeply embedded attitudes and structures of racism and closely connected to the interactions that students have with their schools, families and community. Academic identity is thus fundamentally affected (and, in part, determined) by the cultural competence and practices of teachers, parents and other adults "to create a supportive cultural, social and intellectual environment for learners of color grappling with the formation of their academic identities" (Murrell, 2007, p. 98).

What do we imagine when we think of an excellent teacher in urban American schools of the 21st century? We view the cultivation of both *resilience* and *resiliency* as the cornerstone of accomplished practice for promoting school success and identity development. Resilience is the capacity of individuals to both negotiate and navigate adversity; *navigate* their way to the psychological, social, cultural and physical resources that sustain their well-being *and* their capacity individually and collectively; and *negotiate* for those resources to be provided in culturally meaningful ways. Those called upon to serve these children and their families need to be fully committed to the development of resilience in children in all manner of in-school and out-of-school settings.

The core aims of the teacher must be to foster agency and success in a complex environment through a concerted cultivation of resiliency. The *excellent teacher* is, therefore, one who brings all of his or her personal resources, skills and character together with those of other adults responsible for raising healthy, successful children—one who, in concert with these other adults, grounds practice in the cultural and historical context and meets the true developmental needs of each student. We call this kind of teacher the *community teacher*.

Contrast this conception of the *community teacher* with the contemporary paradigm of teaching emanating from what is essentially a *factory model* carried over from the 19th century. In this view, the role of the teacher is a processor of children in batches and in lock-step assembly-line fashion. Developing teachers in the old paradigm sees the function of teachers to be that of filling children with information that they purportedly need to be good "products"—managing their behavior while doing so—and using standardized tests to determine how they measure up to minimal criteria.

We have found that accomplished teachers become *community teachers* as they begin to critically interpret, from real experience, the ways in which this old paradigm falls short in actually developing the intellectual and personal abilities of their students. They recognize that the best teachers care deeply for their students and have the expertise, the knowledge and the skills to educate them with that caring. They understand that under-resourced schools, poor physical conditions and unqualified teachers create conditions within which children develop a sense of themselves that is disabled, disenfranchised and disengaged. Finally, they enter into a *developmental alliance* with young people, joining them "in their developmental processes and, in doing so, not only contribute to their growth but grow as educators through that experience as well" (Nakkula & Toshalis, 2006, p. xii).

As Michelle Fine and others discovered in a series of interviews with public school children, adverse external conditions "moved into the skin; ... shame, filth, and state neglect crossed membranes from what was outside the child, in the building, to what was the child" (Fine and Ruglis, 2009). Low expectations seep through these "membranes" as well, giving children damaging messages about who they are and what they are capable of. *Community teachers* see this and want to be part of a transformation of their school communities—to seek the *moral will* and the *moral skill* (Schwartz & Sharpe, 2010) to do something different in their own classrooms and to build with like-minded adults the kind of school community that will nurture students' highest and best growth and development. Often, however, their professional training for teaching has not fully prepared them for the challenges they face, nor has it exposed them to the learning opportunities the community has to offer. This teacher immersion project seeks to remedy this with a program for developing *community teachers*—educators who are passionate about transforming the educational lives of children and families in city environments. More importantly, they are individuals who develop the practical wisdom of learners' academic identity development.

The *community teachers'* framework expects that teachers will know their students, mobilize families and stakeholders in student success and partner with students and families to reflect on students' progress. Each of these dimensions of teacher practice affects students' academic identity and is strengthened by strong relationships with families and knowledge of community, history and culture. The stronger the link to the community and the more deeply rooted classroom practice is in time-honored cultural traditions and collective wisdom, the more resilient and competent the academic identity that emerges will be (Perry, Steele, & Hilliard, 2003). And the stronger the development of academic identity in the context of high academic expectations, the more engaged and successful the student is likely to be. The teacher development intervention we describe is shaped by the theory that knowledge of community context is gained in direct relationship and shared work, not simply in an activity of *studying* the community. It is in the daily interaction, side-by-side focus and development of a common set of understandings and activities that teachers can develop deep understandings of the context within which their instructional practice emerges (Murrell, 2001; Zygmunt-Fillwalk, Clark, Clausen, & Mucherah, 2012).

As other chapters in this volume attest, quality field-based practice in the community context is an essential formative experience for teacher candidates. One of the most powerful examples of innovative practice in community immersion can be found at Teachers' College at Ball State University. There, undergraduate students can opt to spend an entire semester, encompassing all of their credits, working off campus in the local African American community. They spend the mornings in classrooms at the elementary school or early childhood education center; the middle of the day in collective and individual study and reflection; and the afternoons, evenings and weekends working in community programs, meeting families, being guided by community mentors and learning directly from families and leaders in the neighborhood. Steeped in a participatory anthropological experience of their students' daily lives, these teacher candidates gain insight into the context for learning that is impossible to achieve from books and classroom experience. Results have been tremendous (Zygmunt-Fillwalk et al., 2012). The model described in this chapter is the in-service analog of this immersive experience, created in partnership with community-based agencies and city schools.

One of these agencies, the Alliance for Community Teachers and Schools (ACTS), has participated in the development of this model over the past 2 years, a model that was intellectually based on the *community teacher* and what it takes to mold one. The challenge we have taken up is to adapt this approach to the context of current teachers and their deeper and broader development of practice. Teachers in urban schools today most often do not come from the communities their children are growing up in—and rarely have they experienced the kind of immersion in the community that Ball State's graduates may have experienced. Many urban teachers have no practical field experience at all, since so many come to the classroom through so-called fast-track programs such as Teach for America and teacher residencies.

The Baltimore City Public Schools and two community-based agencies—Park Heights Renaissance Corporation (PHR) and ACTS—have partnered to accomplish this immersive experience. PHR was developed to implement Baltimore City's Park Heights neighborhoods master plan, a blueprint that details the city-wide planning for land and economic development, along with human development and development of human capital, as transformative elements that identify this community. The stated mission of PHR is to transform Park Heights to land development, economic development and, most importantly, human development. Working closely with community residents, government partners and other stakeholders, PHR strives to revive this once-thriving area and create vibrant, sustainable neighborhoods (Park Heights Renaissance Corporation Master Plan, 2006). PHR is working to rebuild the community by combining strategies for housing and community development with the improvement of local schools.

ACTS is focused contextually on the development of the whole urban school. Therefore, it is of critical interest to us to design professional development that also collectively transforms the school's climate, culture and competence. Given the framework of resiliency described previously, we seek to tie teacher development to a focus on the healthy and resilient identity of the school's children through aspects of community connectedness and collaboration. The result of this marriage has been the deployment of two projects of teacher immersion—LIFTT and LINC.

LIFTT: Project Description and *Community Curriculum*

The *community curriculum* is based on the concept of the community teacher. A *community teacher* is defined as "one who possesses contextualized knowledge of the culture, community, and identity of the children and families he or she serves and draws on this knowledge to create the core teaching practices necessary for effectiveness in diverse settings" (Murrell, 2001, p. 52). In addition, the *community teacher* sees himself or herself as integral to the circle of support for each child, along with the family, community residents, social workers, health care providers and social, cultural and recreational leaders.

Of all those who come into contact with a child besides the parents or care-giver, few will have a more reliable and steady presence in the child's life than the child's teacher. The teacher has a great responsibility and opportunity to affect the child's optimal development—not simply cognitively but socially, emotionally and spiritually as well.

Just as vital as the teacher's professional and pedagogical knowledge in their success in city contexts is the quality of the inter-relationship among the child's teachers and family and the practical knowledge for promoting the development of students within a seamless social network (Bronfenbrenner, 1979). The impor-tance of Bronfenbrenner's (1979) theoretical framework is how it contextual-izes school life within the out-of-school experiences of the child so that we as educational professionals can take into account those experiences and dynamics that influence a child's development as much—if not more than—events directly encountered in the school.

The integration and collaboration of the teachers, parents and caregivers in the fabric of the child's life are essential to the development and education of that child. It is when the educational process is authentically situated in the com-munity context that the child has the opportunity for a rich social context of *concerted cultivation* of both academic and personal abilities (Lareau, 2011). Teachers and caregivers need to construct the experiential lives of children so that they realize their identities as achievers and persons of substance and purpose. This kind of teaching can only emerge in the context of a school that is organized around civic responsibility and development, partnership, shared accountability and respect. Unfortunately, most urban teachers are not *of the community* nor even very knowledgeable about the community and families from which their children arrive in the classroom. They are ill-equipped to either build on the strengths or understand the entirety of challenges that their students bring to their studies.

The LINC project immerses the development of a select number of urban teachers within the community contexts of that development. This initiative offers teachers an intensive experience of training by placing them in community-based programs for a 6-week internship while guiding them through reflection, con-ceptual development and self-cultivation. Before the internship, project teams and the school's leadership engage in outreach and partnership development with community organizations. Following the internship experience, teachers bring their host organizations into meaningful partnerships within their school communities. Both the community organizations and teachers should experience significant development of their effectiveness and mutual cognizance. Following the summer internship, LINC teachers are charged with applying their insights and new competencies in new classroom practices.

These newly engaged and connected teachers understand the community, the families, their history and heritage and their values and concerns in ways that classroom or workshop professional preparation and development cannot possibly provide. In the Whitely community of Muncie, IN, where the Ball State program develops its teacher candidates, student teachers come to recognize and revere the deep cultural and historical wisdom of the community's leaders. They learn what it took to overcome oppression and build a vibrant community, how history has placed invisible and explicit challenges in front of them and how they have changed systems. Armed with this kind of knowledge, student teachers approach their classroom practice in new ways, even working with community residents to select the literature curriculum, for example, and using local stories of courage to engage and inspire their students (Zygmunt-Fillwalk et al., 2012).

In the LINC project, teachers are further encouraged to explore how chronic challenges can be addressed collaboratively with community-based partners. They are charged with bringing the relationships they have developed into the school in meaningful ways. By building the school into a *community school* from the inside out, so to speak, each and every intervention, service and programmatic opportunity is grounded in a deep appreciation for the children's developmental needs and the interests and aspirations of their families. Teachers become the drivers for linking community contributions to the pedagogy, curriculum and school climate in demonstrable ways.

The Family and Community Engagement Curriculum

A critical component of the community immersion approach to teacher development is the improvement of skills related to productive family engagement in education. The LINC project has been built in concurrence with LIFTT, a peer education program in its pilot phase in six Baltimore schools. In this program, parents and teachers are paired as peer educators, are trained to work together in classrooms, and form a leadership team that addresses collective challenges in the school community. This experience for the first cohort will lay the groundwork for the family and community engagement curriculum for subsequent cohorts. Participation in LIFTT serves as the teacher's initial year of LINC—providing a deep grounding in the community gained through the development of a close working relationship with a parent peer educator. Furthermore, it is envisioned that each LINC teacher will be assigned a family mentor in the community at whose home and in whose community activities the teacher will develop authentic relationships and experience something of life in the community in an intimate and honest encounter.

There is extensive research on the importance of family engagement in student success and related research on the potentially transformative role of the teacher as the key lever for engaging parents in their children's success (Henderson & Mapp, 2002; Warren & Mapp, 2012). There is also clear evidence that children in low-income communities are being educated by teachers who often do not reflect the race, language or communities with which they are familiar (National Center for Education Statistics [NCES], 2011). Most teachers begin teaching with little cultural or racial expertise or knowledge or operational awareness of perspectives and sensibilities to any groups outside their own cultural–political group—mostly white middle- or upper-middle class (e.g., Noguera, 2003; Darling-Hammond, 2010).

There are promising examples in the literature of improvements in teacher practice that provide teachers with immersive experiences in those communities beyond the walls of the schoolhouse, as mentioned previously (Zeichner, 2010). However, this approach has not yet been used systematically in any urban school district as a way to help new and experienced teachers gain deep cultural competence. There is also increasing attention in the research to ways in which "building powerful forms of family and community engagement in schools can play an essential role in creating desperately needed reform in public education and contributing to healthier communities for children and young people" (Warren & Mapp, 2012; Shaakir-Ansari & Williams, 2009).

Without an intimate understanding of the child's socio-cultural context, the teacher cannot guide this development through genuine engaged practice (Perry et al., 2003). The historic disconnect of school from community has resulted in the dominance of the *missionary model* of teaching in which the instructor arrives from a *foreign* place and knows more about the information she wants to transmit than she does about the children before her. Rather than utilizing deep knowledge about the environment to guide a child through the process of learning, the contemporary missionary teacher seeks to *civilize* students by bringing them out of their culture, which is seen as deficient, and into her own, which is perceived as superior. The new turn in recognizing the social and cultural situativity of human development is a major foundation of successful urban teaching and learning. The result of this conception of teaching is to reduce the impact of the nascent culture of drill-and-test that has so overwhelmed the American classroom and to challenge the structural inequity of a system that rewards the students who are most culturally familiar to educators and disadvantages those whose cultures are devalued. We have coined the term *community teacher* to connote the individual whose practice is shaped by these ideas.

The *community teacher* finds himself or herself in continuous development of practice. No two students and no two classrooms are the same, and each interaction is both a teaching and a learning opportunity. The identity of both teacher and child is developed in part during those accumulated interactions and relies upon the deepening of understanding and engagement. Becoming a better teacher is not accomplished simply by becoming more proficient at certain procedural tasks needed for the transmission of information but in the ability to use all of one's knowledge of the students to create activity settings that engage their interest, curiosity and critical capacities. The *community teacher* seeks to know as much as possible about the context with which his or her students are growing and forming their identities as learners and seeks to situate their learning process in the strongest elements of social, historical and political culture. Ongoing historical and cultural study is critical, but there is no substitute for personal, immediate, sustained experience.

Murrell's (2001) framework of the community teacher, coupled with the writings of Wenger (1998) and Bronfenbrenner's (1979) ecological systems theory, constitutes the groundwork for the pedagogical structures for professional learning. Wenger's (1998) social theory of learning expresses the key components of how learning is structured within this field-based, collaborative learning community. The key components of this paradigm are illustrated in Figure 8.2.

Our work also rests on the social network theory that underpins traditional community organizing, which is necessary to collaborate with community-based agencies. Social network research suggests that informal webs of relationships are often the chief determinants of how well and quickly change efforts take hold, diffuse and sustain. Focusing on the structure of the relationship network first represents a shift in the way we approach change. Usually, a change effort begins with an overall articulation of the strategy, including the components of the effort, necessary resources, assessment tools, timelines and personnel. In the best situations, these elements are integrated, but more typically they are layered onto existing efforts without systematic attention to the structure of the underlying informal network or established relationships (Daly, 2010).

Employing Wenger's (1998) theory of collective action, the collaboration of teachers and parents will help each school grow as a community of practice. Communities of practice provide a context for collaborative and supportive work. Those working within a community of practice share common values and work toward the same designated goal(s). Communities of practice often bring about hard-to-attain, high-quality collaboration. They arise from the joining of three elements: mutual engagement (building trust, improving communication, developing habits of collaboration, relying upon one another); shared productive enterprise (improving student learning in the classroom and out, designing and leading a school-wide campaign); and shared *tools* (ways of teaching and learning that are based on excellent practice, developmental skill sets and themes that enrich

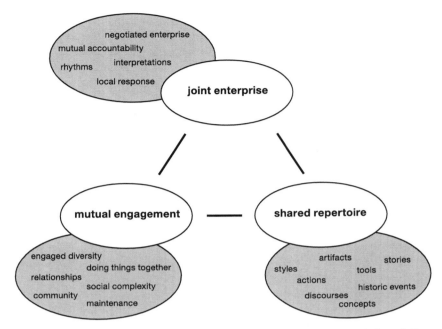

FIGURE 8.2 Dimensions of practice as the property of community (adapted from Wenger, 1998, p. 73)

cultivation of student capacities, etc.). Our cultural value is that everyone gets better all the time, and this is both a shared and a mutual responsibility. We can count among the outcomes for the project elements of social, cultural and political capital, which will be clearly observable in a campaign (a collective shared enterprise) but also in the wider social effects of the team's developing relationships.

By fully participating in practices that offer mutual support for continuous development, each parent and teacher will find himself or herself becoming more proficient in the functions they need to perform—they get more done together, and they do it better.

Community Immersion through Engagement and Collaboration

The project team proposes a community immersion program for new and experienced teachers that connects them to deeply rooted community organizations for a period of 6 weeks in the summer, with continued connection at a lesser intensity throughout the following school year. This intensive, practical engagement, through which the teacher works alongside community members and providers, will be guided by experienced teacher educators (the project team), who will provide the theoretical grounding and an ongoing opportunity for reflection and self-cultivation. Participants will examine at the deepest level what their purpose is as an educator; where their misconceptions and biases may be responsible for blind spots or missed opportunities; and how they can improve their communications, relationships and teaching practices once informed by enhanced familiarity with the social context.

While adding value in community-based organizations (CBOs) by providing experienced and professional support, they will be exposed to the networks of mutual support, traditions and practices that make this community work. They will become familiar in a more immediate way with the strong principles and character of community residents, including the families of their students, and will grapple reflectively with some of the challenges those families face. Each will be assigned a community mentor and a resident mentor family (in some cases, these will be the same), who will let the educator into their lives for genuine friendship, understanding and engagement.

Teachers will be challenged to create pathways for increased school–community partnerships. In the year following their community internships, the participants will generate significant *activity settings* for their own continued development and opportunities for sharing their insights and experiences with other teachers. Projects that reflect genuine community solutions, engaged learning opportunities for students and connections with families will extend the impact of the LINC initiative beyond the individual teacher and create a framework for whole-school climate and culture development. Also, during the school year following this intensive engagement, monthly meetings of the cohort and self-directed continued engagement in the community will deepen and extend the application of new knowledge in the classroom and in the role the teacher plays in the school's development. Given sufficient funding, teacher coaches will visit cohort members in their classrooms for collaborative coaching, and cohort members may also choose to visit one another for ongoing constructive observation and support. Pre-development for this project will: (1) involve engagement with school leaders to determine which schools are the best candidates for the project and (2) facilitate partnership development between school leaders and the community organizations identified for prospective placements. The relationship between the school and CBO is envisioned to extend beyond the 6-week internship, as indicated previously; therefore, the relationship should be placed on a firm footing of collaboration and mutual understanding.

Implementation—Overlapping Projects

The LINC framework requires collaborative program development in consultation with families and school leadership, which is promoted by the LIFTT project. The development of the clinical curriculum in the practical wisdom of local funds of knowledge is the work of the participating cohorts of teachers in the program. The cohort of six teachers for each of the six schools was recruited based on members' interest in enhancing their professional knowledge and skill with regard to family and community engagement. They were offered the opportunity to increase their professional development and work collaboratively with a team of parents from their schools.

In the pilot year for this project, the cohort of teachers are the pioneers: the project team will recruit those who are interested not only in participating in the program but also in the work of developing it, meeting its challenges and making it work. The greater demands of the Common Core State Standards make it more important than ever that families be aware of, support and contribute tangibly to the academic aspirations and habits of learning that are fundamental to student achievement—from regular attendance to reinforcing homework to providing practical opportunities to learn at home. At the same time, the district is preparing to put into place a new teacher effectiveness framework, tied to evaluation and compensation, which specifically incorporates parent and community engagement as a core element of teacher practice in multiple aspects of the framework. Many schools are not prepared to offer opportunities like LINC to their teachers, as these new demands in evaluation are arising.

The LIFTT project generates and develops schools' family and community engagement practices through the work of the team of six teachers and six parents. Engagement processes are part of creating a *community of practice* for whole-school improvement toward a fully functioning community school. The framework for intervention involves creating developmentally nurturing environments that are designed to be safe spaces for children; attuned to their needs; and co-created with families, staff and community constituencies. Through this lens, parents and teachers are viewed as co-educators who share the responsibility for raising healthy, successful children. This project is based in part on the Parent Mentor Project of the Logan Square Neighborhood Association (LSNA) in Chicago. Since 1996, the LSNA has recruited a team of parents at each of their partnering schools, provided self-development and leadership training and placed them in classrooms to support the teachers. Their parent mentors develop as school leaders, deepen their understanding of the education process, build closer relationships with teachers, engage other parents and address challenges and improvements they observe.

The collaborative approach to monitoring and evaluation is rooted in the theoretical approach of participatory action research (PAR). This approach is also referred to as collaborative inquiry, action learning and contextual action research. In PAR, "there is a dual commitment in action research to study a system and concurrently to collaborate with members of the system in changing it in what is together regarded as a desirable direction" (Whyte, 1989). Those involved in monitoring and evaluation will collect, analyze and present information/data on an ongoing and cyclical basis. For the purposes of the program, parents, teachers and other involved parties will include in their regular meetings a structured assessment of progress toward objectives that have been specified at the beginning of their work together. In the case of each objective, one or more agreed indicators will be selected by the team, and discussions will both quantify and describe incremental progress made and areas in need of improvement, with the aim of determining what really works. Through cyclical monitoring and evaluation and collective documentation, the system/program will constantly be improving and growing. Such "collective action for social change" is at the heart of this proposed project (Fox et al., 2010).

Evaluation will include an analysis of how well this model can be implemented in schools that are community resources schools and those that are not and significant differences in success and the timeline of development. The analysis will include cost comparisons and lessons for possible expansion and scale-up.

References

Boyle-Baise, L., & McIntyre, D.J. (2008). What kind of experience? Preparing teachers in PDS or community settings. In M. Cochran-Smith, S. Feiman-Nemser, & D.J. McIntyre (Eds.), *Handbook of research on teacher education* (3rd ed.). (pp. 307–330). New York, NY: Erlbaum/Routledge.

Bronfenbrenner, U. (1979). *The ecology of human development: Experiment by nature and design.* Cambridge, MA: Harvard University Press.

Cooper, J. (2007). Strengthening the case for community-based learning in teacher education. *Journal of Teacher Education, 58*(3), 245–255.

Daly, A. (2010). Mapping the terrain: Social network theory and educational change. In A. Daly (Ed.), *Social network theory and educational change* (Chapter 1, pp. 1–16). Harvard Education Press.

Darling-Hammond, L. (2010). *The flat world and education: How America's commitment to equity will determine our future.* New York, NY: Teachers College Press.

Fine, M., & Ruglis, J. (2009). Circuits and consequences of dispossession: The racialized realignment of the public sphere for U.S. youth. *Transforming Anthropology, 17*(1), 20–33.

Fox, M., Mediratta, K., Ruglis, J., Stoudt, B., Shah, S., & Fine, M. (2010). Critical youth engagement: Participatory action research and organizing. In L. Sherrod, J. Torney-Puta, & C. Flanagan (Eds.), *Handbook of Research on Civic Engagement in Youth.* (2010). Hoboken, NJ: Wiley.

Henderson, A.T., & Mapp, K.L. (2002). *A new wave of evidence: The impact of school, family, and community connections on student achievement.* Austin, TX: Southwest Educational Development Lab.

Henderson, A.T., Mapp, K.L., Johnson, V.R., & Davies, D. (2007). *Beyond the bake sale: The essential guide to family-school partnerships.* New York, NY: The New Press.

Lareau, A. (2011). *Unequal childhoods: Class, race and family life.* Berkeley, CA: University of California Press.

Marks, M.H., Louis, K.S., & Printy, S.M. (2000). The capacity for organizational learning. In K. Leithwood (Ed.), *Understanding schools as intelligent systems* (pp. 239–265). Stamford, CT: JAI Press.

McLaughlin, M.W., & Talbert, J.E. (2001). *Professional communities and the work of high school teaching.* Chicago, IL: University of Chicago Press.

McLaughlin, M.W., & Talbert, J.E. (2006). *Building school-based teacher learning communities: Professional strategies to improve student achievement.* New York, NY: Teachers College Press.

McLaughlin, M.W., & Talbert, J.E. (2007). Building professional communities in high schools: Challenges and promising practices. In L. Stoll & K. Seashore Louis (Eds.), *Professional learning communities: Divergence, depth and dilemmas* (pp. 151–165). Berkshire, United Kingdom: Open University Press.

Murrell, P. (2001). *The community teacher: A new framework for effective urban teaching.* New York, NY: Teachers College Press.

Murrell, P. (2009). Identity, agency, and culture: Black achievement and educational attainment. In L.C. Tillman (Ed.), *The SAGE handbook of African American education* (pp. 88–106). Thousand Oaks, CA: SAGE Publications, Inc.

Murrell, P.C., Jr. (2007). *Race, culture, and schooling: Identities of achievement in multicultural urban schools.* New York, NY: Lawrence Erlbaum.

Nakkula, M.J., & Toshalis, E. (2006). *Understanding youth: Adolescent development for educators.* Cambridge, MA: Harvard Education Press.

National Center for Education Statistics (NCES) (2011). *The National Assessment of Educational Progress (NAEP) report card in reading.* Retrieved from http://nces.ed.gov/nations reportcard/pubs/dst2011/2012455.asp

Noguera, P. (2003). *City schools and the American dream: Reclaiming the promise of public education.* New York, NY: Teachers College Press.

Park Heights Renaissance Corporation Master Plan (2006). Park Heights Renaissance Corporation, p. 11. Retrieved from http://boldnewheights.org/wp-content/uploads/2013/06/Master-Plan-Final-Amended-Version.pdf

Perry, T., Steele, C., & Hilliard, A., III (2003). *Young, gifted and black: Promoting high achievement among African American students.* Boston, MA: Beacon Press.

Santiago, E., Ferrara, J., & Quinn, J. (2012). *Whole child, whole school: Applying theory to practice in a community school.* New York, NY: Rowman & Littlefield.

Schwartz, B., & Sharpe, K. (2010). *Practical wisdom: The right way to do the right thing.* New York, NY: Penguin.

Shaakir-Ansari, Z., & Williams, O. (2009). Parent power in New York City: The coalition for educational justice. *Communities and Schools, 23,* 36–45.

Warren, M.R., & Mapp, K.L. (2011). *A match on dry grass: Community organizing as a catalyst for school reform.* New York, NY: Oxford University Press.

Wenger, E. (1998). *Communities of practice: Learning, meaning, and identity.* Cambridge, United Kingdom: Cambridge University Press.

Whyte, W.F. (Ed.). (1989). Action research for the twenty-first century: Participation, reflection, and practice. *American Behavioural Scientist, 32*(5), 499–623.

Zeichner, K. (2010). Rethinking the connections between campus courses and field experiences in college- and university-based teacher education. *Journal of Teacher Education, 61*(1–2), 89–99.

Zygmunt-Fillwalk, E., Clark, P., Clausen, J., & Mucherah, W. (April 13–17, 2012). *Teacher education redefined: Contextual cognizance and the promise for community impact.* Paper presented at the American Educational Research Association (AERA) Conference. Vancouver, British Columbia, Canada.

Zygmunt-Fillwalk, E., Malaby, M., & Clausen, J. (2010). The imperative of contextual cognizance: Preservice teachers and community engagement in the schools and communities project. *Teacher Education Quarterly, 37*(2), 53–67.

PART III

Assessing and Improving Teacher Preparation

The estimated national high school graduation rate is higher than it has ever been: 80 percent in the 2011–2012 school year. This means that nearly four out of five students who enter ninth grade graduate from high school in 4 years. However, recent reports on the academic performance of students in the nation's public schools clearly indicate the need for improving learning outcomes. Data from the 2013 National Assessment of Educational Progress (NAEP) report show that only 26 percent of 12th graders performed at or above the proficient level, and only 38 percent performed at the proficient level in reading. Seven percent of African Americans and 12 percent of Hispanics were proficient in mathematics. Sixteen percent of African Americans and 23 percent of Hispanics were proficient in reading. Performing at the proficient level is defined as "solid academic performance for each grade level assessed" (National Center for Education Statistics [NCES], 2013, Glossary). The American Promise Alliance 2014 Annual Report indicated that in 2012, across the nation, there were 1,359 high schools labeled "dropout factories" where the graduation rate was 60 percent or less. This was down 32 percent from the 2,007 high school dropout factories identified in 2002. The students attending these high schools were disproportionately low-income and ethnic minority. Further, the Bureau of Labor Statistics reported that 65.9 percent of students who graduated from high school in 2013 were enrolled in a college or university in the fall of 2013; however, "nearly 60% of first-year college students discover that, despite being fully eligible to attend college, they are not academically ready for postsecondary studies. After enrolling, these students learn that they must take remedial courses in English or mathematics, which do not earn college credits" (Bureau of Labor Statistics, 2014).

The underperformance of the public school system has resulted in a dependence on other countries for supplying workers with expertise in particular occupations and professions, while many of our own citizens are unemployed or locked into low-wage jobs because of a lack of academic and professional preparation. The Department for Professional Employees, AFL–CIO, reported in 2013 that:

> There are a staggering number of skilled guest workers in the U.S.; estimates are as high as 900,000. In the broad occupation groups that make up the science, technology, engineering, and mathematics (STEM) workforce (business and financial operations, computer and mathematical science, architecture and engineering, and life, physical, and social science occupations), there were 1,050,377 non-U.S. citizens employed (nearly 15 percent of workers) in June 2013.
>
> (p. 3)

The condition of public education has a significant impact on the income of individuals and on the economic conditions in local communities, states and the nation. It is evident that low-performing schools contribute to unemployment and crime in poor urban communities (McKinsey & Company, 2009). According to the Alliance for Excellent Education (2013), over 5,000 students drop out of high school every day. These students are at risk for unemployment, government assistance and incarceration in the prison system. Further, high school dropouts earn 29 percent less than high school completers. Unless high school graduation rates improve, it is estimated that nearly 12 million students will drop out over the next 10 years, with a loss of $1.5 trillion for the nation's economy (http://impact. all4ed.org/#potential/income/united-states/all-students/).

Policymakers have responded to the underperformance of students in the nation's public schools with more rigorous standards for accountability and increased monitoring. The No Child Left Behind (NCLB) Act required that, beginning in 2003, each state develop a definition of adequate yearly progress toward 100 percent of students reaching proficiency by 2013–2014, with a valid and reliable accountability system for assessing 95 percent of students in each subgroup in the areas of reading/language arts and mathematics, including high school graduation rates. Additionally, states and school districts have developed more rigorous teacher evaluation systems, and some states have significantly modified or eliminated teacher tenure. Further, beginning in 2003, Title II of the Higher Education Act requires three annual reports on the quality of teacher preparation, which includes certification/licensure requirements, pass rates on state assessments disaggregated by institutions and other program data.

The demand for greater accountability for the preparation and performance of preservice teachers entering the field has fueled a new round of testing and assessment. The extent to which these new accountability mandates will result in improved learning outcomes in P–12 schools—or better teacher preparation and better pedagogical practices—is influenced by the extent to which P–12 students have access to meaningful and productive learning experiences. Presently, there are frequent complaints about the rigid adherence to scripted curriculum, pacing guides and the preparation of students for high-stakes tests. Further, there is a fear that teacher educators will continue traditional practices for preservice teacher preparation but might feel pressured by new demands for accountability to describe traditional practices in ways that appear to meet the new mandates without making substantive changes to improve teacher preparation. This could seriously compromise the preparation of the next generation of teachers for improving the academic and intellectual development of students from different cultural and experiential backgrounds.

The first chapter in this third section of the book is concerned with recent calls for reform in preservice teacher preparation, emphasizing clinical experiences and preservice assessment of readiness for professional teaching practice. The authors compare and contrast teacher preparation and licensure with that of two other service professions, describe the emerging trend toward preservice performance assessment, discuss the potential for embedding a common performance assessment within clinical experiences and identify the benefits and pitfalls of the new preservice assessment. The authors bring attention to the need for "authentic improvement" in the preparation of teachers for students from different cultural and experiential backgrounds.

The authors of the second chapter of this part of the book are concerned with developing an approach to authentic and continuous improvement in teacher education through the use of network improvement communities (NICs). NICs bring together teacher educators across university campuses and other stakeholders using an approach that provides a structure for identifying and solving problems in preservice teacher preparation. The authors describe work done in response to an initiative from the American Educational Research Association, Division K—Teaching and Teacher Education, where a study group approach was used to identify the challenges faced by teacher educators in developing meaningful and productive clinical experiences for learning to teach. This approach engaged teacher educators, practitioners, researchers and program administrators in interactive sessions at professional meetings for the purpose of developing an NIC. The intent for using this approach was to examine challenges in the field, generate interest in related research and elicit suggestions for designing a research agenda. The authors report on the outcomes for this attempt to develop an NIC.

References

Alliance for Excellent Education (2013). *Education and the economy: Boosting the nation's economy by improving high school graduation rates.* Washington, DC: Author.

Balfanz, R., Bridgeland, J.M., Fox, J.H., DePaoli, J.L., Ingram, E.S., & Maushard, M. (2014). *Building a grad nation: Progress and challenge in ending the high school dropout epidemic.* Washington, DC: The American Promise Alliance.

Bureau of Labor Statistics (2014). *College enrollment and work activity of 2013 high school graduates.* Retrieved from http://www.bls.gov/news.release/hsgec.nr0.htm

Department for Professional Employees, AFL–CIO (2013). Guest worker visas: The H-1B and L1. Washington, DC: Author.

McKinsey & Company (2009). The economic impact of the achievement gap in America's schools. Author.

National Assessment of Educational Progress (NAEP) (2013). *The nation's report card: Are the nation's 12th-graders making progress in mathematics and reading?* Washington, DC: Institute of Education Sciences, U.S. Department of Education.

National Center for Education Statistics (NCES) (2013). *Are the nation's 12th graders making progress in mathematics and reading?* Washington, DC: Institute for Education Sciences, U.S. Department of Education.

No Child Left Behind Act of 2001 (January 8, 2002). Public Law 107–110, 107th Congress.

9

TEACHER PERFORMANCE ASSESSMENT

Readiness for Professional Practice

Jamy Stillman, Gisele Ragusa and Andrea Whittaker

Introduction

As others in this volume have illustrated, teacher education programs (TEPs)—especially those sponsored by colleges and universities—are experiencing unprecedented scrutiny and criticism from both policymakers and the public at large. Secretary of Education Arne Duncan (2009), for example, has argued that "by almost any standard, many if not most of the nation's 1,450 schools, colleges, and departments of education" are "doing a mediocre job of preparing teachers for the realities of the 21st century classroom" (Duncan, 2009). Criticisms such as these have led to increased pressure on university-based TEPs to demonstrate their value. In particular, calls for TEPs to use value-added modeling (VAM) to provide empirical evidence of individual graduates' impact on K–12 students' standardized tests scores have become relatively commonplace (U.S. Department of Education, 2011). Meanwhile, the advocacy group National Council on Teacher Quality (NCTQ, 2013) has designed its own program evaluation instrument and used that instrument, despite its demonstrated limited validity (American Association of Colleges for Teacher Education [AACTE], 2013a), to evaluate and offer widespread criticism of university-based TEPs nationwide.

Notably, the assumptions underlying these criticisms and calls for evaluation of university-based teacher education reflect broader reform efforts (e.g., GREAT Act, 2013) aimed at privatizing K–12 schooling and deregulating teacher education; they also reflect the long-standing push by those outside teacher education to narrowly frame the learning to teach process as merely involving the acquisition of technical skills, absent an "understanding of the historical, cultural, political, economic, and social contexts in which [teachers'] work is embedded" (Zeichner,

2012, p. 380). As a result, such criticisms and calls for evaluation typically fail to recognize important features of quality TEPs and thus may push programs to reform in ways that are unlikely to lead to authentic improvement, especially concerning the preparation of teachers to serve students from historically underserved communities.

Unfortunately, teacher educators have struggled to quiet the cacophony of criticisms, the calls for particular kinds of evaluation and the accompanying reforms. The body of empirical work documenting teacher education's contribution to K–12 student learning, particularly at the scale that policymakers demand, remains modest and thus offers little defense. In addition, agreement remains elusive across the profession about what constitutes good practice. The resulting absence of a shared language or structure for talking about teaching practice further contributes to the profession's vulnerability and its struggle to respond to criticism in agentive and productive ways (Ball & Forzani, 2009; Grossman, 2011; Levine, 2006).

Nonetheless, there are a handful of responses gaining widespread attention. Some leaders in the field, for example, have begun to identify and recommend core or *high-leverage* practices that they argue will improve teachers' instruction and bring much-needed cohesiveness to the profession (Ball & Forzani, 2009; Darling-Hammond, 2012; Grossman, 2011; Lampert & Graziani, 2009; Windschitl, Thompson, & Braaten, 2011). Although promising for its potential to ground teacher education in practice—an approach lauded by scholars for more than a century (e.g., Ball & Cohen, 1999; Dewey, 1904/1965; Grossman, 2011)—the identification of high-leverage practices also runs the risk of reinforcing rather than disrupting technical notions of teaching competence. In particular, the assumption that certain instructional practices can and should be replicated in all settings and with all students may lead practitioners to overlook the role that context and culture play in teaching and learning, a tendency that research has shown to further disadvantage the most underserved students (Hollins, 2011; Stillman & Anderson, in press; Zeichner, 2012). Recommendations for the implementation of teacher performance assessments (AACTE, 2013b; Council of Chief State School Officers [CCSSO], 2012) and growing emphasis on "clinically rich" preparation (AACTE, 2010; National Council for Accreditation of Teacher Education [NCATE], 2010; National Research Council [NRC], 2010) represent additional efforts to improve university-based teacher education by moving it closer to teaching practice. While it is still too early to know with certainty how these reforms will play out, there is little doubt that they will impact TEPs significantly.

Though the growing use of teacher performance assessment and the charge to make teacher education more clinically rich are not without flaws, we take the perspective in this chapter that these two reform emphases—particularly if they are thoughtfully brought into conversation with one another—may offer teacher educators an opportunity to authentically improve university-based teacher education. In particular, we demonstrate how embedding common teacher performance assessments within clinical experiences across programs might help to increase the likelihood that clinical field experiences assess and cultivate candidates' readiness for teaching practice. In this chapter, we describe how similar practices are currently and successfully used to ensure quality in other professions. We compare such practices to the current and potential future state of practice in teacher education.

Importantly, this is not to suggest that policy initiatives themselves will necessarily generate positive outcomes, even if similar efforts have worked with some success in comparable professions. To the contrary, the charge to make teacher education more clinical, including policymakers' emphasis on identifying associated *best practices* that can be scaled up and applied universally, could easily lead programs to make technical changes that do little to deepen preservice candidates' deep and applied learning. The widespread implementation of teacher performance assessment could pose similar risks, given the well-documented tendencies of those under pressure to respond to top-down reforms, like high-stakes assessments, in ways that privilege compliance over more adaptive responses (Campbell, 1976; Nichols & Berliner, 2007; Rennert-Ariev, 2008). That effective leadership, particular structural changes and resources are required preconditions for approaching such mandates from an inquiry orientation may add to these risks as well (Peck, Gallucci, & Sloan, 2010; Peck & McDonald, 2013; Whittaker & Nelson, 2013).

In light of these issues, we argue the importance of teacher educators making sense of and instantiating these reform initiatives on their own terms and in alignment with local program goals and values. In doing so, we make the case for a profession-wide cohesiveness that builds upon the success of assessment work in comparable professions *and* grows out of teacher educators' efforts to engage with similar tools and structures, but in adaptive and context-sensitive ways.

The chapter opens with a review of how other *helping* professions, such as medicine and social work, treat preservice clinical experiences, assessment, accountability and advancement into the profession (Corey, Corey, & Callanan, 2011; Zelner, 2007). We then compare these approaches with those typically employed in teacher education; we do this with the intent of drawing on what has worked in other professions to inform renewal in teacher education. This comparison is followed by a discussion of teacher performance assessment and its current role in teacher education's efforts to define the profession's knowledge base and "take responsibility for its own professional accountability" (Falk, 2013, p. 1). Drawing on what we know about the relationship between clinical experiences and performance assessment in medicine and social work, we then consider some possible affordances of embedding a common teacher performance assessment within clinical experiences during preservice teacher preparation, focusing on the potential benefits of this relationship for both teacher candidate and P-12 student learning. We conclude with some general comments about the importance of teacher educators having the latitude to respond to reform initiatives in contextually sensitive ways, thus staying true to program-specific goals while situating their work meaningfully within the profession at large.

Performance Assessment and Readiness for Practice

Although there are substantive differences between the medical, social work and teaching professions, each profession is concerned primarily with providing services that intend to support individuals and contribute to the overall health of communities and society at large. In addition, each of these professions is responsible for serving diverse populations, including those individuals representing society's most vulnerable subgroups (e.g., children, the elderly, the poor, the ill, etc.). These professions have in common a required professional licensure and a set of preservice *clinical experiences* that serve as precursors to advancement into the profession. As we describe in the following sections, both medicine and social work have also widely used formative procedures and associated benchmark assessments during the preparation process, as well as standardized, summative assessments of readiness for professional practice that we argue offer actionable insights for the teaching profession.

Clinical Experiences and Associated Benchmark Assessment

Although widely used within medical, social work and teaching graduate programs, formative and *benchmark* assessments vary greatly across the three professions. While all three professions require courses and preservice clinical experiences, the structure, time frame, supervision and assessments associated with these experiences vary significantly. For example, medical students enroll in highly specified technical courses that are tightly aligned with preservice clinical experiences and that extend beyond coursework into the medical *residency*—a highly practical, guided clinical preservice experience required for all medical subfields. These clinical experiences (both within courses and during residency) are closely monitored and assessed formatively by medical school faculty, most of whom are also practicing physicians and/or active medical researchers. Such monitoring is accomplished through a process by which the preservice medical student first shadows a full- or part-time medical school faculty member, who gradually releases responsibility to the student while providing ongoing clinical supervision (Krasne, Wimmers, Relan, & Drake, 2006). In other words, for the entirety of his or her graduate school experience, the medical student is treated as an apprentice whose developing practice is carefully guided by practicing physicians and clinical faculty.

Importantly, there are several steps in medical students' preservice experience that serve as benchmarks in the physician preparation process. During clinical experiences, for example, medical students receive daily verbal and written feedback on their medical case notes, on their interactions with patients and guided diagnoses, and in relation to their treatment of patients, both from medical school faculty and the medical residents with whom they interact regularly (Pelgrim et al., 2012). Upon successful completion of coursework and early clinical experiences, medical students prepare for the medical board examination (a nationwide required benchmark assessment), graduate from medical school, take a state-specific medical board examination and, upon passing, obtain the title of medical doctor. Additionally, during the final year of medical school, medical students apply to *match* with a medical residency program. This constitutes a second critical benchmark for medical students.

Once graduated from medical school and matched as a resident, physician candidates must engage in additional supervised clinical experiences for between 3 and 7 years, depending on the area(s) of chosen medical specialization. Only after residency—and, in some cases, medical fellowship—can physician trainees advance as independent, practicing physicians.

In total, medical school preparation takes 4 to 5 years of pre-medical preparation, another 4 years of medical school and 3 to 7 years of residency to advance to independent practice. Benchmark assessments, both in the form of formal clinical feedback and in medical board and residency matching, provide important feedback to physician candidates during training. Perhaps even more importantly, these benchmark assessments serve as preservice checkpoints for determining one's professional readiness for becoming a practicing physician.

Similar to medicine, all Master of Social Work (MSW) programs require candidates to complete supervised clinical experiences that are aligned with their graduate courses. While the graduate coursework required of a social worker trainee is roughly half of that of a physician in training (2 years rather than 4), clinical field experiences are extensive, supervised and formatively assessed. Earning the MSW degree accepted by the National Association of Social Workers (NASW) requires 1,500 hours of clinical supervision during the master's program. Following this, graduates must complete a minimum of 1,500–3,000 additional hours of supervised practice in order to receive licensed clinical social worker certification, with hours varying within this range from state to state (NASW, 2013). Also similar to medicine, during clinical experiences, social work students shadow licensed, practicing social workers who systematically debrief with them at least weekly (and often daily) (Spence, Wilson, Kavanagh, Strong, & Worrall, 2001), focusing on continuous improvement and anticipatory guidance of client and trainee needs (Tsui, 2005). As is the case with medical students and residents, social work students take on the role of apprentice and, in this capacity, receive support and guidance for the entirety of their preparation.

Research conducted on the clinical supervision of developing social workers and others in the mental health professions sheds light on some of the features that are critical to such experiences' effectiveness (Pajak, 2002; O'Donoghue, 2004). In particular, results of such research underscore the importance of *guided* experiential learning that provides social work trainees with targeted professional feedback and personal support. Importantly, in the context of the social work profession, the aim of providing personal support is not simply to encourage trainees. Rather, within the context of debriefing, social work trainees are required to describe their affect in relation to what is heard during therapeutic sessions with clients and to reframe it in accordance with relevant theory-to-practice strategies. The extensive number of required hours of clinical supervision reflects the widely accepted value of such field experiences for social work trainees (Munson, 2004). Notably, however, social work research, and in particular therapeutically focused social work research, has indicated that it is not simply the *number* of hours of clinical supervision that matters. Rather the types and contexts of clinical supervisors' formative feedback have been found to be more consequential for trainees' preparation (Munson, 2004).

Formative feedback and associated benchmark assessments during trainees' clinical experiences vary across programs and depend upon the type of practice trainees intend to engage in. Across most programs and forms of practice, however, most formative benchmarks are embedded within the clinical debriefing process, which is recognized as a best practice by the NASW (2013). The position of the NASW, along with insights from research, emphasizes the importance of clinical debriefing sessions, including collaborative review of case records and written narrative reports in addition to guided review of audio- and videotaped client–social work trainee sessions and role-plays of pertinent scenarios in trainees' local practice (NASW, 2013). Most importantly, scenario-based role-play and guided review of videotaped client–social worker sessions have been found to be especially supportive of preservice social work candidates' success (Mead, 1990; Munson, 2004; NASW, 2003). These two formative practices may provide insights that can inform the supervision of preservice teacher candidates' clinical experiences.

Similar to those preparing to be physicians, individuals intending to become licensed clinical social workers must pass their respective state's board examination before engaging in independent, unsupervised practice. This summative examination focuses on the various aspects of social work practice and therapeutic intervention with diverse populations and is required for school social work practices in some states and for various healthcare-related social work practices nationally.

Requirements for Advancement into the Professions: Impacts and Influences of Professional Organizations

As previously described, both medicine and social work require professional licensure obtained via passage of a summative state board examination. Similarly, teaching requires professional certification and, in many states, a summative examination. The differences lie in the examinations' content. In social work and medicine, summative examinations focus both on content and professional practices; at present, there is no nationally *required* summative examination for teacher candidates that focuses on instructional practice to the same degree.

Another important difference between the two aforementioned professions and teaching pertains to the role of professional organizations in affecting licensure and monitoring the behavior of independent practitioners. In medicine, the American Medical Association (AMA), the American Association of Medical Colleges (AAMC), the Accreditation Council for Graduate Medical Education (ACGME), the Federation of State Medical Boards (FSMB) and each state's medical board set policy and practice both for medical schools and practicing physicians. Each state board offers and administers the medical board examination that students must pass before practicing (beginning during residency) and complete periodically to renew their medical license. The initial medical license is typically based on graduation from a medical school accredited by the Liaison Committee on Medical Education, completion of at least 1 year of graduate medical education in a residency program accredited by the ACGME and passing either the National Board of Medical Examiners Examination(s) or the Federal Licensing Examination. Renewal of the medical license requires completion of a specific number of units of continuing medical education (prescribed by the physician's practicing state and varying across specializations but ranging from 100–160 units per professional category) (AMA, 2012). If the licensing board determines that physicians are unethical, impaired or incompetent, it can restrict, suspend or revoke their licenses.

In addition to achieving the general medical license, physician candidates may also be certified by medical specialty boards. Private organizations have established graduate medical educational (residency) requirements and administer examinations to determine whether a licensed physician has met medical specialty standards. Other credentials exist as well. For example, physicians may complete a course of study that *certifies* them to provide particular services or perform specific procedures, such as cardiopulmonary resuscitation or advanced cardiac life support. These specialty certifications enable the physician candidate to meet the particular needs of the populations they may serve.

Similarly, in social work, the NASW and the American Board of Examiners in Clinical Social Work have nationally recognized professional standards and established guidelines for advancement into the profession. The NASW Credentialing Center administers NASW Professional Social Work Credentials (membership required), NASW Advanced Practice Specialty Credentials (available to all qualified social workers) and national certification through the Academy of Certified Social Workers (recognized by Congress).

This is not to suggest that teacher education operates without influence from professional organizations. Like medicine and social work, there are several professional organizations, including the American Association of Colleges for Teacher Education (AACTE), the Association of Teacher Educators (ATE) and the National Council for Accreditation of Teacher Education (NCATE), soon to be the Council for the Accreditation of Educator Preparation (CAEP), that weigh in on issues such as accreditation and, more recently, professional assessment. Additionally, there are various professional organizations for practicing teachers, such as the National Science Teacher Association (NSTA), the National Council of Teachers of Mathematics (NCTM) and various other specialty organizations that provide advice and resources for university-based TEPs, as well as forums for teachers working in specialty areas. However, unlike in medicine and social work, teacher education and teacher organizations do not govern or greatly influence the licensure of teachers. Rather, each state department of education or licensure board governs and issues teacher licenses (sometimes referred to as teaching credentials). NCATE, for example, offers accreditation for university and alternative certification programs, has an established set of professional standards for TEPs and recently has begun to work with state agencies in order to offer joint accreditation. Worth noting, however, is that colleges and universities operating preservice TEPs are not required to earn NCATE accreditation. In addition, organizations like NCATE typically do not monitor the professional behavior of practicing teachers once they have completed their preservice preparation. As such, national examinations are not currently required for teacher certification or recertification. Monitoring and initial practice assessment in teaching occur state by state, and many states do not accept other states' preservice program requirements, examinations and associated licensure. In other words, a teacher candidate (or practicing teacher) who has completed a preservice program in one state and passed the state's subject matter competence examination may be required to complete additional courses and examinations in a different state in order to become eligible to teach there. Most importantly, as previously described, the current examinations for teacher licensure in most states assess only a teacher candidate's content knowledge (or subject matter competence) without also assessing the candidate's instructional practice or teaching performance. This missing component is what makes assessments of competency for the teaching profession different—and, some would argue, less informative, consistent or rigorous—than those employed in medicine and social work.

Considerable differences clearly exist between the preparation of medical and social work practitioners and the preparation of teachers, particularly with regard to the kinds and amounts of supervision provided to trainees during clinical experiences and in relation to the assessment of trainees' readiness for practice. Given these differences and the increasing pressure for teacher education to become both more cohesive and more rigorous, many argue that the profession would stand to benefit from the establishment of an assessment of readiness for teaching practice—an assessment that TEP graduates must pass in order to advance as independent practitioners—and from a tighter connection between assessment and teaching candidates' experiences in the field (e.g., Darling-Hammond, Newton, & Wei, 2012; Snyder, 2009; Zeichner, 2010).

Over the last decade, National Board Certification has been the assessment considered by the teaching profession to be the most rigorous and the most attentive to both subject matter knowledge *and* teaching performance. Notably, National Board Certification, while itself a performance assessment, is not required and cannot be completed until a teacher has been teaching independently for at least 3 years. Accordingly, this process does not serve as a nationwide summative teacher assessment or as a gatekeeper for the profession. As a result, the advent of contemporary teacher performance assessment, which we describe next, may hold promise as a means of raising the level of rigor and oversight at the national level in alignment with comparable professions.

Teacher Performance Assessment: Readiness for Practice

In line with the medical and social work professions, recent policy recommendations by the American Federation of Teachers (AFT, 2012) and the Council of Chief State School Officers (CCSSO, 2012) endorse the use of performance-based assessments within TEPs and as a basis for licensure decisions. In addition, the NCATE now requires that performance-based data of actual teaching practice—rather than simply subject matter competence—be used as metrics in the national accreditation system. Performance-based assessments are also being touted as tools that can inform faculty inquiry and program renewal. Darling-Hammond (2010), for example, offers teacher performance assessments (TPAs) as levers for change in teacher preparation and clinical field experiences. She argues that while input measures such as grade point average, coursework, seat time and subject matter exams may explain some of what teacher candidates experience in and acquire through their programs, they have limited power to assess teacher candidates' capacities to facilitate student learning or to inform how TEPs can prepare teachers more effectively. Research additionally suggests that tracking graduates' student achievement data—for example, by using VAM approaches—likewise fails to provide direct or diagnostic feedback to programs (Darling-Hammond, Amrein-Beardsley, Haertel, & Rothstein, 2010).

Similar to clinical examinations in medicine and social work, performance-based measures of teaching can also serve a formative purpose in supporting candidates' development. In particular, by examining candidates' actual performance as they attempt to facilitate K–12 students' learning, such measures may provide useful insights that can inform changes to curriculum, lead to improvements in clinical field experiences and help hone faculty focus.

Within this chapter, we choose to use edTPA as an example of a teacher performance assessment that stands to shape teacher education in consequential ways, both because it will be the first teacher performance assessment to become nationally available and because it is being used widely and with high stakes attached to it. (For example, Washington, Minnesota and New York have been using edTPA to determine program completion, licensure and/or program review and accreditation since January 2014; Illinois, Wisconsin, Georgia, Oregon and Alabama have policies that require the use of edTPA beginning in 2015 or beyond.) Meanwhile, California, Hawaii, Tennessee and Iowa have policies that allow the use of edTPA in lieu of other required assessments. While other high-quality TPAs (e.g., Cal TPA, Performance Assessment for California Teachers (PACT) and Kansas Performance Teaching Portfolio) have been in play at the state level for some time, most—including Teacher Work Sample (Girod, 2002; Schalock, Schalock, & Girod, 1997) and others developed by the Renaissance Project—have been developed for local evaluation and formative campus-based feedback to candidates and are typically decoupled from state licensure requirements or program accreditation. Or, as is also the case for California, teacher performance assessments (PACT and Cal TPA) have been evaluated without centralized scoring, primarily because of mandates against candidate fees that would be necessary to support external scoring. Although there are clear benefits to using more localized evaluation tools (e.g., the ability to have such tools closely reflect program goals and values; the opportunity for faculty with context-specific expertise to score candidate performance), there are also possible affordances to using a common assessment tool, including the positioning of teacher educators to respond to some of the criticisms—described previously—that have been directed at the profession.

In this section of the chapter, we provide an overview of edTPA development history, its design framework, the constructs measured by the assessment and its potential for educative use by teacher candidates and faculty in supporting teacher education renewal. We close this section of the chapter with a brief discussion of the tensions and questions that emerge in bringing an assessment of this nature to national scale.

edTPA History and Educative Design Framework

edTPA stems from a 25-year lineage of teacher performance assessment development led by Linda Darling-Hammond and Raymond Pecheone at Stanford University. This lineage begins with their influence in the development of the National Board for Professional Standards portfolio, followed by the Interstate Teacher Assessment and Support Consortium (InTASC) portfolio, Connecticut's Beginning Educator Support and Training (BEST) assessment during induction and, most recently, PACT. All are subject-specific assessments of teaching that address content pedagogy and pedagogical content knowledge within grade-level spans (e.g., elementary, middle, secondary). In addition, all share common architectural elements—for example, using both artifacts (e.g., lesson plans and instructional materials) and commentaries to document and explain a teacher's instructional intentions, using video clips to provide evidence of enacted teaching and using student work samples as the subject of analysis. Perhaps most importantly, each requires that teachers focus on *student* learning and reflect on their teaching effectiveness and next steps for instruction.

edTPA is the latest assessment tool to emerge from this evolution of TPAs. Its development has included hundreds of teacher educators and P–12 teachers on subject-specific design teams and in content validation processes, benchmarking, scoring and bias review activities. Nearly 30 versions of the assessment—addressing subject-specific initial licensure fields within early childhood, elementary, middle childhood and secondary grade-level spans—have undergone extensive field testing over the past three years (AACTE, 2013b). All edTPA versions share a common architecture, yet emphasize key elements of subject-specific pedagogy and subject-specific learning for students, as described in the following paragraphs.

One of edTPA's core design principles is that it aims to support an educative process for campuses, faculty and candidates and to serve as a summative measure for external accountability. The design—using authentic artifacts of teaching practice, analytic rubrics measuring teaching behaviors associated with student learning and an integrative, multiple-measures assessment of teaching—is intended to support candidates to learn about their practice by engaging with the assessment. The design also invites programs to examine candidate performance in ways that research suggests can lead to program renewal (e.g., Peck et al., 2010).

As mentioned previously and shown in Figure 9.1, at the core of edTPA architecture is a focus on student learning. In contrast to generic evaluations of teaching behaviors, the three tasks that make up edTPA—planning, instruction and assessment—document evidence of candidates' engagement in a cycle of inquiry addressing their students' subject-specific learning. Throughout these three tasks, candidates are expected to:

- provide a rationale for and examine the effectiveness of their teaching in reference to the strengths and learning needs of their students.
- reflect on student engagement in subject-specific learning (not merely participation, classroom management or getting through the lesson).

Candidates document and justify a cycle of teaching by planning for, enacting and analyzing student learning within a short *learning segment* of 3–5 instructional hours that addresses a subject-specific learning focus. Candidates document their teaching of the learning segment through artifacts, including lesson plans, instructional materials, student assignments, samples of completed student assessments and video recordings. Further, candidates are prompted to justify their instructional decision making, analyze evidence of student learning and reflect upon their teaching effectiveness through commentaries associated with each task. Candidates are additionally expected to utilize student assessments to justify further planning of instruction, thereby using student assessment as a feedback loop for iterative processes of instructional planning (Mayer, 2011).

edTPA directs candidates to develop the learning segment in accordance with major student learning outcomes within their particular licensure field as promoted by the national subject matter organization standards and the Common Core State Standards. For example, the subject-specific learning emphasis for mathematics (elementary, middle childhood and secondary licenses) requires that candidates support students to demonstrate mathematical practices as they develop procedural fluency, conceptual understanding and problem-solving and reasoning skills. While the particular content (e.g., linear equations or equivalent fractions) varies by grade level, student readiness or local curriculum, all teacher candidates are expected to address a full array of student learning outcomes for mathematics and to tailor their instruction to reflect their knowledge of students' prior academic learning, knowledge and experiences.

In addition, teacher candidates are expected to plan for and analyze the degree to which their teaching facilitates students' development and use of academic

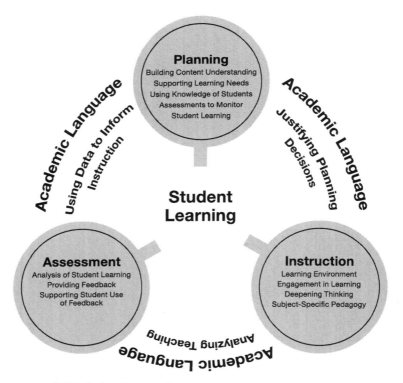

FIGURE 9.1 edTPA design framework

language in support of deep content learning. edTPA's attention to academic language as the language of the discipline and key language functions (e.g., argue, explain, infer, interpret, etc.) is consistent with expectations articulated in the Common Core State Standards for English Language Arts & Literacy in History/ Social Studies, Science and Technical Subjects (Common Core State Standards, 2010) and intends to leverage teaching practices associated with closing the academic achievement gap for English language learners and all students learning the language of school (Stanford Center for Assessment, Learning and Equity, 2012).

Lastly, edTPA requires that teacher candidates attend to student learning within socio-cultural/experiential contexts. Rather than expecting candidates to demonstrate specific *high-leverage* teaching behaviors, edTPA prompts candidates to justify how selected teaching approaches reflect their knowledge of learners. edTPA prompts ask candidates to describe what they know and understand about their students' lived experiences and assets (including personal, cultural, community and developmental strengths) and students' varied learning needs and to "consider the variety of learners ... who may require different strategies/support (e.g., students with Individualized Education Programs (IEPs), English language learners, struggling readers, underperforming students or those with gaps in academic knowledge and/or gifted students)" (Stanford Center for Assessment, Learning and Equity, 2012, p. 9) as justification for the design of instructional approaches and assessments of student learning and in determining next steps for instruction following their analysis of student performance.

The 15 rubric constructs of edTPA were designed to examine elements of planning, instruction, assessment, analysis of teaching and academic language support and were developed in reference to the InTASC standards and national subject matter organization pedagogical standards. As designed, subject matter experts (teacher educators and P–12 teachers) who are calibrated and certified to score in a standardized process use these rubrics to evaluate candidates' teaching performance along a five-level scale, representing a continuum of developing practice from early novice (not ready to teach) to proficient beginning-level practice to accomplished beginning practice. The rubrics are meant to support teacher educators in determining candidates' expanding repertoire of skills and strategies within a learning progression from fragmented or indiscriminant practice to intentional, integrated and well-executed practice; they are also meant to support the examination of candidates' deepening rationale and reflection based on knowledge of students. The upper ends of the rubrics and associated tools were designed with the goal of privileging knowledge of students as the basis for instructional decisions and interpretation of student learning in reference to prior academic learning and students' strengths, socio-cultural assets and particular needs (Stanford Center for Assessment, Learning and Equity, 2012).

edTPA presents a challenging set of tasks and demands intended to be used summatively such that candidates have opportunities to integrate the knowledge and skills developed throughout the entirety of their preparation programs. In addition, programs using edTPA are encouraged to develop curriculum-embedded signature assessments for use prior to and during field experiences to provide formative opportunities to engage in practice teaching that reflects the outcomes measured by edTPA, as well as other valued knowledge and skills reflected in individual programs.

A major goal of edTPA is to document and describe novice teachers' actual teaching practice while they are engaged in clinical practice and to determine their readiness for independent teaching responsibilities. The assessment is intended to serve as *one* component of a program's or state's multiple-measures assessment system, which may include one more of the following: ongoing observations and evaluations during clinical experience (e.g., cooperating teacher feedback, supervisor ratings); course-embedded assignments or assessments (e.g., case studies, analysis of instructional materials or curriculum units, etc.); and standardized measures of subject matter knowledge and basic skills (e.g., Praxis, California Subject Examinations for Teachers [CSET], etc.). Similar to the treatment of assessment in the medical and social work professions, developers of edTPA designed the summative assessment to contribute to licensure decisions within a multiple-measures assessment system. As such, and similar to medicine and social work, edTPA was not designed to replace formative clinical evaluations conducted by local actors (e.g., course instructors, university field supervisors, cooperating teachers, etc.) who also contribute to recommendations for licensure. That being said, in a growing number of states, teacher candidates who do not pass edTPA will not be granted teaching licenses, even in cases where they perform and score well on local assessments.

Within a multiple-measures system, data from performance-based assessments can provide evidence of candidate strengths and needs that can inform faculty inquiry about curricular or programmatic change (Peck et al., 2010; Whittaker & Nelson, 2013). Research on PACT use in California offers some examples of this possibility. Following a series of *mock scoring* events examining PACT portfolios, for example, faculty at a large California state university developed and revised a collection of embedded signature assessments to improve program coherence, provide formative opportunities for candidates to practice planning instruction responsive to students' needs and address valued program outcomes not adequately measured by PACT (e.g., creating and sustaining positive learning environments). Researchers additionally reported that discussions among faculty, which included clinical faculty responsible for field supervision, led to greater articulation of the goals and content of foundations, methods and clinical seminar courses in support of program improvement and candidate performance (Peck et al., 2010). We further discuss the potentially educative use of teacher performance assessment in the following sections; first, however, we examine tensions that may arise in bringing a teacher performance assessment like edTPA to scale and for use in high-stakes decisions.

Bringing Teacher Performance Assessments to Scale

As described previously, medicine and social work have a long history of shared expectations and standards for licensure and systems of standardized, externally administered and scored examinations. Shulman (1998) has long argued that key changes necessary for establishing teaching as a profession include the adoption of common definitions for and shared approaches to monitoring practice within the professional community. Darling-Hammond (2010) extends this argument to propose a valid and reliable *system* of performance assessments to determine readiness for licensure, to support state and local accreditation, and to allow for mobility across states. If edTPA fulfills its own promises, it could be a tool that supports the profession in these ways. Despite these potential benefits, however, it is also important to consider what may be sacrificed when TPAs are scaled up, as is currently occurring with edTPA.

One of the more contested topics surrounding the widespread adoption of edTPA is the assessment's operational partnership with *Evaluation Systems*, a subsidiary of the assessment and publishing company Pearson. Based on the company's history supporting licensure assessment and following an open selection process, Stanford University established a partnership with Evaluation Systems to enable scalability of edTPA to a national audience and to provide opportunities for centralized scoring—an approach intended to increase reliability and comparability of judgments about candidate performance across programs and states, as is the case in other professions with required licensure. Scalability and use of standardized assessments for state licensure exams of other types typically include administrative management by similarly large testing companies.

Stanford's agreement with Evaluation Systems delineates the roles and responsibilities of each partner. Stanford continues to exclusively own the intellectual property rights and is responsible for working with the profession to develop all edTPA handbooks and assessment rubrics, scorer training design and materials and implementation support resources. Evaluation Systems provides the infrastructure to manage official edTPA submissions, scoring and score reporting functions at local, regional, state and national levels. This includes hiring teacher educators and K–12 educators who are subject matter experts and who work with beginning teachers as scorers, assigning them to score individual edTPA submissions and compensating them for their work.

The opportunity for centralized scoring addresses a number of important concerns, including policy demands for common standards of performance and accountability, local budget concerns (candidate fees for external scoring offset campus scoring costs for paying faculty or building it into the workload) and psychometric concerns about assessment reliability and validity. However, exclusive use of external scoring also raises questions about the degree to which and how programs can make sense of and implement edTPA adaptively and in ways that support local goals and respond to local contexts and conditions—all of which are critical to any performance assessment maintaining its educative value. While the outsourcing of scoring may be a necessary component of bringing assessment to scale, it is essential that local faculty be engaged in some capacity to evaluate their own candidates' work to help interpret and/or critique externally provided results and to ensure consistency in scoring. Recent attention to scoring/reporting errors made by Pearson in relation to standardized student assessments reminds us that external scoring processes are not foolproof (Baker, 2013). Indeed, for any high-stakes assessment, it is crucial that all involved are vigilant that scoring and reporting processes are carried out with transparency and rigor. For the teacher education community, for example, such vigilance might include participating in the external scoring processes as official scorers and/or in conducting local evaluations to ensure consistency of interpretation of candidate performance. Along these lines, some states will likely opt for a newly established combination of regional/local scoring training and opportunities for faculty to score some portion of their candidates' portfolios.

External scoring is not the only potential concern with high-stakes use of performance assessments of teaching. Some teacher educators have also suggested that the use of common assessment tools like edTPA may lead to rigid implementation approaches, reduce program autonomy and narrow or standardize the teacher education curriculum. Others have raised questions about and offered solutions for how programs and state agencies might protect against an approach to edTPA implementation that privileges compliance and implementation *fidelity* over more authentic, inquiry-oriented use. In addition, questions remain about the roles that faculty and P–12 partners might play in efforts to balance external accountability with local program improvement efforts. For example, will programs new to performance-based assessment develop and sustain faculty engagement, especially in examining candidate performance to inform program renewal? In what ways will programs provide candidates with formative opportunities to develop practices associated with performance assessment constructs without *teaching to the test*? What can be done to ensure that the implementation process focuses on local responsiveness rather than universalism? And what can be done to ensure that implementation does not undermine program capacity or opportunities for faculty to draw on their professional expertise and engage in adaptive practice? In subsequent sections of this chapter, we return to these important questions as we examine the potential benefits and pitfalls of embedding large-scale and local teacher assessment within clinical field experiences.

Embedding Teacher Performance Assessment within Clinical Field Experiences

Alongside efforts to make teacher performance assessment a core component of university-based TEPs are calls to move such programs closer to the practice of teaching. As a number of scholars have illustrated, clinical field experiences—and particularly those considered high-quality—are critically important to teacher candidates' successful development of teaching practice (Boyd et al., 2009; Ronfeldt & Reininger, 2012; Zeichner & Conklin, 2005). Indeed, teaching's context-specific nature and ill-defined structure make it difficult to imagine how novices could possibly learn the essential dimensions of teaching practice without opportunities to engage in high-quality, school-based learning experiences. Yet despite increasing evidence that strong clinical experiences matter a great deal, simply calling on teacher education to provide learning experiences that are clinically rich does little to ensure that field experiences will indeed lead to improvements in teacher candidate and P–12 student learning.

Challenges to Organizing Educative Clinical Field Experiences

For one, even the most strident calls to make teacher education more clinically rich offer limited criteria to guide teacher educators' programmatic and instructional decisions. Calls for more and better clinical experiences that *do* include specific criteria, on the other hand, tend to emphasize student teaching's technical and structural dimensions (e.g., location, duration, division of labor) while underplaying—and even overlooking—the features (e.g., quality teacher educator mediation, coherence between program values and school-based approaches, etc.) known to be most consequential for teacher candidates' development of effective practice (Anderson & Stillman, 2011; Grossman, McDonald, Hammerness, & Ronfeldt, 2008; Valencia, Martin, Place, & Grossman, 2009; Zeichner, 2010). Thus, while the contemporary discourse about clinical experiences may encourage teacher educators to incorporate more and lengthier school- and practice-based components, there is little reason to believe that this will be enough to overcome the considerable variation in clinical experience quality that currently exists across programs (Clift & Brady, 2005).

Additionally, there are significant gaps in our understandings regarding the kinds of clinical experiences that are, indeed, educative for teacher candidates. With the exception of a handful of recent studies that shed some light on key features of effective clinical experiences, including the contexts (Anderson & Stillman, 2011; Ronfeldt, 2012), specific learning experiences (e.g., Brock, Moore, & Parks, 2007; Parks, 2008) and program structures (e.g., Grossman et al., 2008) that seem to bolster and/or impede teacher candidates' learning, our knowledge base on teacher candidates' *learning* through clinical experience is relatively thin. Teacher education's historical dearth of agreed-upon, practice-based assessments that could provide information about candidates' field-based learning contributes to this limited understanding as well.

In addition, a recently published review of research on teacher candidates' learning in and from clinical placements situated in urban and/or high-needs schools, specifically, suggests that many such studies offer limited insights when it comes to the contributions of clinical experiences to candidates' teaching readiness (Anderson & Stillman, 2013). For example, the reviewed studies focused predominantly on teacher candidates' belief and attitude changes (e.g., Knoblauch & Woolfolk-Hoy, 2008; Pohan & Adams, 2007; Walker-Dalhouse & Dalhouse, 2006, etc.), with far fewer offering insights regarding candidates' development of teaching practices and facilitation of student learning (e.g., Brock et al., 2007; Buehler, Gere, Dallivas, & Haviland, 2009; LaBoskey & Richert, 2002; Lloyd, 2007; Merino & Holmes, 2006, etc.). In addition, few studies shed light on what *leads* to teacher candidate learning; this is the case when it comes to the contributions of teacher educator guidance (e.g., Brock et al., 2007; Buehler et al., 2009; Parks, 2008), despite research identifying frequent, targeted mediation as a critical feature of educative field experiences (Anderson & Stillman, 2011; Stillman & Anderson, 2011; Valencia et al., 2009; Zeichner, 2010).

Together, these well-documented problems of practice and imbalances in the knowledge base raise questions about how programs ought to reorganize clinical field experiences, including the support provided therein. In light of this uncertainty, we draw on what we know about assessment approaches employed by comparable professions and their role in clarifying guidelines for apprenticeship and increasing profession-wide cohesiveness and accountability. More specifically, we highlight some features of teacher performance assessment that we argue hold promise for supporting teacher educators' efforts to make clinical experiences more conducive to teacher candidate learning and, more broadly, for strengthening the profession.

Using Teacher Performance Assessment to Strengthen Teacher Candidates' Field-Based Learning

There is considerable agreement that learning to teach requires that novice teachers have opportunities to observe and reflect upon classroom teaching, engage in classroom teaching themselves, receive anticipatory guidance and quality feedback on their emerging practice and develop a readiness to teach that corresponds with their capacity to promote student learning (e.g., Feiman-Nemser & Buchmann, 1987; Hollins, 2011; Zeichner, 2010). We additionally know that in order to ensure that teacher candidates emerge from programs ready to teach, those charged with supporting teacher candidates' field-based learning (e.g., course instructors, cooperating teachers, university field supervisors) must understand and support candidates' movement toward agreed-upon learning goals (e.g., Anderson & Stillman, 2011; Stillman & Anderson, 2011; Valencia et al., 2009).

As described previously, edTPA—used as an example in this chapter because of its status as the most widely used teacher performance assessment in preservice programs today—is a performance-based assessment that measures individual teacher candidates' competencies in relation to student learning in multiple areas and within a variety of subject areas. Early research on PACT (which shares architecture and lineage with edTPA and the National Board portfolio, as noted previously) suggests that the performance-based data that is collected as candidates complete the assessment—including artifacts of candidates' instruction and critical reflections on this instruction—can provide faculty with critical information about candidates' teaching readiness (Pecheone & Chung, 2006), insights regarding program strengths and weaknesses and direction for program improvement efforts (e.g., Bunch, Aguirre, & Téllez, 2009; Peck et al., 2010).

What has been discussed far less, however, is performance-based assessment's untapped potential as a tool for strengthening clinical field experiences—one that could be used to *mediate* teacher candidate learning in addition to evaluating it. Indeed, teacher performance assessment instruments have the potential to address many of the issues (described previously) that are known to make the development and sustenance of optimal clinical field experiences so challenging (Zeichner, 2010). For example, although most TEPs have been designed to reflect established professional standards, edTPA's 15 rubrics may serve as useful tools for delineating such standards using a common language and structure while also offering a general sense of how a teacher candidate's knowledge, understandings and skills/ practices are likely to manifest at different stages of development. In this respect, as described previously, TPAs may support faculty to come together around a clear set of learning goals to organize complementary and outcome-focused learning experiences across courses and field settings. This represents one possible means of addressing common struggles with program coherence, both among university-based faculty and between actors situated in university- and field-based contexts (Feiman-Nemser & Buchmann, 1987; Grossman et al., 2008; Valencia et al., 2009).

Teacher performance assessment might also be used formatively to supplement locally designed formative or transition point assessments. This could support teacher educators to gather information about teacher candidates' developing practice and understandings in relation to program-specific *and* profession-wide goals, which could then be drawn upon to inform future instruction and facilitate inter- and intra-program discussions about candidate development. That TPAs typically evaluate multiple competencies additionally stands to support TEPs' efforts to monitor candidates' overall readiness to teach and potentially lessens the possibility of privileging one competency (e.g., belief and attitude change) over another (e.g., development of teaching practice).

Performance assessment's focus on teacher candidates' capacities to facilitate student learning in context, including prompts designed to help candidates grapple with the relationship between what they teach and what students learn, similarly stands to advance practice and the profession in important ways. Hollins

(2011), for example, has argued that in "exemplary" schools, teachers' talk about instruction is seamlessly connected to conversations about learners and authentic learning. Zeichner (2010) has similarly underscored the importance of linking assessments of candidates' readiness with their capacities to promote student learning, a charge that most valid performance-based assessments—given their near-universal requirement that candidates collect and analyze student work produced during their instruction—can support. A common, cross-program tool like edTPA could press all teacher candidates to scrutinize various dimensions of their practice (e.g., planning, enactment and assessment of their own instruction) in relation to different learners' responses to it.

By design, a performance assessment tool wouldn't advance a particular set of instructional strategies (e.g., *high-leverage* practices). However, embedding a widely used teacher performance assessment within clinical field experiences might support teacher educators in designing structured opportunities for developing among candidates what Hollins (2011) has referred to as "epistemic practices"— a shared discourse or "grammar of practice" that could transcend the confines of individual programs and states (Grossman, 2011). Just as importantly, requirements that candidates critically analyze, interpret and reflect upon their instruction's impact on student learning could assist teacher educators in pushing candidates toward developing an inquiry stance, which has been shown to be key to facilitating learning among students from historically underserved groups in particular (e.g., Cochran-Smith, 1991). Indeed, such reflective practice, particularly when mediated by a faculty or clinical supervisor, has proven to be effective in fields like social work as well (Tsui, 2005). That most TPAs require candidates to anchor their commentaries and reflections in a theoretical or philosophical perspective additionally has the potential to strengthen the development of equity-minded teachers who aim to serve students from underserved communities (Gay, 2010; Hollins, 2011; Zeichner, 2012). In essence, when used thoughtfully, TPAs are well positioned to help ensure that clinical field experiences are guided and reflective learning experiences rather than opportunities wherein candidates are expected to learn simply by spending extended time in schools and/or engaging in independent practice teaching, with little sense of—or feedback in relation to—what the field and faculty agree is most critical to learn.

Targeted and thoughtful feedback that teacher educators offer candidates in relation to their developing practice is also an essential ingredient of clinical field experiences that are meant to serve as opportunities for *guided practice*. Situating teacher performance assessment within clinical experiences may offer helpful direction in this regard as well. More specifically, teacher performance assessment tools can provide teacher educators with guidelines for ensuring that their mediation of candidates' learning is tied to established and agreed-upon learning goals rather than treated as an opportunity to, for example, offer general encouragement—a tendency that has been shown to limit candidates' learning

(Anderson & Stillman, 2011; Valencia et al., 2009). To be sure, our exploration of medicine and social work suggests that while more hours spent in clinical experience may be helpful, it is the guidance, shadowing, debriefing and critical reflection about such experiences that has assisted these professions in preparing candidates for practice (Krasne et al., 2006; Munson, 2004; Pelgrim et al., 2012). Requirements that candidates describe their planning, enactment and assessment of instruction, as well as demonstrate competency in multiple areas (e.g., understanding learners in a social context, teaching academic language, etc.), additionally provide teacher educators with a common structure for offering feedback that is varied, comprehensive and tied to candidates' practice and its impact on student learning.

Teacher performance assessment tools can also serve as a foundation for the important yet often marginalized work that is required to prepare cooperating teachers and university field supervisors to mediate candidates' field-based learning. In addition to providing data on candidate development that university- and field-based teacher educators can gather around, such tools can also communicate program goals in clear terms, potentially decreasing the likelihood of the "two-worlds pitfall" (Feiman-Nemser & Buchmann, 1985, p. 53).

Certainly, as the previous examples suggest, embedding teacher performance assessment tools within clinical field experiences holds promise for helping ensure the strength of individual TEPs and the learning experiences offered therein. Using a *common* assessment tool that was developed within the profession across programs additionally holds promise for strengthening the profession more broadly, in particular, by helping teacher educators develop a more unified vision of what constitutes readiness to teach, a greater sense of responsibility for holding our own graduates accountable for meeting learning goals and a more cohesive discourse for talking about teaching and the learning-to-teach process. This coming together could bolster the profession's capacity to take a more agentive role in public discourse and policy discussions surrounding teaching and teacher education, similar to that which is presently afforded other professions.

And yet despite these potential benefits of embedding a common teacher assessment instrument in clinical field experiences across programs, there are notable risks involved with using one tool to determine a candidates' readiness to teach. In particular, using one assessment tool to evaluate teacher candidates' learning could increase the likelihood that program-specific competencies (e.g., the ability to facilitate learning among students representing non-dominant groups) are assessed inaccurately or overlooked altogether. At the same time, using only one assessment tool may also *decrease* possibilities for triangulating assessment data, leaving candidates vulnerable to potential scorer subjectivity and other possible inaccuracies (Sandholtz & Shea, 2012). Indeed, now that some TPAs like edTPA use centralized scoring systems in addition to local evaluators, teacher educators may need to become even more vigilant about such possibilities. The narrowing—even standardization—of the curriculum that can emerge when instructors use only one assessment instrument to drive rather than simply guide instruction is perhaps the most likely risk (e.g., Berlak, 2003; Kornfeld, Grady, Marker, & Ruddell, 2007), particularly when a single assessment is tied to high stakes such as licensure. For these reasons, we argue the importance of teacher educators implementing common assessment tools in combination with multiple measures and doing so adaptively—that is, with thoughtful attention to the context, goals and values of their respective programs and the contexts of the schools in and for which they prepare teachers to work.

Using Teacher Performance Assessment in Adaptive, Context-Specific Ways

Even as we write this chapter about the generative possibilities of embedding teacher performance assessment in clinical field experiences, we find ourselves struggling with the tensions surrounding our recommendations. In particular, we hope that it is evident to readers that we are also concerned—as are many of our colleagues—about the profession becoming more standardized and about other unintended consequences of a *best practices* approach to teacher education reform. In particular, we know that increased standardization can compromise the inclusion of multiple perspectives (e.g., Sleeter & Stillman, 2005) and other coursework features that aim to develop candidates' multicultural competencies, specifically (e.g., Berlak, 2003; Sleeter, 2003). We also know that the practices often considered *best* tend to be monocultural practices, or practices that treat learners and learning as culture-free (Goodwin, Cheruvu, & Genishi, 2008). Accordingly, we emphasize the importance of teacher educators using any tool—including performance assessment tools—thoughtfully and in ways that do not compromise individual program values nor ignore the contexts where candidates are learning to teach. Recent studies of PACT use by California teacher educators offer actionable insights regarding adaptive approaches to teacher performance assessment implementation that we believe are useful to consider in relation to edTPA's current scaling-up efforts and in light of the potential pitfalls we've raised.

Existing research on PACT implementation in California suggests that there are various ways of approaching implementation of teacher performance assessment adaptively. Several scholars, for example, have underscored the particular value of teacher education faculty approaching mandated teacher performance assessment from an inquiry stance rather than as an exercise in compliance (e.g., Peck et al., 2010; Peck & McDonald, 2013; Whittaker & Nelson, 2013). In one study, Peck et al. (2010) found that faculty engagement in conversations about PACT data seemed to aid them in articulating "program-wide valued outcomes" and ideas about how such outcomes "might be enacted through a more pervasively shared practice" (p. 459). Related to this, other studies point to possibilities for using program-specific values to guide faculty analysis of performance assessment data. One study, for example, illustrates how faculty representing a program that aims to prepare all of its candidates to work with English-language learners approached PACT data with the goal of gathering previously unavailable information about candidates' learning to teach this population of students (Bunch et al., 2009). This information allowed faculty to grapple openly with the goals they held for candidates and to consider how their program might better support teacher candidates to serve these students.

Taking this a step further, other accounts of PACT implementation offer insights regarding approaches for augmenting the actual performance assessment *instruments* in efforts to ensure that the teaching competencies deemed most critical by program faculty are not supplanted by—and are evaluated as carefully as—externally derived goals. To date, the concern that seems to have generated the most discussion is the relationship between PACT (and now edTPA) and teacher candidates' capacities to teach students from culturally and linguistically diverse backgrounds in culturally responsive, equity-minded ways (Hyler, Yee, Barnes, & Carey, 2012; Stillman et al., 2014). Such concerns are warranted, particularly given past tendencies in teacher education for top-down reforms to lead to the marginalization of program components geared specifically toward developing candidates' multicultural competencies (Berlak, 2003; Sleeter, 2003; Zeichner, 2012).

Take, for example, one group of teacher educators representing three California TEPs aimed at preparing teachers for urban schools specifically who expressed concern that existing PACT rubrics might not be able to fully capture candidates' knowledge about and capacities to serve students from historically underserved communities. That the one PACT component requiring candidates to provide an account of the social context of their K–12 learners (called the Context Commentary) is not formally scored added to these teacher educators' concerns (Stillman et al., 2014). In light of these concerns, these teacher educators analyzed sample PACT artifacts and commentaries from across their programs in relation to both program goals and PACT rubrics. Drawing on what they learned from this focused inquiry, faculty developed a supplemental matrix, designed with the explicit intention of examining candidates' knowledge about and ability to enact *contextualized practice*. Accounts of the process by which PACT was analyzed and adapted illustrate the potential benefits—including faculty learning and program improvement—that can emerge when faculty approach mandated teacher performance assessment as a tool that can be used *in the service of* established learning goals rather than as a goal in and of itself. In another example, Hyler et al. (2012) engaged in a similar process, ultimately identifying features of edTPA prompts and rubrics that aligned most with program goals and values, particularly those related to candidates' commitments to and capacities for recognizing and building upon students' knowledge, interests and experiences in their attempts to facilitate students' learning.

In each of these examples, faculty engaged with performance assessment tools and data in ways that challenged compliance-oriented responses, thereby reducing the likelihood that the assessment tools they were charged with using would become the goals toward which all teaching and learning were geared. Existing research suggests that this kind of work is essential for avoiding the kinds of technical changes known to contribute little to the generation of authentic, context-sensitive change (Zeichner, 2010, 2012). Although programs and states are likely to implement teacher performance assessment with different orientations toward fidelity, we hope that teacher educators will seek out the time and space to engage in this kind of adaptive, inquiry-oriented work. Although such work would likely occur at a small scale and within local contexts, we believe that teacher educator agency of this sort may be one of the more powerful approaches for reclaiming the profession.

Summary and Conclusions

In this chapter, we have highlighted some potential affordances of using teacher performance assessment, particularly as a tool that is embedded within clinical field experiences. More specifically, we have argued that the growing use of teacher performance assessment may not only begin to respond to the call for an internally developed, valid means of assessing teacher candidates' readiness to teach (Zeichner, 2010), but that it might also serve as a tool for addressing some of the challenges that have been shown to accompany efforts to create and sustain educative, carefully guided clinical field experiences.

Additionally, we have considered the potential benefits of teacher educators from across states and programs using a *common* teacher performance assessment instrument as a means of cultivating cohesiveness in the profession, particularly with regard to the learning-to-teach process and the development of a shared discourse and common understanding of practice. Such cohesiveness stands to strengthen the profession, both by documenting systematically that those who matriculate through university-based programs have the knowledge, skills and dispositions needed to facilitate learning among P–12 students across settings and by supporting the profession to respond productively and proactively to external criticisms and demands. Scaling common assessments across programs and states also stands to elevate the reputation of the teaching profession, including preservice teacher preparation, to the level of respect experienced by other professions.

At the same time, we have highlighted some of the potential pitfalls of placing too much stock in any single measure or approach to assessment, including the risk of program standardization. To be sure, research demonstrating that there is no one assessment instrument that can or should do everything (Sandholtz & Shea, 2012) and other professions' reliance on multiple assessments, including formative benchmark assessments, presses teacher educators to consider the serious implications for both teacher and student learning of relying too heavily on one instrument to define program goals, guide learning experiences or evaluate teacher candidate learning. Research that illustrates the ill effects of lock-step, technical responses to reform initiatives should give teacher educators additional pause, particularly in situations where pressure to comply threatens to undermine TEP goals and values (e.g., Kornfeld et al., 2007). This is especially important given teacher education's documented record of responding to new standards and/or assessments by marginalizing and/or treating as *add-ons* courses that aim to develop candidates' cultural competence and capacities to facilitate learning among historically underserved youth (Berlak, 2003). Indeed, as Zeichner (2012) has argued, while developing greater professional coherence and a stronger sense of internal accountability is important, "there is much more involved in improving educational outcomes for the many students who are now underserved by our public schools than [these developments] can alone provide" (p. 381).

Also worth mentioning are the local challenges (e.g., resources necessary for managing assessment logistics, costs shouldered by teacher candidates, etc.) that can accompany the implementation of a scaled-up assessment like edTPA. In light of ongoing divestment in the public universities that prepare the majority of the nation's teachers, programs and states must allocate the resources necessary for supporting the local labor that accompanies using an assessment well, including maintaining its educative purpose.

To be sure, these tensions are at the heart of debates currently surrounding the widespread use of edTPA. For example, some leaders in the field have taken the position that edTPA adoption stands to strengthen individual TEPs and the profession more broadly by providing teacher educators with important information on candidates' learning and teaching ability (Hollins, 2013; Peck, 2013) and by "assur[ing] that . . . educators meet a defined standard of expertise . . . before they assume responsibility for children's lives" (Falk & Snyder, 2013, p. 1). In addition, some have demonstrated why edTPA is a smarter investment in teacher quality than other forms of teacher evaluation, particularly VAM. Specifically, VAM has been shown to provide inconsistent measurements of teacher quality, primarily because of its sole focus on student standardized test scores and an inability to sort out the different factors that influence student progress (Darling-Hammond et al., 2010; NRC, 2009). On the other hand, teacher performance assessment—for reasons discussed in this chapter—is better positioned to provide programs with actionable insights about their candidates' readiness to teach, both in accordance with agreed-upon, internally derived professional standards and in relation to local contexts and student learning. Meanwhile, others, including 30 of 85 faculty members from Columbia Teachers College, have raised questions about the New York State implementation timeline for edTPA (and edTPA's partnership with Pearson's *Evaluation Systems*) for its potential to compromise TEPs' abilities to maintain ethical relationships with schools serving historically marginalized youth (Sawchuk, 2013).

In light of these potential benefits and pitfalls, we've made the case for teacher educators to treat performance assessment instruments as *tools* that are *meant* to be critically analyzed and implemented in light of local goals, conditions and contexts rather than as goals unto themselves. This adaptive implementation work is critical at a time when calls to make teacher preparation clinically rich and the increasing use of teacher performance assessment could easily become another cycle of compliance-oriented reforms that end up addressing the technical dimensions of teacher education rather than building upon the features most essential to teacher and student learning. In addition, engaging with reforms adaptively and with an inquiry stance models for teacher candidates the complex nature of educators' work in today's policy context and the importance of engaging in principled practice, regardless of where the winds of reform may blow.

References

American Association of Colleges for Teacher Education (AACTE) (2010). *Reforming teacher education: The critical clinical component.* Washington, DC: Author.

American Association of Colleges for Teacher Education (AACTE) (2013a). Experts cite lack of research, dismiss credibility of state policy report on teacher preparation. Press Release, Friday, January 25, 2013. Retrieved from http://aacte.org/news-room/press-releases/experts-cite-lack-of-research-dismiss-credibility-of-state-policy-report-on-teacher-preparation.html

American Association of Colleges for Teacher Education (AACTE) (2013b). edTPA. Retrieved from http://edtpa.aacte.org/

American Federation of Teachers (2012). *Raising the bar: Aligning and elevating teacher preparation and the teaching profession.* Retrieved from http://www.aft.org/pdfs/highered/raisingthebar2012.pdf

American Medical Association (2012). Medical licensure: State medical licensure requirements. Retrieved from http://www.ama-assn.org/ama/licensure

Anderson, L., & Stillman, J. (2011). Student teaching for a specialized knowledge base?: Opportunities to teach and learn in urban, high-needs schools. *Journal of Teacher Education, 62*(5), 446–464.

Anderson, L., & Stillman, J. (2013). Student teaching's contribution to preservice teacher development: A review of research focused on the preparation of teachers for urban and high-needs contexts. *Review of Education Research, 83*(1), 3–69.

Baker, A. (2013). More in New York City qualify as gifted after error is released. *The New York Times.* Retrieved from http://www.nytimes.com/2013/04/20/education/score-corrections-qualify-nearly-2700-more-pupils-for-gifted-programs.html

Baker, A. (2013). More in New York City Quality as Gifted after error is Released. *The New York Times,* April 19, 2013. Retrieved May 13, 2013: http://www.nytimes.com/2013/04/20/education/score-corrections-quality-nearly-2700-more-pupils-for-gifted-programs.html

Ball, D., & Cohen, D. (1999). Developing practice, developing practitioners: Toward a practice-based theory of professional education. In L. Darling-Hammond & G. Sykes (Eds.), *Teaching as the learning profession: Handbook of policy and practice* (pp. 3–32). San Francisco, CA: Jossey-Bass.

Ball, D., & Forzani, F. (2009). The work of teaching and the challenge for teacher education. *Journal of Teacher Education, 60*(5), 497–510.

Barnes, C. (2006). Preparing preservice teachers to teach in a culturally responsive way. *The Negro Educational Review, 57*(1–2), 85–100.

Berlak, A. (2003). Who's in charge here?: Teacher education and 2042. *Teacher Education Quarterly, 30*(1), 31–40.

Boyd, D.J., Grossman, P.L., Lankford, H., Loeb, S., & Wyckoff, J. (2009). Teacher preparation and student achievement. *Educational Evaluation and Policy Analysis, 31*(4), 416–440.

Brock, C.H., Moore, D.K., & Parks, L. (2007). Exploring pre-service teachers' literacy practices with children from diverse backgrounds: Implications for teacher educators. *Teaching and Teacher Education, 23*(6), 898–915.

Buehler, J., Gere, A., Dallivas, C., & Haviland, V. (2009). Normalizing the fraughtness: How emotion, race, and school context complicate cultural competence. *Journal of Teacher Education, 60*(4), 408–418.

Bunch, G.C., Aguirre, J.M., & Téllez, K. (2009). Beyond the scores: Using candidate responses on high stakes performance assessment to inform teacher preparation for English learners. *Issues in Teacher Education, 18*(1), 103–128.

Campbell, D.T. (1976). *Assessing the impact of planned social change.* Hanover, NH: The Public Affairs Center, Dartmouth College.

Castro, A.J. (2010). Negotiating challenges in teaching for multicultural citizenship: Student teaching in an accountability driven context. *Action in Teacher Education, 32*(2), 97–109.

Clift, R.T., & Brady, P. (2005). Research on methods courses and field experiences. In M. Cochran-Smith & K.M. Zeichner (Eds.), *Studying teacher education: The report of the AERA panel on research and teacher education* (pp. 309–424). Mahwah, NJ: Lawrence Erlbaum.

Cochran-Smith, M. (1991). Learning to teach against the grain. *Harvard Educational Review, 61*(3), 279–310.

Common Core State Standards (2010). *Common Core State Standards for English Language Arts and Literacy in History/Social Studies, Science and Technical Subjects.* Retrieved from http://www.corestandards.org/assets/CCSSI_ELA%20Standards.pdf

Corey, G., Corey, M.S., & Callanan, P. (2011). *Issues and ethics in the helping professions* (8th ed.). Independence, KY: Cengage Learning.

Council of Chief State School Officers (CCSSO) (2012). *Our responsibility, our promise: Transforming educator preparation and entry into the profession.* Retrieved from http://www.ccsso.org/Documents/2012/Our%20Responsibility%20Our%20Promise_2012.pdf

Darling-Hammond, L. (2010). *Evaluating teacher effectiveness: How teacher performance assessments can measure and improve teaching.* Washington, DC: Center for American Progress.

Darling-Hammond, L. (2012). The right start: Creating a strong foundation for the teaching career. *Phi Delta Kappan, 94*(3), 8–13.

Darling-Hammond, L., Amrein-Beardsley, A., Haertel, E., & Rothstein, J. (2010). Evaluating teacher evaluation. *Phi Delta Kappan, 93*(6), 8–15.

Darling-Hammond, L., Newton, S.P., & Wei, R.C. (2012). Developing and assessing beginning teacher effectiveness: The potential of performance assessments. Policy Brief, Stanford Center for Policy in Education. Retrieved from http://edpolicy.stanford.edu/publications/pubs/657

Dewey, J. (1904/1965). The relation of theory to practice in education. In M. Borrowman (Ed.), *Teacher education in America: A documentary history* (pp. 140–171). New York, NY: Teachers College Press.

Duncan, A. (October 22, 2009). Teacher preparation: Reforming the uncertain profession. United States Department of Education. Remarks of Secretary Arne Duncan at Teachers College, Columbia University. Retrieved from http://www2.ed.gov/news/speeches/2009/10/10222009.html

Falk, B. (2013). Lessons from the Performance Assessment for California Teachers (PACT). *The New Educator, 9*(1), 1–2.

Falk, B., & Snyder, J. (2013). Continuing controversy over new teacher test. Letter to the Editor. *Rethinking Schools Online, 27*(3). Retrieved from http://www.rethinkingschools.org/archive/27_03/27_03_letters.shtml

Federation of State Medical Boards (2013). State licensure and continuing education in medicine. Retrieved from http://www.fsmb.org/for-medical-professionals.html

Feiman-Nemser, S., & Buchmann, M. (1985). Pitfalls of experience in teacher preparation. *Teachers College Record, 87*(1), 53–65.

Feiman-Nemser, S., & Buchmann, M. (1987). When is student teaching teacher education? *Teaching and Teacher Education, 3*(4), 255–273.

Gay, G. (2010). *Culturally responsive teaching.* New York, NY: Teachers College Press.

Girod, G. (Ed.). (2002). *Connecting teaching and learning: A handbook for teacher educators on teacher work sample methodology.* Washington, DC: AACTE Publications.

Goodwin, A.L., Cheruvu, R., & Genishi, C. (2008). Responding to multiple diversities in early childhood education: How far have we come? In C. Genishi & A.L. Goodwin (Eds.), *Diversities in early childhood: Rethinking and doing* (pp. 3–10). New York, NY: Routledge.

GREAT Teachers and Principals Act (2013). Retrieved from http://www.newschools.org/wp/wp-content/uploads/GREAT-Act-6-21-11.pdf

Grossman, P. (2011). A framework for teaching practice: A brief history of an idea. *Teachers College Record, 113*(12), 2836–2843.

Grossman, P., McDonald, M., Hammerness, K., & Ronfeldt, M. (2008). Constructing coherence: Structural predictors of perceptions of coherence in NYC teacher education programs. *Journal of Teacher Education, 59*(4), 273–287.

Hollins, E. (2011). Teacher preparation for quality teaching. *Journal of Teacher Education, 62*(4), 395–407.

Hollins, E. (2013). Finally a truly promising new approach to improving teacher preparation. Retrieved from http://edtpa.aacte.org/wp-content/uploads/2012/09/Hollins-edTPA.pdf

Hyler, M.E., Yee, L.S., Barnes, S.R., & Carey, R.L. (November 2, 2012). Opportunities for demonstrations of equity-centered pedagogy in edTPAs. Paper presented at the Annual edTPA Implementation Conference, University of San Diego, San Diego, CA.

Knoblauch, D., & Woolfolk-Hoy, A. (2008). "Maybe I can teach those kids": The influence of contextual factors on student teachers' efficacy beliefs. *Teaching and Teacher Education, 24*(1), 166–179.

Kornfeld, J., Grady, K., Marker, P.M., & Ruddell, M.R. (2007). Caught in the current: A self-study of state-mandated compliance in a teacher education program. *Teachers College Record, 109*(2), 1902–1930.

Krasne, S., Wimmers, P., Relan, A., & Drake, T. (2006). Differential effects of two types of formative assessment in predicting performance of first-year medical students. *Advances in Health Science Theory and Practice, 11*(2), 155–171.

LaBoskey, V.K., & Richert, A.E. (2002). Identifying good student teaching placements: A programmatic perspective. *Teacher Education Quarterly, 29*(2), 7–34.

Lampert, M., & Graziani, F. (2009). Instructional activities as a tool for teachers' and teacher educators' learning. *Elementary School Journal, 109*, 491–509.

Levine, A. (September 2006). *Educating school teachers.* The Education Schools Project. Retrieved from http://www.edschools.org/teacher_report.htm

Lloyd, G. (2007). Strategic compromise: A student teacher's design of kindergarten mathematics instruction in a high-stakes testing climate. *Journal of Teacher Education, 58*(4), 328–347.

Mayer, R.E. (2011). *Applying the science of learning.* Boston, MA: Pearson Education.

Mead, D.E. (1990). *Effective supervision: A task-oriented model for the mental health professions.* New York, NY: Brunner/Mazel.

Merino, B.J., & Holmes, P. (2006). Student teacher inquiry as an "entry point" for advocacy. *Teacher Education Quarterly, 33*(3), 79–96.

Munson, C.E. (2004). The evolution of protocol-based supervisory practice. In M.J. Austin & K.M. Hopkins (Eds.), *Supervision as collaboration in the human services: Building a learning culture* (pp. 85–96). Thousand Oaks, CA: Sage.

National Association of Social Workers (NASW) (2003). *Guide for Clinical Practices, 3*(2), 2–4.

National Association of Social Workers (NASW) (2013). NASW professional credentials and advanced practices. Retrieved from http://www.naswdc.org/credentials/default.asp

National Council for Accreditation of Teacher Education (NCATE) (2010). *Transforming teacher education through clinical practice: A national strategy to prepare effective teachers (Report of the Blue Ribbon Panel on clinical preparation and partnerships for improved student learning).* Retrieved from http://www.ncate.org/LinkClick.aspx?fileticket=zzeiB1OoqPk%3d&tabid=715

National Council of the Accreditation of Teacher Education (NCATE) (2013). Quick facts. Retrieved from http://www.ncate.org/Public/AboutNCATE/QuickFacts/tabid/3

National Council on Teacher Quality (NCTQ) (2013). *Teacher prep review 2013 report.* Retrieved from http://www.nctq.org/dmsView/Teacher_Prep_Review_2013_Report

National Research Council (NRC) (2010). *Preparing teachers.* Washington, DC: National Academies Press.

National Research Council (NRC) Board on Testing and Assessment (2009). *Letter Report to the U.S. Department of Education.* Washington, DC: Author.

Nichols, S.L., & Berliner, D.C. (2007). *Collateral damage: How high-stakes testing corrupts America's schools.* Cambridge, MA: Harvard Education Press.

O'Donoghue, K. (2004). Social workers and cross-disciplinary supervision. *Social Work Review, 16*(3), 2–7.

Pajak, E. (2002). Clinical supervision and psychological functions: A new direction for theory and practice. *Journal of Curriculum and Supervision, 17*, 177–189.

Parks, A.N. (2008). Messy learning: Preservice teachers' lesson study conversations about mathematics and students. *Teaching and Teacher Education, 24*(5), 1200–1216.

Pecheone, R. L., & Chung, R. R. (2006). Evidence in teacher education: The Performance Assessment for California Teachers. *Journal of Teacher Education, 57*(1), 22–36.

Peck, C. (2013). edTPA: Voices from the field. Retrieved from http://edtpa.aacte.org/voices-from-the-field

Peck, C., & McDonald, M. (2013). Creating "cultures of evidence" in teacher education: Context, policy and practice in three high-data-use programs. *The New Educator, 9*(1), 12–28.

Peck, C. A., Gallucci, C., & Sloan, T. (2010). Negotiating implementation of high-stakes performance assessment policies in teacher education: From compliance to inquiry. *Journal of Teacher Education, 61*(5), 451–463.

Pelgrim, E., Anneke, A.M., Kramer, W.M., Henk, G.A., Mokkink, C., & Van der Vleuten, P.M. (2012). Quality of written narrative feedback and reflection in a modified mini-clinical evaluation exercise: An observational study. *Biomed Central: Medical Education, 12*(97), 1–6.

Pohan, C.A., & Adams, C. (2007). Increasing family involvement and cultural understanding through a university-school partnership. *Action in Teacher Education, 29*(1), 42–50.

Rennert-Ariev, P. (2008). The hidden curriculum of performance based teacher education. *Teachers College Record, 110*(1), 105–138.

Ronfeldt, M. (2012). Where should student teachers learn to teach? Effects of field placement school characteristics on teacher retention and effectiveness. *Educational Evaluation and Policy Analysis, 34*(1), 3–26.

Ronfeldt, M., & Reininger, M. (2012). More or better student teaching? *Teaching and Teacher Education, 28*(8), 1091–1106.

Sandholtz, J.H., & Shea, L.M. (2012). Predicting performance: A comparison of university supervisors' predictions and teacher candidates' scores on a teaching performance assessment. *Journal of Teacher Education, 63*(1), 39–50.

Sawchuk, S. (2013). Columbia university profs raise concerns about certification test. *Education Week, Teacher Beat*. Retrieved from http://blogs.edweek.org/edweek/teacher-beat/2013/01/columbia_university_profs_rais.html

Schalock, H.D., Schalock, M., & Girod, G. (1997). Teacher work sample methodology as used at Western Oregon State College. In J. McMillan (Ed.), *Grading teachers, grading schools: Is student achievement a valid evaluation measure?* (pp. 15–45). Thousand Oaks, CA: Corwin Press.

Shulman, L. (1998). Theory, practice and the education of professionals. *The Elementary School Journal, 98*(5), 511–526.

Sleeter, C. (2003). Reform and control: An analysis of SB 2042. *Teacher Education Quarterly, 30*(1), 19–30.

Sleeter, C., & Stillman, J. (2005). Standardizing knowledge in a multicultural society. *Curriculum Inquiry, 35*(1), 27–46.

Snyder, J. (2009). Taking stock of performance assessments in teaching. *Issues in Teacher Education, 18*(1), 7–11.

Spence, S.H., Wilson, J., Kavanagh, D., Strong, J., & Worrall, L. (2001). Clinical supervision in four mental health professions: A review of the evidence. *Behaviour Change, 18*(3), 135–151.

Stanford Center for Assessment, Learning and Equity (SCALE) (2012). *edTPA English language arts handbook*. Stanford, CA: Stanford University.

Stillman, J., & Anderson, L. (2011). To follow, flip or reject the script: Preparing teachers to manage instructional tension in an era of high-stakes accountability. *Language Arts, 89*(1), 422–437.

Stillman, J., & Anderson, L. (in press). Minding the mediation: Examining one teacher educator's mediation of two preservice teachers' learning in context(s). *Urban Education*.

Stillman, J., Anderson, L., Arellano, A., Wong, P. L., Berta-Ávila, M., Alfaro, C., & Struthers, K. (2014). Putting PACT in context and context in PACT: An account of teacher educators' collaboration and adaptive response to policy mandates. *Teacher Education Quarterly 40*(4), 135–157.

Tsui, M.S. (2005). *Social work supervision: Contexts and concepts.* Thousand Oaks, CA: Sage.

U.S. Department of Education (2011). *Our future, our teachers: The Obama administration's plan for teacher education reform and improvement.* Washington, DC. Retrieved from http://www.ed.gov/sites/default/files/our-future-our-teachers.pdf

Valencia, S.W., Martin, S.D., Place, N.A., & Grossman, P. (2009). Complex interactions in student teaching. *Journal of Teacher Education, 60*(3), 304–322.

Walker-Dalhouse, D., & Dalhouse, A. (2006). Investigating white preservice teachers' beliefs about teaching in culturally diverse classrooms. *The Negro Educational Review, 57*(1–2), 69–84.

Whittaker, A., & Nelson, C. (2013). Assessment with an "end in view." *The New Educator, 9*(1), 77–93.

Windschitl, M., Thompson, J., & Braaten, M. (2011). Ambitious pedagogy by novice teachers. *Teachers College Record, 113*(7), 1311–1360.

Zeichner, K. (June 17, 2010). The importance of strong clinical preparation for teachers. Paper presented at a U.S. Congressional Briefing organized by the American Association of Colleges for Teacher Education, Washington, DC.

Zeichner, K. (2012). The turn once again toward practice-based teacher education. *Journal of Teacher Education, 63*(5), 376–382.

Zeichner, K., & Conklin, H. (2005). Teacher education programs. In M. Cochran-Smith & K. Zeichner (Eds.), *Studying teacher education.* Washington, DC: American Educational Research Association.

Zelner, D. D. (2007). Teaching to prevent burnout in the helping professions. *Analytic Teaching, 24*(1), 20–25.

10

BUILDING A RESEARCH AGENDA AND DEVELOPING SOLUTIONS FOR CHALLENGES IN CLINICAL EXPERIENCES

Amy Bacevich, Stephanie L. Dodman, Lena "Libby" Hall and Meredith Ludwig

In the past 5 years, research has helped create a more precise understanding of the relationship between teacher preparation and PK–12 success, pointing to three critical indicators: content knowledge, field experience and quality of teacher candidates (Boyd, Grossman, Lankford, Loeb, & Wyckoff, 2009). The second of these—field or clinical experience—is widely acknowledged by both teacher educators and novice teachers as critically important, yet the field has struggled to ensure that clinical experiences truly prepare novices for the work of teaching. With clinical experience at the fore in the national conversation on teacher preparation reform, this chapter addresses efforts to develop a research agenda that could engage the community in re-envisioning clinical experience as an effective centerpiece of teacher preparation.

Defining the Problem of Clinical Experience

Clinical experience is a traditional component of teacher preparation in which preservice teachers study, attempt and refine the practice of teaching, most often in PK–12 classrooms. Clinical experience is considered an essential component of teacher preparation, evidenced by its inclusion as a requirement in virtually every preparation program (American Association of Colleges for Teacher Education [AACTE], 2013). It seems that teacher educators largely agree that novices need opportunities to learn teaching in *real* settings. But the field's agreement appears to end there, with vast differences among programs in terms of the purposes of clinical experiences, the design of clinical experiences and the roles of those invested in clinical experiences. Given this variability, it is little wonder that clinical experience has come under fire as one component of the "confusing patchwork" of the teacher education curriculum (Levine, 2006, p. 26; see also National Council on Teacher Quality [NCTQ], 2013; Council of Chief State School Officers [CCSSO], 2012; National Council for the Accreditation of Teacher Education [NCATE], 2010).

One major issue related to clinical experience is that of its purposes. The possible purposes are many, and a single program would likely claim myriad purposes for its clinical experiences. These purposes include learning about the teacher's job; developing skills of instruction and classroom management; putting principles and concepts from coursework into practice; and developing attitudes and beliefs about teaching, learning and subject matter (Wilson, Floden, & Ferrini-Mundy, 2001). The literature also emphasizes the role that clinical experience plays in enabling novice teachers to examine their deep-seated beliefs and preconceptions related to teaching (e.g., Cole & Knowles, 1993; Rosaen & Florio-Ruane, 2008). Despite the many—and potentially conflicting—purposes for clinical experience, the purpose frequently goes unexamined or unstated when teacher preparation programs create requirements for clinical experience. Clarity about purpose is critical in designing appropriate opportunities for novices' learning about teaching (Darling-Hammond & Hammerness, 2005).

Design is a second key issue related to clinical experience. Looking across preparation programs, design might be described as haphazard at best: Clinical experiences vary in terms of the contexts in which candidates are placed; the content addressed; the degree of responsibility taken by the novice; and the purpose, duration and sequence within the program (Cruickshank & Armaline, 1986; Zeichner & Conklin, 2008). Among these elements of design, teacher education programs can most readily control the structural issues of duration and sequence, often touting a certain number of clock hours that preservice teachers spend in PK–12 classrooms as an indicator of quality. The other, more qualitative aspects of design are elusive; the program may prescribe them, but their realization depends on the attitudes, preparation and practices of those most directly involved in clinical experiences (novice teachers, cooperating teachers and university supervisors) (Knowles & Cole, 1996). As a result, novices within the same preparation program may have vastly different opportunities to learn teaching within clinical experiences. This lack of consistency raises questions about what principles drive the design of clinical experiences and how best to identify and leverage the scarce resources (both material and human) that are needed to ensure high-quality clinical experiences for all.

A third issue relates to who is supporting novices' learning in clinical settings and how the support is provided. Much has been written about the qualifications of those who work most directly with novices in PK–12 classrooms, with those supervisors often characterized as well intentioned but ill prepared (Guyton & McIntyre, 1990; Zeichner, 2010). Researchers have long emphasized the importance of strong relationships among "the triad" (the novice teacher, the PK–12 cooperating teacher and the university supervisor) (Guyton & McIntyre, 1990;

Knowles & Cole, 1996). To a lesser degree, the literature has attended to the pedagogy of clinical experience—the instructional activities in which "the triad" engages (e.g., Feiman-Nemser, 2001; Feiman-Nemser & Beasley, 1997; Stanulis, 1994). Notably, the questions of who teaches and how they teach lead to questions about the role of technology in extending, enhancing or even replacing *live* clinical experiences (Hixon & So, 2009). For example, preservice teachers' study of video recordings of teaching can provide time to reflect, as well as opportunities for collegial study and finer-grained analysis of teaching (Sherin, 2004). On the whole, this issue of who teaches and how they teach shifts the focus from clinical experiences as settings in which experiences occur to instructional opportunities (Ball & Forzani, 2009; Zeichner, 1996), but additional work is needed to understand how these opportunities can be best realized.

This brief review hints at the growth of the body of literature on clinical experience in the past 30 years. In this time, the field has transitioned from acknowledging clinical experience as an important component of teacher preparation to recognizing that it is perhaps *the most* important aspect of teacher preparation; some have recently conceptualized clinical experience as the centerpiece of teacher education reform efforts (Hollins, 2011; NCATE, 2010; Zeichner, 2012). Through strategically designed clinical experiences, "novices can work directly with the elements of infrastructure that are taking shape in many districts; the curriculum of training may be grounded in the curriculum of practice; and grooming and preparing teachers can be linked more directly to recruitment, induction, and placement" (Sykes, Bird, & Kennedy, 2010, p. 470). Some scholars and researchers have called for extensive, deliberately designed and intensely supervised clinical experiences that are closely integrated with the other components of preparation (Darling-Hammond, 2006b; Zeichner, 2006). Others have gone further, building on Ball and Cohen's (1999) call for "learning about practice *in* practice," which laid the conceptual groundwork for the notion that clinical experience should be the primary—or even exclusive—focus of all teacher preparation (Ball & Forzani, 2009).

The problem of clinical experience and its role in teacher preparation reform has certainly occupied researchers and scholars in teacher education but has also captured the attention of national organizations and policymakers. In 2010, two published reports called for a focus on clinical experience as a necessary component of a national research agenda on teacher preparation (Committee on the Study of Teacher Preparation Programs in the United States, 2010; NCATE, 2010). The NCATE Blue Ribbon Panel, especially, established a challenge for the teacher preparation community: turn teacher preparation on its head—in essence, build the program around clinical experience. The report called for the creation of "an entire system of excellent programs, not a cottage industry of pathbreaking initiatives" (NCATE, 2010, p. ii). In short, the Blue Ribbon Panel advocated innovative, transformative efforts to develop clinically based teacher preparation in a systematic manner among institutions.

Designing the Study Group

Simultaneous to these calls to action, Division K of the American Educational Research Association (AERA) issued a call for the development of study groups focused on problems in teacher preparation, with the goal of stimulating new lines of research for doctoral students and newly hired faculty. As teacher educators, researchers and program leaders, we took up this challenge and proposed a yearlong study group addressing the problem of clinical practice opportunities. The proposal for a study group was submitted to Division K and approved, with a planned session at AERA Vancouver. Our goal, to fulfill the charge from Division K, was to (1) explore what the field is thinking about studying clinical practice by engaging colleagues in a networked improvement community (NIC), (2) generate interest in conducting research on clinical practice and (3) elicit suggestions for a research agenda.

The study group members proposed to engage teacher educators, practitioners, researchers and program administrators in interactive sessions at professional meetings with a long-term goal of building an NIC. In an NIC, it is assumed that varied types of expertise about a problem are likely to be located in different but related institutions. The NIC brings together this expertise, purposefully crossing boundaries. The NIC participants know that there is improvement activity (i.e., research and experimentation) occurring in their field and that it is likely that someone has started to work out solutions to various components of the problem of practice. Bringing together many individuals with various areas of expertise improves the chances for the overall community to make progress quickly, leading to desired improvements. In an NIC, a common compelling problem serves as a unifying force for the group; there is a set of common indicators that point to the need to address the problem; and there is a set of common protocols for inquiry. These principles and the approach to develop an NIC are outlined in a paper by Bryk, Gomez, and Grunow (2011).

The Division K study group on clinical practice believed that this NIC framework was a good fit with the challenge of addressing clinical practice. We believed that (1) the problem could be clearly stated, (2) many teacher preparation programs are already implementing innovative practices and (3) the AERA is an organization suited to engage these innovators in conversations about their efforts and ways to pursue meaningful research on clinical practice.

On the basis of the principles in the Carnegie paper (Bryk et al., 2011), the goals of our envisioned NIC were to:

1. Capture practitioner knowledge and bring it into the professional knowledge base.
2. Develop an improvement map with detailed characteristics of system elements that operate and produce outcomes.
3. Prepare a description of challenges.

4. Develop a research agenda.
5. Engage participants in support of model prototyping and focused studies (i.e., designing new approaches to clinical experience and studying these approaches).
6. Engage participants in the support of graduate student (and new faculty and practitioner) research.

Developing the Networked Improvement Community

Planning the NIC

The study group read and discussed *Getting Ideas into Action: Building Networked Improvement Communities in Education* (Bryk et al., 2011) and held several conference calls during which we discussed the components of the process to build an NIC. In these discussions, we wrestled with the terminology associated with improvement research (Bryk et al., 2011), especially the terms *root causes, drivers* of the problem of practice and the steps leading to the production of a *driver diagram*. We also considered how to develop a statement that described the problem of clinical practice. We knew that the statement would need to be based on evidence (research) and that we would need to identify areas for improvement and indicators that would represent improvement.

Dr. Alicia Grunow of the Carnegie Foundation for the Advancement of Teaching graciously agreed to help us dissect the content of the Bryk et al. (2011) paper, and she explained how we could apply the precepts. Our study group designed an agenda for the AERA Vancouver meeting, which Dr. Grunow helped translate into a facilitator's guide. As the prospective facilitators in the study group, we acknowledged some challenges that would likely influence the success of implementing the process and the goal of achieving a research agenda—one that authentically emerged from the meetings we hoped to facilitate. The potential challenges to our work were as follows:

1. **Ensuring that a diversity of practice would be represented.** As seasoned members and participants in past AERA meetings, we were well aware that we could not predict the number of attendees at a session, but we knew that there would be a great variety of experience represented given the diversity of meeting participants.
2. **Supporting continuous dialogue.** There was also some uncertainty about extending the study group meetings throughout the year. In an NIC, as conceptualized in the Carnegie paper, the communities would meet across an extended period.
3. **Defining and setting goals.** This was a new effort within Division K; we were charting a new course and adapting a methodology that had not been previously used. We decided to treat the Vancouver session as if it might be our

only opportunity to meet as an NIC. We knew that we could not accomplish all of the goals in one 90-minute session, so we chose to focus on three goals: gaining consensus from participants on our research-derived problem statement, discussing improvement goals and learning as much as possible about the participants' research initiatives. In the end, we were able to address these goals in sessions at three different professional meetings (AERA Vancouver, AACTE Orlando and AERA San Francisco).

4. **Visualizing a product.** We reported the results of the first meeting back to our sponsoring AERA division, and when it became clear that we would have two more meeting opportunities during that year, we began to visualize the product as a research agenda. Our concept of a research agenda emerged from examples in commission reports (e.g., NCATE, 2010): It would reflect identified gaps in information and highlight areas where research would move the knowledge in the field ahead or at least in tandem with the innovations occurring. We recognized that it would be beyond our scope to implement an NIC after this year or to implement innovations and conduct research on them. These initiatives would have to be carried out by members of the teacher preparation community.

Forming the NIC

From April 2012 to April 2013, the study group conducted sessions at three meetings: at AERA in Vancouver, at AACTE in Orlando and at AERA in San Francisco. During the course of the three sessions, the NIC worked toward the goal of developing a research agenda for improving clinical experience in teacher education. Table 10.1 summarizes the purpose, activities and outcomes for each session.

Our session at AERA in Vancouver drew 20 individuals from a variety of colleges and universities. The session began with an explanation of the NIC process. Dr. Grunow stressed the value of a networked approach from which parallel efforts would benefit as members learned from one another. The following problem statement, initially generated by the study group, was presented to AERA attendees for review and confirmation: *Clinical opportunities in teacher preparation programs do not adequately prepare teachers for the first years of teaching.* The attendees participated in discussions, lending their views to the formalized statement of the problem, commenting on the way the problem is measured and suggesting root causes. At AACTE in Orlando, eight participants representing eight different colleges and universities reviewed the prior work on the problem statement and root causes. The group worked to identify research directions for the study of clinical practice in teacher preparation, with particular emphasis on innovative ways to study the problem or its causes. They discussed a key question: Based on the problem and considering new ways to think about clinical practice, what directions for research are indicated? The result was attendees' identification of key concepts,

TABLE 10.1 Summary of NIC Meetings

Session	Purpose	Activities	Outcomes
AERA Vancouver	Goal setting	Discussion of problem statement	Root causes of problem Innovative redesigns
AACTE Orlando	Research direction	Identification of areas of inquiry	Big questions regarding clinical practice focus Innovative redesigns
AERA San Francisco	Propose research agenda	Discussion: Research underway Research needs	Research questions Research approaches

innovative practices and challenges to innovation related to clinical practice based on their own research and their knowledge of the field. Finally, the third session in San Francisco was planned as an opportunity to build a research agenda to fulfill our goal as a study group with members of AERA. Beginning with the set of topics (areas of inquiry) that emerged from the AACTE meeting, the 20 attendees discussed the following questions in small groups:

1. In your own context, what research do you know of, and what are you and your colleagues doing?
2. What research evidence or practices are important to you in being able to work on this problem or solve it?
3. What kind of research would you suggest needs to be conducted?

Table 10.2 displays the results of the three sessions (organized by session focus), the challenges raised by participants in each session, the outcomes of each session, the innovations reported by participants and the next steps for the NIC. The information encompasses work related to clinical experience currently being conducted by NIC participants and the areas of research they perceived as being critical to better understanding clinical experiences. The NIC participants used their experiences in tandem with the literature to begin crafting a research agenda (described in the next section) aimed at supporting innovation and effectiveness in the ways clinical experiences are conceptualized, designed and assessed.

Recommended Research Agenda

Our goal, to fulfill the charge from Division K, was to (1) explore what the field is thinking about studying clinical practice by engaging colleagues in an NIC, (2) generate interest in conducting research on clinical practice and (3) elicit

TABLE 10.2 Summary of Meeting Focus, Challenges, Outcomes and Next Steps

Meeting Feature	Vancouver	Orlando	San Francisco
Focus	Problem statement presented and confirmed: Clinical opportunities in teacher preparation programs do not adequately prepare teachers for the first years of teaching.	▪ Research conducted ▪ Research evidence or practices that are important ▪ Research needs	▪ Research conducted ▪ Research evidence or practices that are important ▪ Research needs
Challenges	Challenges raised centered on the statement of the problem: 1. Clarifying the scope (first year or early career) and responsibility of teacher preparation for courses and clinical practice. 2. Interest in, including references to, quality and addressing the improvement of the quality of clinical opportunities. 3. Changing the tone to phrase the statement more positively or even in the form of a question (although this may move the problem statement more toward a research question). For example, "What types of clinical opportunities adequately prepare teachers for the first year of teaching?"	Challenges raised were related to the research enterprise as it addresses the problems in teacher education: 1. In education, we tend to differentiate between evaluation and research—would it be beneficial to see these as interrelated, as in the public health field? 2. How can (or should) research designs for studying clinical practice better incorporate formal evaluation, mixed methods, replicable design, etc.? 3. What is lost with the current focus on practice, especially if it has a technical meaning (or is understood to have such a meaning)? What about teacher thinking, planning, etc.?	Challenges raised were focused on the limitations of research thus far conducted to provide direction for the reform of clinical experience: National reports confirm that we have invested a great deal in research, but we still lack important knowledge—for example, in defining a successful clinical experience, a model for clinical supervision and knowledge about what it takes to be a supervising teacher (i.e., motivation, dispositions)

(Continued)

TABLE 10.2 (Continued)

Meeting Feature	Vancouver	Orlando	San Francisco
	4. Considering context: How do we prepare teachers for working in several different types of education settings but also ensure that they have rich experiences?	4. How should the first years of teaching be designed to continue the preparation begun in preservice education? 5. Who is doing the teaching of teachers? How can we be deliberate about ensuring that they have the necessary qualifications, experiences and coaching skills? 6. What evidence do we need to demonstrate the effectiveness of clinical practice in teacher education? What evidence do we already have that can be knit together to demonstrate effectiveness?	
Outcomes	Root causes identified: 1. Clinical experiences lack coherence. 2. Clinical experiences have insufficient or inconsistent resources. 3. Clinical experiences have inconsistent quality with respect to cooperating teachers.	Research topics in an agenda should be organized by level of concern. National level 1. Examine the impacts of high-stakes assessments for teachers in the design of student teaching. Program level 1. Examine how key themes identified across programs within one institution (through a transformational initiative study) fit together with the current emphasis on practice.	Research topics proposed were somewhat traditional, but this reflects a lack of answers to persistent problems and unchanging methods. 1. What is the role and impact of policy on teacher candidate development and clinical experience? 2. How are schools and universities working together for teacher candidate development? What are the outcomes of this alignment?

Meeting Feature	Vancouver	Orlando	San Francisco
		2. Determine the optimal amount of experience in teaching and education needed for an effective field supervisor; determine whether use of *experienced* educators (i.e., retired principals) as field supervisors makes a difference.	3. How does or can technology facilitate teacher candidate development during clinical experience? 4. What relationships exist between teacher candidates and K–12 student outcomes? 5. What relationships exist between mentors and teacher candidate outcomes? 6. How do we develop a high-quality mentorship model? 7. What types and locations are ideal for teacher candidate development? 8. How do we ensure consistency within a program?
Innovative structures, program components or practices	• Coauthoring a system of evaluation of clinical practice • Coplanning program structure with principals and teachers	• Including a community-based sequence (i.e., drawing deliberately on community action groups and school contexts) • Institutionalizing a model of practice-based coaching (including instructor modeling and guided practice for preservice teachers)	• Technology-mediated instruction, supervision and mentoring for teacher candidates in clinical practice
	• Systematizing the clinical component's timing, duration and evaluation	• Transitioning from a one-semester to a one-year post-baccalaureate secondary program; identifying models that respond to the specific demands of secondary education	

TABLE 10.2 (Continued)

Meeting Feature	Vancouver	Orlando	San Francisco
Next steps	1. Present and discuss root causes. 2. Seek examples of research addressing the root causes. 3. Formulate research questions about the root causes.	1. Continue to identify research underway. 2. Identify research that is needed. 3. Suggest research questions indicating a direction for a research agenda.	Propose new approaches to answering the persistent questions: 1. Seek opportunities for collaborative research (K–12 and teacher preparation). 2. Conduct focused, short-term studies of innovative use of technology to inform the field. 3. Conduct case studies of first-year teachers, candidates counseled out and successful clinical teachers supervising candidates. 4. Explore variation in experiences across different cohorts of candidates. 5. Explore approaches used in other fields in which field experience involves rotations and increasingly challenging conditions.

suggestions for a research agenda salient for new faculty in teacher preparation and for doctoral students. The experience designing and managing a short-term NIC was intellectually stimulating and achieved substantially more than we had anticipated.

Our meetings brought us in contact with a group of colleagues who are dedicated to exploring the challenges of clinical practice and are conducting investigations and exploring practices new to us. Our contact with educators was enhanced by contact with graduate students and new faculty who were beginning their research and seeking support and ideas for direction. We hope that individuals in our profession will continue to discuss and refine these or propose new questions and approaches, especially in light of the changing landscape in which teacher preparation programs reside.

The NIC approach introduced an opportunity for participants to spend a full meeting session grappling with ideas and challenges. It started with their own experiences, not with a particular paper, which is a somewhat different format than the typical session in many professional meetings. The questions and approaches to research that emerged represent what our session participants believe to be important.

In this section, we lay out the recommended research agenda by identifying several questions borne out of the NIC's work, briefly discussing how these questions have been explored in the recent research literature to date and offering ideas for how these questions can be further researched for the benefit of clinical experiences. In some ways, this list reflects the kinds of questions raised by teacher educators and researchers during the past 30 years as the field has sought to conceptualize key outcomes, relationships and models. We believe that these questions should be considered anew, however, in light of ongoing innovative design of programs and practices related to clinical experience.

What Is the Role and Impact of Policy on Teacher Candidate Development and Clinical Experience?

Over the past 10–15 years, national education policy has become increasingly invested in teacher accountability structures that rely on assessment of student learning (Lewis & Young, 2013). These policies have affected several levels of education. For example, at the PK–12 instructional level, this "age of accountability" (Cochran-Smith, 2003) has resulted in changes to the curriculum. Due to the high-stakes pressures associated with current accountability policies, teachers and schools are finding themselves narrowing their instructional content and practices to what is being tested (and how it is being tested) by annual standardized tests of achievement (Berliner, 2011). Research has examined experienced and novice teachers' navigations regarding the effects of accountability on their curriculum (see, e.g., Crocco & Costigan, 2007; Haydar, 2008), but the body of research on the effects of this curriculum narrowing on teacher candidate development is limited and worth expanding. Given our awareness of the strong influence of the mentor teacher (Ronfeldt & Reininger, 2012; Rozelle & Wilson, 2012), how might teacher candidates' clinical experiences be affected by narrowed conceptualizations of teaching and learning? How are candidates negotiating theory to practice in this environment? In what high-leverage teaching experiences are candidates authentically engaging during their clinical experiences, and what teaching experiences are included in their typical instruction during clinical experiences? What does the role of cooperating teacher look like in this policy context? Have cooperating teacher roles changed as accountability pressures have grown, and what impact has that had on candidates' clinical opportunities? The NIC indicated that examining these kinds of questions, with sharp analysis of the context for clinical practice, was important in understanding how we can design clinical experiences that are effective within the current context of PK–12 teaching, not in spite of that context.

In addition to this increased pressure on in-service teachers, there have been increasingly louder calls for accountability of the preservice programs that prepare them (Lewis & Young, 2013). Policies aimed at teacher quality have become intertwined with teacher accountability (Cochran-Smith, 2003), and it is still unclear how such policies aimed at preparation programs affect clinical opportunities. The preparation programs that will soon be using edTPA—the first national teacher candidate performance assessment (http://www.edtpa.com/ developed by Stanford University, AACTE and Pearson Education Inc.)—provide opportunities to investigate these effects. For those preparation programs that adopt edTPA, some questions to pose are: How does it constrain or enhance the clinical experiences of candidates? Are the results used to revise components of teacher preparation programs? How are teacher effectiveness policies being considered and utilized by preparation programs and by states in their efforts to meaningfully improve the clinical preparation of teachers? Rich case studies of programs that attempt to strengthen their clinical practice experiences within current policy contexts could offer a starting point. This research must also include rigorous study of candidates within their clinical experiences and focus on the opportunities and constraints they now face.

What Are Effective Ways to Assess Program Outcomes and Teacher Candidate Development?

As Berry (2005) claimed, "teaching will not be a profession, and teacher education will not earn its rightful status in the university, until practitioners link teacher learning to student learning" (p. 277). The NIC asserted that teacher education must seek that link with its candidates while also attending to teacher thinking, beliefs and actions. In addition to the aforementioned performance assessments, there is much to be gained by using multiple measures to assess program outcomes (Darling-Hammond, 2006a). Data regarding changes in the perceptions, knowledge and performance of both teaching candidates and their PK–12 students can offer a triangulated approach to determining the outcomes of clinical experiences. In addition, case studies of graduates in their first year or candidates counseled out of their student teaching can offer insight into the design of clinical opportunities (Grossman, 2010). Integrating the performance data of graduates is not without its difficulties and will benefit from further research that investigates fair and accurate measures that go beyond test scores (Henry, Kershaw, Zulli, & Smith, 2012); such measures should provide relevant data for improving clinical experiences.

How Are Schools and Universities Working Together for Teacher Candidate Development?

According to AACTE (2010), teacher preparation is "now increasingly recognized as an academically taught, clinical practice profession, such as nursing, clinical psychology, and medicine" (p. 6). Universities and schools must be, and are increasingly, partners in teacher development. This partnership must not be only in name or setting but must truly value both academic and practitioner needs and expertise. In her examination of the common components of powerful teacher preparation, Darling-Hammond (2006a) found that programs that were effective in preparing candidates for success with all students had strong partnerships between university- and school-based faculty. These partners authentically shared knowledge and beliefs related to teaching and learning and had a strong commitment to students; both sets of stakeholders had voices within the program, and there was regular collaboration. Zeichner (2012) asserted that "moving teacher education closer to the work of teaching" (p. 377) means that teacher education must take place on both university and school campuses; however, what happens on those campuses must prepare candidates to enact high-leverage instructional practices (i.e., the mere physical location of a class is not in itself representative of a partnership).

Lab schools, professional development schools (PDSs) and teacher residencies are three large-scale models of school–university partnerships that have been formed in part to support high-quality clinical experiences. In terms of PDSs, a good deal of research to date describes the relationships of the institutions and partners involved (see, e.g., Neopolitan, 2011), but this research needs to be expanded across all clinical practice settings to examine the outcomes of school-to-university alignment in terms of resources and coherence. The research must ask: How is coherence between the two settings sustained over time? How are these partnerships being creatively approached in our current policy and economic context (Wiseman, 2011)? What resources are needed and created by such partnerships? Are certain candidate development activities best conducted in school settings or in university settings? How do we foster the sustained development of desired candidate perceptions, attitudes and skills across settings over time (Jacobbe, Ross, & Hensberry, 2012)? The NIC stated that investigating these questions of partnership as part of a rigorous *collaborative* research agenda for clinical practice will aid the development of clinical experiences that meaningfully prepare candidates for their first years of teaching.

What Are Some Examples of Programs in which Coherence, Consistency and Resources Support High-Quality Models of Mentorship and Clinical Practice?

Related to the previous question, case studies are needed to address ways that programs with a strong clinical focus ensure coherence and consistency across settings and also within the program itself. AACTE (2010) provided snapshot examples of programs that exemplify "the essential linking of course work with clinical work" (p. 6)—that is, they have been judged as high-quality, clinically focused models. These profiles offer summary descriptions of 60 programs that include overviews of the candidates' clinical opportunities and summary data demonstrating outcomes. In AACTE's report (2010), outcome evidence varies by institution. Most schools offer evidence of impact on candidates prior to graduation, such as successful completion of student teaching and mentor teacher perceptions of candidate skills, while some schools offer evidence of impact that includes post-graduation outcomes, such as employer perceptions and impact on their students' learning during their first years of teaching. These snapshots might be considered starting points for what is needed on a much grander scale: clinical descriptions that can demonstrate both the nuances of the clinical experiences and the impact on candidate outcomes (including their actual teaching performance).

The NIC also raised important foundational questions related to clinical practice that might be illuminated by additional case studies of high-quality, clinically focused programs, both in teacher preparation and in other professions (e.g., Grossman et al., 2009). These questions included: What constitutes a successful clinical experience? What outcomes are valued, and what actions in the clinical setting lead to them? Would this be defined differently by each teacher preparation program or *within* a teacher preparation program? Most studies and program descriptions to date tend to speak in generalities about clinical experiences (Anderson & Stillman, 2013; Rozelle & Wilson, 2012). These generalities can mask the assumptions that underlie the design of clinical opportunities and can omit important considerations that impact program coherence and consistency. Program selection of candidate clinical mentors, which includes cooperating teachers and internship supervisors, is a frequent research omission. The questions of what mentor qualities and activities contribute to candidate development and how those characteristics and skills can be fostered within and across clinical opportunities are questions about which we know surprisingly little. As a result, a clinical practice research agenda requires more investigation into

- The indicators of a successful clinical experience;
- The features of a high-quality mentorship model; and
- The dispositions, training and instructional skill set of a successful mentor.

How Does or Can Technology Facilitate Teacher Candidate Development during Clinical Experience?

As teacher preparation programs seek to improve their clinical opportunities for candidates, technology is being increasingly utilized for coaching, reflection and assessment. Technology can serve to extend *live* field experience or provide opportunities for vicarious experience through the study of recordings of teaching and the use of simulated environments (Hixon & So, 2009). In one study of technology-enhanced clinical experience, Kopcha and Alger (2011) examined the eSupervision instructional program. eSupervision is a series of online modules designed to support candidates, their cooperating teachers and university supervisors. Candidates participate in the modules with their mentors and also with other candidates and their mentors. Modules contain activities such as discussion forums, lesson plan creation and feedback and video reflection. The eSupervision program acts as a supplement to the face-to-face observations and interactions that candidates have with their assigned mentors, although candidates did receive fewer site visits from university supervisors than a control group. Kopcha and Alger (2011) found that, as compared with a control group in the same program, the eSupervision students scored as well on the Performance Assessment for California Teachers (PACT) and higher than the control group on the Teachers' Sense of Self-Efficacy Scale at the conclusion of the experience.

The NIC described a good deal of innovative practice related to using technology to support clinical experience, including initiatives related to real-time coaching and virtual supervision. The research investigating such initiatives is still limited and often highly descriptive; the field would benefit from focused, short-term case studies of innovative uses of technology that focus on various outcomes related to candidate development, including perceptions, beliefs and teaching performance.

Next Steps

We believe that the work of the NIC, as reported herein, is only a starting point for building a professional community that is collectively focused on developing effective, clinically based teacher preparation. To progress toward the long-term goal of building and sustaining the NIC, we recommend that the next steps involve:

1. Leveraging technology to maintain and sustain an ongoing dialogue with the community (e.g. www.preserviceteachered.com).
2. Seeking resources and funding opportunities to support the NIC and its efforts.
3. Constructing a national collaborative focused on the research necessary to address these research questions.
4. Encouraging the AERA, AACTE and Association of Teacher Educators (ATE) to create special interest groups around the NIC and its research agenda.
5. Seeking support from national-level policy groups such as the Council of Chief State School Officers, the National Governors Association and the National Commission on Teaching and America's Future to influence policy

changes that recognize the challenges associated with providing high-quality clinical opportunities for all teacher candidates.

Concluding Thoughts

In the process of engaging researchers and practitioners, we found that broader questions emerged about the purpose and direction of teacher education. To stimulate further discussions across the division, we offer these questions and some additional thoughts from the study group.

- What research results will be meaningful to future clinical practices if the context in which we prepare new teachers remains the same? What if the context changes?
- Can we learn more about preparing educators from studying first-year teachers than from clinical experience in the final year of an undergraduate program?
- What is lost with the current focus on practice, especially if it has a technical meaning (or is understood to have such a meaning)? What about candidates' thinking, beliefs and planning? We must make sure that these elements of candidate development do not get lost in the process.
- Who is doing the teaching of teachers? How can we be deliberate about ensuring that they have the necessary qualifications, experiences and coaching skills?

Our NIC conversations about the current state of teacher preparation prompted us to further rethink the purpose of teacher education. Instead of turning teacher education upside down, as the NCATE Blue Ribbon Panel suggests, why not consider the following: reframe the first year of teaching by creating collaborative ventures between teacher preparation programs and the hiring PK–12 school systems. Leveraging the resources of both teacher preparation programs and school systems maximizes the ability to study in depth the design, implementation and ongoing assessment of what does and does not work. As long as we continue to study what is, rather than exploring what could be, we risk continuing to repeat the processes and methods that fail to yield data and provide answers that make little impact on the problems of clinical practice.

References

American Association of Colleges for Teacher Education (AACTE) (2010). *Reforming teacher preparation: The critical clinical component.* Washington, DC: Author.

American Association of Colleges for Teacher Education (AACTE) (2013). *The changing teacher preparation profession.* Washington, DC: Author.

Anderson, L.M., & Stillman, J.A. (2013). Student teaching's contribution to preservice teacher development: A review of research focused on the preparation of teachers for urban and high-needs contexts. *Review of Educational Research, 83*(1), 3–69.

Ball, D.L., & Cohen, D.K. (1999). Developing practice, developing practitioners: Toward a practice-based theory of professional education. In L. Darling-Hammond & G. Sykes (Eds.), *Teaching as the learning profession: Handbook of policy and practice* (pp. 3–32). San Francisco, CA: Jossey-Bass.

Ball, D.L., & Forzani, F. (2009). The work of teaching and the challenge of teacher education. *Journal of Teacher Education, 60*(5), 497–511.

Berliner, D. (2011). Rational responses to high stakes testing: The case of curriculum narrowing and the harm that follows. *Cambridge Journal of Education, 41*(3), 287–302.

Berry, B. (2005). The future of teacher education. *Journal of Teacher Education, 56*(3), 272–278.

Boyd, D., Grossman, P., Lankford, H., Loeb, S., & Wyckoff, J. (2009). Teacher preparation and student achievement. *Educational Evaluation and Policy Analysis, 31*(4), 416–440.

Bryk, A.S., Gomez, L.M., & Grunow, A. (2011). *Getting ideas into action: Building networked improvement communities in education.* Retrieved from http://www.carnegiefoundation.org/sites/default/files/bryk-gomez_building-nics-education.pdf

Cochran-Smith, M. (2003). The unforgiving complexity of teaching: Avoiding simplicity in the age of accountability. *Journal of Teacher Education, 54*(1), 3–5.

Cole, A., & Knowles, J.G. (1993). Shattered images: Understanding expectations and realities of field experiences. *Teaching and Teacher Education, 9*(5–6), 457–471.

Committee on the Study of Teacher Preparation Programs in the United States—National Research Council (2010). *Preparing teachers: Building evidence for sound policy.* Washington, DC: National Academies Press.

Council of Chief State School Officers (CCSSO) (2012). *Our responsibility, our promise: Transforming educator preparation and entry into the profession.* Washington, DC: Author.

Crocco, M.S., & Costigan, A.T. (2007). The narrowing of curriculum and pedagogy in the age of accountability: Urban educators speak out. *Urban Education, 42*(6), 512–535.

Cruickshank, D., & Armaline, W. (1986). Field experiences in teacher education: Considerations and recommendations. *Journal of Teacher Education, 37*(3), 34–40.

Darling-Hammond, L. (2006a). Assessing teacher education: The usefulness of multiple measures for assessing program outcomes. *Journal of Teacher Education, 57*(2), 120–138.

Darling-Hammond, L. (2006b). Constructing 21st-century teacher education. *Journal of Teacher Education, 57*(3), 300–314.

Darling-Hammond, L., & Hammerness, K. (2005). The design of teacher education programs. In L. Darling-Hammond & J. Bransford (Eds.), *Preparing teachers for a changing world* (pp. 390–441). San Francisco, CA: Jossey-Bass.

Feiman-Nemser, S. (2001). Helping novices learn to teach: Lessons from an exemplary support teacher. *Journal of Teacher Education, 52*(1), 17–30.

Feiman-Nemser, S., & Beasley, K. (1997). Mentoring as assisted performance: A case of co-planning. In V. Richardson (Ed.), *Constructivist teacher education: Building new understandings* (pp. 108–125). Washington, DC: Falmer.

Grossman, P. (2010). *Learning to practice: The design of clinical experience in teacher preparation.* Policy Brief, Partnership for Teacher Quality. Retrieved from https://www.nea.org/assets/docs/Clinical_Experience_-_Pam_Grossman.pdf

Grossman, P., Compton, C., Igra, D., Ronfeldt, M., Shahan, E., & Williamson, P. (2009). Teaching practice: A cross-professional perspective. *Teachers College Record, 111*(9), 2055–2100.

Guyton, E., & McIntyre, D.J. (1990). Student teaching and school experience. In R. Houston (Ed.), *Handbook of research on teacher education* (pp. 514–534). New York, NY: Macmillan.

Haydar, H. (2008). "Who's got the chalk?": Beginning mathematics teachers and educational policies in New York City. *Forum on Public Policy Online, 2008*(2). Retrieved from http://forumonpublicpolicy.com/summer08papers/archivesummer08/haydar.pdf

Henry, G.T., Kershaw, D. C., Zulli, R.A., & Smith, A.A. (2012). Incorporating teacher effectiveness into teacher preparation program evaluation. *Journal of Teacher Education, 63*(5), 335–355.

Hixon, E., & So, H.-J. (2009). Technology's role in field experiences for preservice teacher training. *Educational Technology & Society, 12*(4), 294–304.

Hollins, E.R. (2011). Teacher preparation for quality teaching. *Journal of Teacher Education, 62*(4), 395–407.

Jacobbe, T., Ross, D.D., & Hensberry, K.K.R. (2012). The effects of a family math night on preservice teachers' perceptions of parental involvement. *Urban Education, 47*(6), 1160–1182.

Knowles, J.G., & Cole, A. (1996). Developing practice through field experiences. In F. Murray (Ed.), *The teacher educator's handbook* (pp. 648–688). San Francisco, CA: Jossey-Bass.

Kopcha, T.J., & Alger, C. (2011). The impact of technology-enhanced student teacher supervision on student teacher knowledge, performance, and self-efficacy during the field experience. *Journal of Educational Computing Research, 45*(1), 49–73.

Levine, A. (2006). *Educating school teachers.* Washington, DC: The Education Schools Project.

Lewis, W.D., & Young, T.V. (2013). The politics of accountability: Teacher education policy. *Educational Policy, 27*(2), 190–216.

National Council for the Accreditation of Teacher Education (NCATE) (2010). *Transforming teacher education through clinical practice: A national strategy to prepare effective teachers.* Washington, DC: Author.

National Council on Teacher Quality (NCTQ) (2013). *Teacher prep review.* Retrieved from http://www.nctq.org/dmsStage/Teacher_Prep_Review_2013_Report

Neapolitan, J.E. (Ed.) (2011). *Taking stock of professional development schools: What's needed now.* New York, NY: Teachers College and National Society for the Study of Education.

Ronfeldt, M., & Reininger, M. (2012). More or better student teaching? *Teaching and Teacher Education, 28*(8), 1091–1106.

Rosaen, C., & Florio-Ruane, S. (2008). The metaphors by which we teach: Experience, metaphor, and culture in teacher education. In M. Cochran-Smith, S. Feiman-Nemser, & D.J. McIntyre (Eds.), *Handbook of research on teacher education* (3rd ed.) (pp. 706–731). New York, NY: Routledge.

Rozelle, J.J., & Wilson, S.M. (2012). Opening the black box of field experiences: How cooperating teachers' beliefs and practices shape student teachers' beliefs and practices. *Teaching and Teacher Education, 28*(8), 1196–1205.

Sherin, M.G. (2004). New perspectives on the role of video in teacher education. In J. Brophy (Ed.), *Using video in teacher education (Advances in research on teaching, Volume 10)* (pp. 1–27). New York, NY: Elsevier Science.

Stanulis, R. (1994). Fading to a whisper: One mentor's story of sharing her wisdom without telling the answers. *Journal of Teacher Education, 45*(1), 31–38.

Sykes, G., Bird, T., & Kennedy, M. (2010). Teacher education: Its problems and some prospects. *Journal of Teacher Education, 61*(5), 464–476.

Wilson, S., Floden, R., & Ferrini-Mundy, J. (2001). *Teacher preparation research: Current knowledge, gaps, and recommendations.* Seattle, WA: Center for the Study of Teaching and Policy.

Wiseman, D.L. (2011). Response to Section IV: What's needed now: Issues of professional development, school accountability and sustainability in today's complex educational environment. In J.E. Neapolitan (Ed.), *Taking stock of professional development schools: What's needed now* (pp. 567–576). New York, NY: Teachers College and National Society for the Study of Education.

Zeichner, K. (1996). Designing educative practicum experiences for prospective teachers. In K. Zeichner, S. Melnick, & M.L. Gomez (Eds.), *Currents of reform in preservice teacher education* (pp. 215–234). New York, NY: Teachers College Press.

Zeichner, K. (2006). Reflections of a university-based teacher educator on the future of college- and university-based teacher education. *Journal of Teacher Education, 57*(3), 326–340.

Zeichner, K. (2010). Rethinking the connections between campus courses and field experiences in university-based teacher education. *Journal of Teacher Education, 61*(2), 89–99.

Zeichner, K. (2012). The turn once again toward practice-based teacher education. *Journal of Teacher Education, 63*(5), 376–382.

Zeichner, K., & Conklin, H. (2008). Teacher education programs as sites for teacher preparation. In M. Cochran-Smith, S. Feiman-Nemser, & D.J. McIntyre (Eds.), *Handbook of research on teacher education* (3rd ed.) (pp. 269–289). New York, NY: Routledge.

ABOUT THE CONTRIBUTORS

Amy Bacevich is a teacher education consultant whose work addresses clinical practice design issues, including the use of instructional activities, alternative settings and video technology to support novice teacher learning.

Marisa Bier is the program director of the Seattle Teacher Residency in Seattle, WA. She has worked in education for 20 years, beginning her career as a special education teacher. She received her doctorate in education at the University of Washington in 2009 and has worked in teacher education since then.

Rachel Carlson began her work in elementary urban education and has since worked in the field of clinical psychology. Her interests lie in identity development via internal and external factors and through the development of resilience.

Renée Tipton Clift is associate dean and professor of teaching, learning and sociocultural studies at the University of Arizona. Her research investigates the factors that affect the process of learning to teach; her most recent edited book is *Inside the Role of Dean*, to be published in early 2015.

Stephanie L. Dodman is assistant professor in the College of Education and Human Development at George Mason University. She teaches in the advanced studies in teaching and learning program and researches teacher learning across the professional continuum.

Maritza Alcoreza Dominguez is a co-founder and program director at the Alliance for Community Teachers and Schools in Baltimore, MD. She is a community organizer through leadership development in urban schools and communities. She and her team developed an innovative parent–teacher engagement initiative called Learning Ignited by Families and Teachers Together (LIFTT).

Richard K. Gordon is professor of education at California State University–Dominguez Hills and has over 40 years of experience as an urban school teacher and professor of education. His research centers on critical theory and effective instructional models.

Michelle Haj-Broussard is an associate professor at McNeese State University in Lake Charles, LA. She is president of the National Association for Alternative Certification, and her work focuses on alternative certification and immersion language education. She co-authored "Conflicting agendas: Immersion and desegregation in the Deep South," *Research in the Schools* (2012) and "Teach Louisiana Consortium: A fifth year program evaluation," *Journal of the National Association for Alternative Certification* (2012).

Lena "Libby" Hall recently retired after 44 years of serving as an educator at the elementary, secondary, undergraduate, and graduate levels across five states. Most recently, she was a faculty member in the College of Education and Human Development at George Mason University, where she was the director of the Office of Education Services, providing professional development support to school divisions in the Commonwealth of Virginia.

Heidi L. Hallman is an associate professor of curriculum and teaching at the University of Kansas. She is the co-author of *Community Fieldwork in Teacher Education: Theory and Practice*, Routledge, 2015.

Etta R. Hollins is professor and Kauffman Endowed Chair for Urban Teacher Education at the University of Missouri–Kansas City. She is the author of *Learning to Teach in Urban Schools* and *Culture in School Learning*, both published by Routledge.

Jennifer L. Husbands is the executive director of Schools That Can Chicago, an organization that unites leaders to expand quality urban education across sectors. She is a co-author of *Instructional Leadership for Systemic Change: The Story of San Diego's Reform* (Rowman and Littlefield Education 2005).

Belinda Dunnick Karge is a professor at California State University, Fullerton. She is the co-author of "Alternative certification teachers: building partnerships with paraprofessionals," *Journal of the National Association for Alternative Certification* (2011).

Magaly Lavadenz is a professor in the Department of Educational Leadership and founding director of the Center for Equity for English Learners at Loyola Marymount University in Los Angeles. She served as president of the California Council on Teacher Education and is the editor of *Pedagogies of Questioning: Bilingual Teacher Researchers and Transformative Inquiry* (California Association for Bilingual Education, 2011).

Antoinette S. Linton is an assistant professor of secondary education at California State University, Fullerton. Her doctoral dissertation was titled "The Effects of Structured Dialogue Grounded in Socioculturalism as a Tool to Facilitate Professional Development in Secondary Science" and was completed at the University of Southern California in 2011.

Meredith Ludwig is a principal researcher at the American Institutes for Research. She has been conducting research about teacher preparation programs and teacher preparation policy since 1979.

Kimberly Walker McAlister is associate professor and chair of the Department of Teaching, Leadership & Counseling in the Gallaspy College of Education and Human Development at the Northwestern State University of Louisiana. She is the co-author of "Achieving mathematical concepts one word at a time," *Field Experience Journal* (2010).

Marjorie McCabe is a professor in the Department of Special Education, Rehabilitation, and Counseling at California State University, San Bernardino, and the director of the mild moderate disabilities and early childhood special education intern programs. She has been the director of numerous federal- and state-funded grants and serves on state and national boards in the field of alternative certification.

Peter C. Murrell, Jr., is professor of educational psychology and urban education at Loyola University Maryland and was the founding dean of the School of Education. He is the author of *Race, Culture and Schooling: Identities of Achievement in Multicultural Urban Schools* (Lawrence Erlbaum).

John A. Omelan is a senior education specialist for educator preparation solutions at the Region 4 Education Service Center in Houston.

Phyllis Payne is the director of non-traditional educator preparation at the Georgia Professional Standards Commission. She is the co-developer of the Georgia Teacher Academy for Preparation and Pedagogy (GaTAPP), the foundation for the statewide alternative preparation for classroom teachers.

Vickie V. Person is an assistant professor and program chair for the Master of Arts in Urban Teacher Education Alternative Certification Program at Governors State University, University Park, Illinois. She is also president-elect of the National Association for Alternative Certification. Her dissertation was titled "The Impact of School Culture from the Alternative Certified Teacher Perspective" (2010).

Karen Peterson is professor emeritus at Governors State University. She is currently co-director of a teacher quality partnership grant at the university and coordinator of special projects in induction and mentoring and alternative certification.

Gisele Ragusa is a professor of engineering education at the University of Southern California. She is the author of numerous publications on science, technology, engineering and mathematics (STEM) education and student and teacher assessment.

Terri L. Rodriguez is associate professor of education at the College of St. Benedict & St. John's University in St. Joseph, Minnesota. She is the author of "Stories of Self, Stories of Practice: Enacting a Vision of Socially Just Pedagogy for Latino Youth," *Teaching Education* (2011).

Frances O'Connell Rust is a senior fellow and director of teacher education in the University of Pennsylvania Graduate School of Education. She is professor emeritus at New York University's Steinhardt School of Education. She has published widely on topics related to teacher preparation and teacher quality.

Cyndy Stephens is director of educator workforce development at the Georgia Professional Standards Commission. She is a past president of the National Association for Alternative Certification (NAAC) and is the current policy liaison to the board for NAAC. She co-authored 10 years of the annual supply and demand reports of educators in Georgia and the Georgia teacher retention studies.

Jamy Stillman is an assistant professor of education at the University of Southern California's Rossier School of Education. Her research interests include the preparation of teachers to serve historically marginalized populations; the preparation of teacher educators; and the impact of high-stakes accountability on teachers, teaching and learning to teach in urban high-needs schools.

Jessica Strauss is executive director of the Alliance for Community Teachers and Schools, a national model development organization based in Baltimore. She has been a consultant and non-profit leader for 27 years, working with universities, school leaders, parents, teachers and community partners to generate supportive, stimulating learning environments for urban children.

Andrea Whittaker is director of teacher performance assessment at the Stanford Center for Assessment, Learning and Equity (SCALE). For 15 years prior to SCALE, she was professor of education at San Jose State University, serving as faculty in the Departments of Elementary and Secondary Education.

Kenneth Zeichner is professor emeritus of education at the University of Wisconsin-Madison and the Boeing professor of teacher education at the University of Washington. His recent publications include "Venture philanthropy and teacher education policy in the U.S.: The Role of the New Schools Venture Fund," *Teachers College Record*, "The struggle for the soul of teaching and teacher education in the U.S.," *Journal of Education for Teaching*, and "Democratizing teacher education," *Journal of Teacher Education*, with Katie Payne and Kate Brayko Gence.

Preservice Teacher Education Website: www.preserviceteachered.com

INDEX

Note: Page numbers in italic with *f* indicate figures and with *t* indicate tables.

An environmentally friendly book printed and bound in England by www.printondemand-worldwide.com

PEFC Certified

This product is
from sustainably
managed forests
and controlled
sources

www.pefc.org

This book is made entirely of sustainable materials; FSC paper for the cover and PEFC paper for the text pages.

#0193 - 270515 - C0 - 229/152/14 - PB - 9781138823860